Racial Bias in the Classroom

Can Teachers Reach All Children?

Darlene Leiding

Innovations in Education, No. 8

Rowman & Littlefield Education
Lanham, Maryland • Toronto • Oxford
2006

Published in the United States of America
by Rowman & Littlefield Education
A Division of Rowman & Littlefield Publishers, Inc.
A wholly owned subsidary of The Rowman & Littlefield Publishing Group, Inc.
4501 Forbes Boulevard, Suite 200, Lanham, Maryland 20706
www.rowmaneducation.com

PO Box 317
Oxford
OX2 9RU, UK

British Library Cataloguing in Publication Information Available

Library of Congress Cataloging-in-Publication Data

Leiding, Darlene, 1943–
    Racial bias in the classroom : can teachers reach all children? / Darlene
Leiding.
        p.   cm.— (Innovations in education series ; 8)
    Includes bibliographical references.
    ISBN 13: 978-1-57886-390-7 (hardcover : alk. paper)
    ISBN 13: 978-1-57886-391-4 (pbk. : alk. paper)
    ISBN 10: 1-57886-390-2 (hardcover : alk. paper)
    ISBN 10: 1-57886-391-0 (pbk. : alk. paper)
    1. Discrimination in education—United States.   2. Minorities—Education—
United States—Case studies.   3. Multicultural education—United States.
I. Title.   II. Series.
LC212.2.L44   2006
371.829'00973—dc22

                                                                2005031277

Innovations in Education Series
Edited by Robert J. Brown

1. Edward J. Dirkswager, editor. *Teachers as Owners: A Key to Revitalizing Public Education.* 2002.
2. Darlene Leiding. *The Won't Learners: An Answer to Their Cry.* 2002.
3. Ronald J. Newell. *Passion for Learning: How a Project-Based System Meets the Needs of High School Students in the 21st Century.* 2003.
4. Sarah J. Noonan. *The Elements of Leadership: What You Should Know.* 2003.
5. Jeffrey R. Cornwall. *From the Ground Up: Entrepreneurial School Leadership.* 2003.
6. Linda Schaak Distad and Joan Cady Brownstein. *Talking Teaching: Implementing Reflective Practice in Groups.* 2004.
7. Darlene Leiding. *Managers Make the Difference: Managing vs. Leading in Our Schools.* 2004.
8. Darlene Leiding. *Racial Bias in the Classroom: Can Teachers Reach All Children?* 2006.

Contents

Acknowledgments

One person cannot accomplish anything alone. We are all interconnected and it takes many to make anything a reality. This book is no exception.

Credit must go first of all to Dr. Robert Brown, Educational Leadership professor at the University of St. Thomas and my friend. Bob puts up with me, encourages me, and offers invaluable advice. He shared his wisdom and expertise before and during the entire process. He challenged me to strive for professional excellence.

I offer thanks to the American Indian, Hispanic, Asian American, Hmong, African American, Arab American, and new African immigrant community members, parents, and students who shared their ideas, questions, and concerns with me. Their visions became the foundation of the cultural diversity that I explored. I hope this book is of value to them and others committed to sharing their lives with our culturally diverse learners.

Special thanks go out to Bruce Turnbaugh, educator and friend, who provided critical advice and assistance. His 40 years of teaching expertise, patience, and humor helped make this endeavor an enjoyable task.

Two close friends have inspired and encouraged me. Both are in education and have been part of my life for over 30 years. Judy Schulze, early childhood educator and Christian youth director, lives down the block; and Jane Deeming, educator and philosopher, lives across the country in Los Angeles. Both have devoted their lives to educating our culturally diverse learners.

I wish to thank Tom Koerner and Rowman & Littlefield Publishing for giving me the chance to share my passion for education and tips for success in the form of this book.

Finally, this book would not have been possible without the support and encouragement of the two most important people in my life, my husband, Marty, and my daughter, Wendy. Marty is my partner, my friend, my confidant, and the one constant in my life. Marty has given me more than 40 years of advice, challenging me and supporting me. He has shared my visions and dreams. Wendy is an inspiration because of her youth, vibrancy, and trust in the educational system. Their love and support fill my life and provide me with the motivation and capacity to reach for my dreams.

Introduction

> It is not easy being a minority in the United States. The crushing
> weight of irrational ignorance is directed toward you.
>
> —Bill O'Reilly, *Who's Looking Out For You?*

A close friend related this scenario: He had flown from Los Angeles to
Charleston, South Carolina, to attend a meeting of hundreds of educators
from across the country. These educators were meeting to discuss the
need for greater cultural diversity in the classroom curriculum. As he
chatted with the taxi driver about the weather and tourists, the driver, who
appeared to be about 40 and was white, asked, "How long have you been
in this country?" My friend replied, wincing, "All my life. I was born in
Los Angeles." With a strong southern drawl, the driver remarked, "I was
wondering because your English is excellent." My friend, as he had so
many times before, explained, "My grandfather came here from Japan in
the 1880s. My family has been here in America for over a hundred years."
To the driver, my friend did not look "American." His eyes and complex-
ion looked foreign.

At that moment, both my friend and the taxi driver became uncomfort-
ably conscious of a racial divide. He did not see my friend as American.
He had a narrow but widely shared sense of the past, a history that has
viewed "American" as European in ancestry. "American" has been defined as "white."

However, America has been racially diverse since its very beginning
when the Spanish founded St. Augustine in 1565, and this reality is
becoming more and more visible. Culturally diverse groups are fast
becoming a majority. These groups already predominate in major cities

across the country: New York City, Chicago, Atlanta, Detroit, Philadelphia, San Francisco, Los Angeles, Miami, and Washington, D.C.

This emerging demographic diversity has raised fundamental questions about America's identity and culture. In 1990, *Time* magazine published a cover story entitled "America's Changing Colors." "Someday soon," the magazine announced, "white Americans will become a minority group." How soon? By 2056, most Americans will trace their descent to "Africa, Asia, the Hispanic world, the Pacific Islands, Laos, Thailand, Arabia, almost anywhere but white Europe" (William, 1990, p. 28).

This dramatic change in our nation's ethnic composition is altering the way we think about ourselves. "The deeper significance of America's becoming a majority nonwhite society is what it means to the national psyche, to individuals' sense of themselves and their nation, their idea of what it is to be an American" (William, 1990, p. 31).

Educators believe we need to know about racial and ethnic diversity. We need to see events from the viewpoint of different groups. We need to reach toward a more comprehensive understanding of American history.

The reality of racial tension rudely woke America like a fireball in the night on April 29, 1992. Immediately after the Los Angeles police officers were found not guilty of brutality against Rodney King, rage exploded in the streets of Los Angeles. During the nightmarish rampage, scores of people were killed, over 2,000 injured, 12,000 arrested, and almost a billion dollars' worth of property destroyed. The live television images mesmerized America. The rioting and murderous melee on the streets resembled the fighting in Beirut and the West Bank. The thousands of fires burning out of control and the dark smoke filling the skies brought back images of the burning oilfields of Kuwait during Desert Storm. Entire sections of Los Angeles looked like a bombed city. "Is this America?" "Can't we all get along?"

One of the lessons of the Los Angeles explosion is the recognition of the fact that we are a multicultural society and that race can no longer be defined in the binary terms of black and white. Hispanic, Asian, American Indian, and Arab also represent our diverse nation, and even though the Rodney King incident represented black and white racial tension, many of these groups have experienced similar explosions of tension.

What is the nature of malevolence? Is there a deep need for group identity rooted in hatred for the other? Is ethnic pluralism possible for America? What does our diversity mean? Where is it leading us?

One way to try to eliminate hatred is for our society's various ethnic groups to develop a greater understanding of each other. For example, how can African Americans and Korean Americans work out their conflicts unless they learn about each other's cultures, histories, and economic situations? Shared knowledge about our ethnic diversity is required. We must step back and look at the rich and complex portrait our culturally diverse students present in the classroom.

On the fringes of most school environments gathers a shadow population of students whose motivation and achievement are stymied. Many of these are culturally diverse students who are not being well served by our public schools. Precious little attention is given either to the needs of these young people or to their assets. They are often viewed as deviants from the "regular" students, outsiders who are not productive members of the learning community. This persistent problem of increasing numbers of students who are not succeeding in the classroom must be attacked because youth who fall on the margins are as deserving as those who thrive in the mainstream.

What is wrong with the following statements?

"LaMar is such a social and active child; if only he would calm down, talk less, and stay out of trouble, he would be a good student. He might be able to be a leader if only he would conform."

"Mai Lee is one of my brightest students, but she has priorities other than school. She belongs to a Hmong community dance group that appears to be her focus. She puts more effort into dancing and performing than into achieving in school."

"Hector shows some promise and wants to become a doctor. He'll never make it because his grades in math and science are less than desirable. He seldom comes to class, and when he does, he is not prepared. The other Hispanic kids seem to be struggling too."

"Thunder's performance is inconsistent. He makes a D as easily as he makes an A. His projects are excellent when he feels motivated, but he does poorly on tests and he seems lazy and uncooperative."

The told and untold stories of many culturally diverse students have not been positive when it comes to education. The above comments come in many guises. Teachers appear to recognize potential, promise, or untapped abilities in these students but are often frustrated by the student's behavior.

Self-esteem and self-concept issues, identity issues, the classroom climate, curriculum and instruction, teacher explanations, peer pressure and relationships, and family concerns inhibit students' motivation and achievement.

The common perception is that students would not have academic issues if they would "just try harder," "pay attention," and "listen." However, it is not that simple. Many culturally diverse students have had little or no early intervention and may lack the basic skills to take advantage of educational opportunities. Reversing underachievement may be especially difficult if it is related to social barriers, such as poverty; or to educational barriers, such as inappropriate curriculum and instruction.

Many of our culturally diverse students become "in-school dropouts" who are disillusioned or disenchanted with school, as reflected by poor motivation, lack of interest, boredom, daydreaming, acting out, tardiness, or truancy. Such students are psychologically distanced from school. Others physically reject schools, as reflected in high national dropout rates. Describing students as lazy, unmotivated, or not interested in school and learning fails to explain why some students flee, mentally and/or physically, from schools and otherwise resist learning opportunities. Focusing on students in isolation from the conditions of their life circumstances provides only a partial picture. This incomplete picture results in piecemeal, futile attempts at intervention.

The result of focusing on a child's perceived deficits, of blaming the victim, is that such students are considered less desirable, less salvageable than other students. Unfortunately, schools are unable to deal with students who deviate too much from the norm. Schools are made for students who are independent learners, those who excel, achieve, and fulfill the expectations of teachers and parents.

Students who underachieve are not born lazy or unmotivated. Many students *learn* to underachieve. For example, because of keen insight, an ability to note inconsistencies, and sensitivity to social injustices, many culturally diverse students are aware of the contradictions between their academic learning and their lived experiences. They grow critical and wary of the meritocratic ideology promoted in schools, and they are cognizant of race and class discrimination in schools and the larger society.

This constant feedback can demotivate culturally diverse students and wreak havoc on their desire to participate in a system perceived as unjust.

For decades educators and researchers have attempted to understand reasons for the high rate of academic failure among culturally diverse youth. Genetic characteristics, racial segregation and discrimination and/ or cultural deprivation were offered as explanations for low achievement. Some educators viewed the school as a panacea for bringing about educational equity; others viewed it as not making a difference.

In the late 1960s and early 1970s, the cultural-difference hypothesis was presented as an alternative explanation for low achievement. The hypothesis attributed poor academic performance to differences between children's home learning methods and environments and those of the school. School culture was alien and often conflicted with the home culture. Two questions kept surfacing: How do students from different cultures prefer to learn, and how do they demonstrate what they have learned?

During the 1980s, educators began looking outside the schools to historical factors that formed and shaped cultural responses to schools. School environment was examined in relationship to the groups' experiences. Language and cultural differences could no longer be ignored. Teachers needed to focus on the in-school factor that could be changed as they interacted with their students.

I believe that people perceive the world in different ways, learn about the world in different ways, and demonstrate what they have learned in different ways. The approach to learning and the demonstration of what one has learned are influenced by the norms, values, and socialization practices of the culture in which the individual has been acculturated.

◄ ►❊◄❊ ►

Writing a book is a little like putting a note in a bottle and casting it out to sea. You have no idea where or when it will land, who will receive it, or what impact it will have. You simply send it out with the hope that someone will read its message, and that one day you might receive a reply.

I put my message in this bottle not only to respond to commonly asked questions about cultural diversity but also to help you see how it impacts all of us. Many educators still look at cultural diversity and think of segregation, economic inequality, racial violence, and racism. A colleague pointed to his own racially mixed community as an example. "Here was a place," he said, "where people of color and white people lived together as neighbors and yet there was little meaningful interaction across racial lines; no dialogue was taking place. No one understood cultural diversity." Change was not happening. As Gandhi once said, we need to "be the change we want to see happen." We are the change agents we have been waiting for.

I spoke about an image of a person putting a note in a bottle. I would like you to now consider a different image.

A young girl was walking along a beach. To her amazement she came upon thousands of starfish. Washed ashore by a storm, the starfish were dying in the hot sun. The girl began to toss starfish back into the sea, one by one. After a while a man approached her. "Little girl," he asked, "why are you doing this? There are thousands of starfish on the beach. You cannot possibly hope to make a difference!" The girl was discouraged and dropped the starfish from her hand. But a moment later, she bent down, picked up the starfish once again, and tossed it as far as she could into the sea. She turned back to the man. Smiling brightly she said, "I made a difference to that one." Inspired, he joined her. A crowd had gathered, and soon others joined in. Before long, there were hundreds of people tossing starfish back into the sea and calling out, "I made a difference to that one!" After awhile the calls subsided. The girl looked up. To her amazement, she saw no starfish on the beach. Each one had been tossed back into the sea.

As the story so beautifully illustrates, each of us has the power to make a difference, and collectively we can create a more just and peaceful society that honors, accepts, and respects cultural diversity.

Educators all across the country, most of whom are white, are teaching in culturally diverse classrooms, daily observing identity development in process, and are without an important interpretive framework to help them understand what is happening in their interactions with students.

Daily news reports tell us of the rising racial tensions in the United States. As our nation becomes more diverse, we need to be able to communicate across social and ethnic lines, but we seem less and less able to do so. We must be aware of what it is like to be a white person or a person of color in a race-conscious society.

My Latino, Asian, American Indian, Arab, and biracial students have taught me that they have a developing sense of racial/ethnic identity, too, and that all of us need to see our experiences reflected back to us.

James Baldwin wrote in his 1981 book, *Go Tell It on the Mountain*, "Not everything that is faced can be changed. But nothing can be changed until it is faced" (p. 15). Cultural diversity is a huge part of our lives. We must face the need for constructive action and meaningful social change.

The impact of cultural diversity begins early. Even in our preschool years, we are exposed to misinformation about people different from ourselves. The early information we receive about "others"—people racially, religiously, or socioeconomically different from ourselves—seldom comes as a result of firsthand information or experience. The secondhand information we do receive has often been distorted, shaped by cultural stereotypes, and left incomplete. The stereotypes we are exposed to become the foundation for adult prejudices that so many of us have.

Sometimes the assumptions we make about others come, not from what we have been told or what we have seen on television or in books, but rather from what we have *not* been told. The historical information about people of color leads young and old to make assumptions that may go unchallenged for a long time.

Stereotypes, omissions, and distortions all contribute to the development of prejudice, a preconceived judgment or opinion usually based on limited information. We teach what we were taught. The unexamined prejudices of the parents are passed on to the children. We must interrupt this cycle. We need to acknowledge that an important part of interrupting the cycle is constant reeducation and sharing what we learn with the next generation.

Who am I? Who am I now? Who was I before? Who will I become? The answer depends on who the world around me says that I am. How am I represented in the cultural images around me?

This book was developed with multiple audiences in mind: educators, counselors, parents, administrators, researchers, and practitioners. It considers the collaborative roles that families, educators, peers, and students themselves must play in promoting the academic, psychological, and socioemotional well-being of culturally diverse students.

Educators have a moral and ethical responsibility to help all children reach their potential in school. No child should sit on the margins, feeling isolated from the rewards of educational challenge and learning. In addition, family-school collaboration is essential to students' academic success. Parents are the child's first teachers; teachers are the child's surrogate parents. Without family involvement, schools and children are less likely to succeed. Racially and culturally diverse students are at the greatest risk of being forgotten in our educational system.

Teachers and other school personnel must acknowledge and appreciate the changing demographics of students and respond by:

- Developing educational programs that are multicultural
- Changing curriculum and instruction to reflect and affirm diversity
- Understanding that racially and culturally diverse students have a number of battles to fight, including such social ills as poverty, racism, prejudice, and stereotypes that disrupt their motivation and inhibit equal and equitable learning opportunities
- Advocating for culturally diverse students

We must continue to be works in progress for a lifetime. We also need to study America's past from a comparative perspective. A broad range of groups has been selected: African Americans, Asian Americans, Hispanics, American Indians, Southeast Asians, new African immigrants, and Arab Americans. Together they help to explain general patterns in our society. Each has contributed to the making of the United States.

The purpose of this book is to provide current knowledge, practices, and beliefs that revolve around issues of diversity. We need to become aware of the needs, expectations, and rights of culturally diverse communities. Intolerance stems from lack of exposure to difference, and to fear. We need to confront intolerance based on stereotypes of youth and families who are culturally diverse. We can celebrate difference by providing an atmosphere where difference is nurtured rather than simply tolerated.

There is no universal formula for working with culturally diverse groups of people. Instead we must provide a framework in which we examine our own biases, attempt to confront them, and empower all concerned.

This book will explore the unique cultures of several groups of students. Who are the American Indian, African American, Hispanic/Latino American, Asian American, Hmong/Southeast Asian American, Arab

American, and the new African immigrants? What is there about their family, concepts of honor, and social life that make them unique? What are the implications for education? What are the goals, concepts, and instructional planning needed for a curriculum that improves school performance? These questions must be addressed if we are to inform and assist those who may be planning a program to answer the cry of culturally diverse youth.

Culturally diverse students are educationally disadvantaged, and their educational needs are not being met. These students are failing in school, and the schools are failing these students. We must explore their rich and varied cultures and accept them for who they are. We must see the person, not the color of their skin.

Some of the information presented in this book has been accumulated through 40 years of personal experience in the classroom and more recently as an administrator in the charter school arena. The information presented in this book includes both identified sources from other writers as well as my experiences and those of my colleagues.

Chapter One

Immigration: Shattered Dreams

The poorest, the most miserable came here because they had no future over there. To them, the streets of America were paved in gold. They had the American fever.

—Andy Johnson, an immigrant

Long before immigrants from other nations arrived on its shores, American Indians called the North American continent their home. Today, the majority of Americans trace their family origins to a country other than the United States. Many of our forebears came to this country seeking greater freedom or an opportunity for a better life. Some of us can trace our roots to ancestors who came against their will and were forced to provide the labor that helped build our nation. Whether they were the native inhabitants of this continent or came from distant shores, the citizens of the United States brought to this nation a pride in their heritage, and distinctive cultural traditions and values.

The United States has been characterized as a "melting pot" in which all ingredients blend into a single dish. Likewise, the United States has been characterized as a "salad bowl" in which each ingredient preserves its own flavor and texture while contributing to the aggregate salad. In a speech at Stanford University in June of 2001, former president Jimmy Carter said it best: "We become not a melting pot but a beautiful mosaic. Different people, different beliefs, different yearnings, different hopes, different dreams."

So, who is an "American"? How do you define an American? Does this definition matter? Why? How does the great cultural diversity of our population influence the life of our nation? How does commonality shape the nation? What are your questions?

1

Most of the population of the United States arrived here through immigration, but many people whose families have been here several generations don't know what it means to be an immigrant. They don't realize what it means to struggle for survival. Nearly half of the current population of the United States can trace their ancestors back to Ellis Island, the famous threshold of arrival in America, located in New York City's harbor. In the peak years of immigration, from 1900 to 1914, the Ellis Island immigration station processed five thousand people a day.

Now, both legal and illegal immigration are topics in the media as people from non-European countries arrive in increasing numbers.

Between 1820 and 1992, some 59,795,158 legal immigrants entered the United States. Most of them (37,400,991, or about 63%) were Europeans who belonged to many different religious, political, and cultural groups (U.S. Department of Justice, 1993).

The making of one society from so many different ethnic and national groups is one of the most amazing chapters in human history. Yet, social scientists, and therefore classroom teachers, have largely ignored the role of ethnicity in U.S. history and modern society. Educators and politicians have been preoccupied with theories of assimilation and the melting pot concept. A significant gap exists between cultural groups and the school curriculum.

Europeans began settling in America in significant numbers in the 1600s. The economic, social, and political conditions in Europe caused many of its inhabitants to cross the Atlantic searching for a new home. Most people were peasants who earned their living by farming. The peasants became landless or feared the loss of land and their place in the social order. They were attracted to the land. Without it, they were unable to make a living or maintain a sense of self.

The early settlers were a diverse group. Many were unable to pay for their passage and became indentured servants to make the journey. However, merchants, artisans, professionals, and laborers made up a small but significant part of the immigrants during the entire colonial period. Vagrants and convicts, who were unwanted by European nations, were also among the first settlers.

Once under way, the immigration movement produced forces that stimulated it. The letters settlers sent back to friends and relatives extolling the opportunities in America attracted more immigrants. Ship companies, eager to get passengers, and U.S. states and railroad companies who wanted to settle sparsely populated areas recruited even more immigrants. The rise of the industrial revolution and scientific farming also stimulated immigration to America.

Although all of these factors contributed to immigration, it was the search for a chance to earn a better living that caused most people to come to the United States. The tide of immigration rose and fell with economic conditions in America. Immigrants came for economic reasons.

Their passage from their homes to American port cities was hard and hazardous. The decision to leave their homes came after much thought. Often, only the threat of starvation or the loss of status compelled the immigrants to attempt the difficult journey.

The first step was to reach, usually by foot, a seaport city from which ships sailed to America. Many who made it to the port cities were tired and battered. Once there, they often had to wait weeks or months for a ship. The ship captains waited until the ships were full of goods and human cargo before they sailed. As each day went by during the long wait, the food the would-be immigrants had stored for the journey dwindled and funds were used to rent rooms.

Finally the day came when the ship sailed for America. The joy at the departure was short-lived. The conditions on board were depressing and harsh. To maximize his profits, the captain packed the people like sardines. Each family had an extremely small space and spent their time in these dark, crowded compartments. Diseases like dysentery, cholera, yellow fever, and smallpox were rampant on the vessels and took many lives. The families barely had enough food to last the journey.

The family structure was disrupted since the traditional role of the father as leader and master was not exercised owing to dependency on the crew. The transatlantic crossings severely strained family relationships.

The immigrants who survived the journey eventually landed at an American port city. The landing was eagerly awaited and celebrated. However, there were still more hurdles to overcome. They had to be checked and questioned by American immigration officials before they could travel freely in America. Wrong answers and poor health led to more questions, a stay in a hospital, or even a trip back to their home country. Early questions focused on the ability to work and on physical health. Later, questions relating to morals and political beliefs were added.

Many of the immigrants were broken both physically and financially when they walked off the boats. Some were the sole survivors of families who started out together. Broken and lonely, some found asylum in poorhouses. Many who had planned to settle elsewhere never left the port cities. Others traveled to, and then stayed in, cities like Milwaukee, Chicago, and St. Louis. Some found work on construction properties in the cities. Railroad construction and factory work became more available. The immigrants were paid low wages and were outrageously exploited by their employers. A few immigrants found their way west and became successful farmers or ranchers.

Urban ghettos developed in most of the larger cities. As the immigrants settled in these cities in the late 1800s, they found themselves living in blighted and dilapidated areas that became ethnic ghettos. When the upwardly mobile left the inner city, their old mansions were converted into multiple-family dwellings. Little was done to make these dwellings comfortable. Profit, not comfort, was what the slum landlord sought. When these neighborhoods were deserted by the old residents, they were also forsaken by the street cleaners and sanitation crews. The smells of garbage were pungent. The immigrants' habit of throwing garbage out of the windows made these communities even more unpleasant. Multistory apartments sprang up. These buildings were crowded and dirty. There were only two toilets on each floor in some buildings.

The immigrants lived for the day when their income would permit them to leave and join the exodus to the suburbs. As one ethnic group vacated the ghetto, another group moved in to replace it.

The early immigrant settlements were highly ethnically mixed. English, Scots-Irish, Germans, French Huguenots, Africans, and Jews were the earliest to arrive in America. Early in American colonial life, non-English groups began to be evaluated negatively. The New England colonies took steps to bar Roman Catholics. Scots-Irish and Germans were victims of English antagonism. The attitude that English culture was superior to all others profoundly shaped American life.

RACE AND THE IMMIGRANT EXPERIENCE

Race assumed a new meaning when the southern and eastern European groups attained acceptable levels of assimilation. All white ethnic groups became one. Racial hostilities now focused on nonwhite groups such as African Americans, Asian Americans, Mexican Americans, and American Indians. Who are some of these early immigrants of color?

The Africans

The colonists of the early 17th century recognized various degrees of freedom and servitude. The duties and rights varied from person to person corresponding to rank and position. The nobles, gentlemen, and merchants occupied places near the top, with yeomen, traders, and artisans below. Still further down were women, children, apprentices, and servants, all subject to the master of the house that they lived in.

By the end of the seventeenth century the white servant who worked for a term and then became free and equal was replaced by the black slave who was a chattel, bound for the whole of his life and whose servitude passed on to his children.

Slave trade soared and the shipment of black slaves became more cruel and merciless as they were crammed by the masses into ships, passengers destined for lifelong labor, cruel treatment, prejudice, and ridicule.

The Mexicans

The conquest of and annexation of the Mexican territory in 1848 by the United States created a situation in which people of Mexican ancestry became subject to white domination. Like African Americans and American Indians, Mexican Americans were initially incorporated into U.S. society against their will. It was the general feeling among white settlers that whites and Mexicans were never meant to live together. Segregated schools, segregated housing, and employment discrimination were the result.

The Chinese

Chinese immigration to the United States was first documented in the early 1700s. This was followed by large-scale immigration in the mid-1800s spurred by the gold rush of the 1840s. These first immigrants were well received by the Americans. The Chinese were wealthy, successful merchants and skilled artisans, fishermen, and hotel and restaurant owners renowned for their hard work. Shortly thereafter came a much larger group called "coolies," unskilled laborers usually working for little pay. The Chinese clustered into enclaves called Chinatowns. These enclaves were found nationwide. It is in these Chinatowns that the Chinese lived, worked, shopped, and socialized. They not only mined for gold but also took on jobs as cooks, peddlers, and storekeepers. They also took jobs that no one else wanted or that were considered too dirty. White prejudice and discrimination soon erupted.

The Japanese

The boom in the Hawaiian sugar industry in the 1870s and 1880s, in contrast to Japan's painful transition to a modern economy, which produced widespread unemployment, bankruptcies, and civil disorders, contributed to a much larger number of Japanese immigrants moving to Hawaii. After the takeover of the Hawaiian Islands by the United States, an even larger number of Japanese workers arrived on the shores of the continental United States. When they arrived, the Japanese gained their initial foothold in agriculture by working for lower wages than whites and then acquiring the land by paying more than whites were willing to pay.

On December 7, 1941, Japan's attack on Pearl Harbor was a traumatic landmark in the history of Japanese-American relations. After the attack, which occurred in the midst of peace talks, anti-Japanese feelings ran high, especially on the mainland. In Hawaii, where many Japanese Americans were killed, fewer than 1,500 were taken into custody as compared to over 100,000 who were interned on the mainland. The economic impact of this was devastating. Businesses built up over many years were liquidated in a matter of weeks with huge losses. Shattered careers were never resumed.

SUMMARY OF IMMIGRATION
IN THE UNITED STATES

Immigration Time Line

1492   Columbus sails from Spain and makes landfall somewhere in the Caribbean, "stumbling" onto present-day America.

1565	Spanish explorers arrive and establish the settlement of St. Augustine in present-day Florida.
1587	English settlers establish the first English settlement in America, the Roanoke Colony, in what is now North Carolina.
1620	Immigration to New England begins with the arrival of Pilgrims, who establish the Plymouth Colony in present-day Massachusetts.
1638–1683	Swedes, Dutch, and Germans arrive along with the first Jewish immigrants.
1700s	Immigrants arrive from Europe in scattered numbers.
1800s	Immigrants from Europe arrive in large numbers.
1862	First restriction on immigration, against the Chinese.
1891	The Immigration and Naturalization Service is created.
1892	Ellis Island opens as a screening station for incoming immigrants.
1921	An immigration quota system is introduced.
1948	The Displaced Persons Act is introduced, allowing people to immigrate if they are driven from their homes by disaster or war.
1990	The Immigration Act of 1990 sets an annual ceiling for the number of immigrants allowed to enter the United States each year.
1995	A maximum of 675,000 people are allowed to enter the United States each year. Preference is shown to the relatives of U.S. citizens, refugees, and people with skills needed in the United States. There is no limit on refugees and immediate family members of those immigrants coming to the country.

Reasons for Immigration

In the early years of settling America (1600–1830) immigrants arrived seeking political freedom, religious freedom, economic opportunities (better life, better job, and more money), family reunification, adventure, a new way of life, and sheer survival.

From 1830 to 1890 land was plentiful and cheap. Jobs were abundant owing to industrialization and urbanization. Political and religious freedom also remained important to many immigrants.

From 1890 to 1924, people arrived for religious freedom (Jewish families), employment opportunities (Italians and Asians), and to escape persecution (Russians). America was touted as the "land of opportunity."

From 1924 to the present the main reason for immigration has been economic opportunity. Professional people from the Philippines (doctors and nurses) and India (doctors, engineers, and scientists) were abundant. Wars, revolutions, and political unrest also brought immigrants from Bosnia, Ethiopia, Iraq, Rwanda, Vietnam, Somalia, and Liberia. Low wages, unemployment, poverty, and the communist takeover of Cuba in 1959 brought many others.

Today the largest groups of immigrants come from Mexico, the Philippines, Vietnam, the Dominican Republic, China, India, Cuba, El Salvador, Jamaica, Haiti, South Korea, and Ukraine. A new wave of Southeast Asians, Arabs, and Africans must also be acknowledged.

Many new arrivals first settle in a community made up of people from their native land or even native village. They keep their old customs and acquire limited knowledge of their new country's language, culture, and values. In time, many immigrants, especially the children, assimilate.

Keep in mind that most people find it very hard to uproot themselves from their native land, no matter what the circumstances, and move to a strange country. But, throughout history, countless millions of people have done so.

Methods of Transportation/Ports of Arrival

From the 1600s to 1830, African Americans came over on ships where they were wedged into holds so tightly that they could hardly move. Vessels of 100 to 200 tons often carried 400 to 500 African slaves, as well as the crew and the provisions. They were cooped up for weeks, lived on meager rations, and were deprived of fresh air. This caused many deaths among the captives.

From 1830 to 1890 most immigrants arrived through the port of New York City. The ships would leave passengers at wharves to fend for themselves. Some of the problems that these newcomers faced were posed by con men, thieves, and thugs. Eventually all immigrants passed through Ellis Island.

From 1890 to 1924 Angel Island in San Francisco and the piers of Seattle were ports for Asians arriving on our shores. Presently most arrive by plane at various entry points.

Process for Entering the United States

From 1607 to 1830, slaves or indentured servants were under the charge of a ship captain for the cost of their passage. Once in New York City or some other East Coast port city, slaves were sold and indentured servants had to work ten years to redeem themselves for their passage.

Prior to 1855 the immigrants were simply left at the wharf. The public feared the diseases many new immigrants brought, and they were ostracized by society in general. Castle Garden, in New York City, became an immigration receiving center so that the government could keep track of the newcomers. Clerks recorded the names, nationalities, and destinations of the immigrants. Physicians gave routine checkups and physical examinations to ensure that the immigrants were healthy.

From 1892 to 1924 all immigrants entered through Ellis Island or Angel Island. They were tested for diseases, had to have documents from their home country, had to be mentally fit, and had to be ready to adapt to life in the United States. This process continued throughout the 1930s, 1940s, and 1950s.

In 1962 all commercial flights from Cuba to the United States were suspended. Nonetheless, 50,000 Cubans entered between 1962 and 1965. Most Cubans sailed secretly from Cuba in small boats. Between 1966 and 1973 the United States and the Cuban government set up an airlift between Cuba and Miami that brought 250,000 Cubans into the United States. Until 1994 the United States welcomed Cuban immigrants as victims of an oppressive regime. In 1994 thousands of Cubans set sail for southern Florida on small boats and rafts to escape oppression and poverty in Cuba. Soon after the influx began, President Clinton announced that the United States would not accept any more refugees. This policy was designed to avoid the cost of settling large numbers of refugees in Florida.

After the Vietnam War ended, a huge influx of refugees once again arrived from Southeast Asia and continues to this day.

Destinations/Places Where Immigrants Settled

From the 1600s to the 1890s European immigrants settled in frontier areas and became farmers or ranchers. Cargoes of African slaves were sent to Virginia, the Carolinas, Georgia, and Maryland. The development of the plantation system created a demand for slave labor. Other immigrants remained in the ports where they arrived. Most were too poor to move inland. By 1950, the Irish made up more than half the population of Boston and New York City.

From 1890 to 1924 immigrants settled in Chicago, Cleveland, Detroit, New York City, and Milwaukee. Presently nearly two-thirds of all Cuban Americans live in Miami. Chinese and Japanese still settle on the West Coast or in Hawaii. Many Southeast Asians have settled in St. Paul, Minnesota; Seattle; and various California cities. The Arab newcomers settled around Detroit and more recently in Minneapolis–St. Paul.

Treatment/Reception by Other Americans

From the 1600s to 1860 African slaves were not treated as equals and often were not even treated like human beings. European whites were settling the country and setting the trend.

From 1830 to 1890 the Irish, in their large numbers, were looked upon as a drain on society. They took jobs away from the general public. Many help-wanted ads included the phrase "Irish need not apply."

From 1890 to 1924 immigrant groups formed their own communities and stayed close to each other because of lack of respect from established Americans.

From the 1930s to the present, immigrants have been willing to work for virtually nothing, and therefore have been said to be taking jobs away from average Americans who were, and are, unwilling to work for such low fees. Also, most early immigrants who came here wanted to assimilate as quickly as possible. They wanted to become American, whatever that meant. It was difficult for Asians to assimilate, and therefore they were discriminated against in many areas. They were paid one-third less than whites. They spent 11-hour working days in sweat shops with horrible conditions. During the late 1800s and the early 1900s, the Chinese would work harder for less and formed their own businesses while white American businesses were unable to compete.

Opportunities for Success

African slaves had no opportunities for education or social mobility. Industrialization caused people to leave agriculture and gravitate toward work in industry. After the Civil War, immigrants were enlisted in what became known as the American industrial army. The Homestead Act of 1862 has been called one of the most important pieces of legislation in the history of the United States. This act turned over vast amounts of the public domain to private citizens. An estimated 10% of U.S. land was claimed and settled under this act. A homesteader only had to be the head of a household and at least 21 years of age to claim a 160-acre parcel of land. Settlers from all walks of life, including newly arrived immigrants, farmers without land of their own from the East, single women, and former slaves, came to meet the challenge of developing this free land. The result was westward movement.

From 1890 to 1924 employment was available in grocery stores, dry-cleaning shops, newsstands, machine shops, and the garment industry. The living conditions were poor and the immigrants lived in slum dwellings. Children received an education, parents and elders received none. Racism took over, and social mobility was nonexistent. Most immigrants had little or no political representation.

From 1968 to the present immigrants have the same opportunity as do native-born Americans to find work. Many day laborers who do not speak English are still able to work for English-speaking business/construction owners, and others find work in their cultural communities.

Assimilation? To What Degree?

Many African Americans in the United States have ancestors who were slaves. They were possessions. They had no choice but to assimilate into American culture. They did not have a chance to go back to Africa, and generations later, when they did have the chance, most were so firmly rooted in American society that they had no desire to do so.

Those immigrants who found it difficult to assimilate were discriminated against because of their culture and traditions. Many immigrants were able to preserve some of their culture and still become Americanized. Other immigrants turned their backs on their own culture and became fully Americanized.

Legal Versus Illegal Immigration and Laws Restricting Immigration

No laws were in place restricting immigration until 1862 when a law restricting Chinese immigration was passed. The Chinese Exclusion Act suspended the entry of Chinese laborers. A law was passed in 1875 prohibiting prostitutes and felons from entering the United States. In the 1880s laws were passed enacting restrictions for those mentally ill or insane, the mentally handicapped, and people who needed public assistance and care. In the 1890s convicts, polygamists, and people suffering from diseases of any sort were excluded. The early 1900s brought quotas affecting Asians, Russians, Middle Easterners, and Pacific Islanders. "America must be kept American," said President Calvin Coolidge when he signed the Immigration Quota Law in 1924.

Laws are pending that will continue to restrict legal immigrants for years to come. Under some of these pending proposals, parents, adult children, and brothers and sisters of U.S. citizens could no longer immigrate at all. Spouses and children of lawful, permanent residents would be limited to 10,000 visas per year. Refugees would be barred in all but extraordinary circumstances. Illegal immigrants would be jailed, prosecuted, and deported.

CURRENT TRENDS

America's changing ethnic and racial makeup will profoundly transform the nation's regional landscape for the next few decades. What looks like a diversified melting pot at the national level takes on a dramatically different look if you zoom in on specific regions and metropolitan areas. Immigrants are settling in New York City, Los Angeles, San Francisco, Chicago, Miami, Washington, D.C., Dallas–Fort Worth, and Minneapolis–St. Paul. For example, a new wave of immigrants is arriving in Minneapolis–St. Paul. Fifteen thousand Southeast Asian refugees, mostly Hmong, still living in a Thai camp, have a shot at U.S. resettlement. While the past waves of Hmong refugees received most of their support through social service agencies, this next wave will depend heavily on relatives, many of whom are struggling to make ends meet. American relatives worry about having more mouths to feed. Sometimes only one family member is working.

Those who come to Minnesota and other states will not find churches as their main benefactors as earlier refugees did. Instead relatives will give the newcomers a place to live, drive them to get medical checkups, enroll the children in school, and make sure they have access to social services and job training.

Each refugee will get $400 in federal money to buy food and clothing. Like their predecessors, the newest arrivals will also be eligible to apply for welfare benefits that now include work-participation requirements (*Minneapolis Star Tribune*, March 2004). The refugees' transition to a new culture will be full of challenges, including language barriers, financial worries, and general culture shock. The schools will be a critical element in helping these and all immigrants in the coming years.

Diverging migration patterns have unevenly distributed racial and ethnic diversity in America's regions. New Mexico, Hawaii, and California stand out as the nation's first states with a nonwhite majority. At the same time, in 15 states culturally diverse groups account for less than 15% of the population.

Arriving immigrants tend to cluster geographically because destination communities provide them with a comfort zone of familiarity. Ethnic enclaves in New York City and Los Angeles contain already established institutions (churches, community centers, stores, neighbors) that make new arrivals feel at home and give them social and economic support. Hispanic immigrants are flocking to Texas, California, Florida, New York, Illinois, and New Jersey. Asian patterns are similar, with new arrivals also going to California, New York, Illinois, Texas, and Washington, D.C. Recent racial and ethnic immigrant patterns show that America has a long way to go before it becomes a coast-to-coast melting pot, with racial and ethnic groups spread evenly across the land.

We can also look at immigration in terms of racism. Globalization not only has created enormous economic hardships through the increasing gap between the so-called Third World and the First World, but it has also given rise to unprecedented immigration. In the past few years, for the first time in history, more than 100 million people immigrated to different parts of the world. This exponential growth in immigration has given rise to a dramatic increase in racism. In France, the ultraright National Front Party has unleashed an incessant attack on immigrants, especially Muslims from the former French colonies. In Germany, there has been a significant increase in neo-Nazi groups that have been responsible for many bomb attacks against Turks and Greeks. In the United States we are witnessing manifestations of racism that range from referenda in California, Arizona, and Massachusetts making it a crime to teach content areas in a language other than English, to the present assault on affirmative action.

English teachers (sometimes unknowingly) are complicit with structures of racism in their eagerness to "save" students from their non-English-speaking status. In other words, English teachers need to understand that while the acquisition of English can empower non-English-speakers, it can also become a weapon that can shame, humiliate, and colonize.

Racism and power intertwine at every level of social interaction, from the classroom to the job site, from the streets to the corridors of government. An understanding of racism helps us comprehend how power functions and reveals embedded hierarchies of privilege that limit the life chances of so many. Ultimately, racism limits the democratic potential that is the core promise of American life. We tend to forget what Franklin D. Roosevelt said during a state of the union speech in 1936: "Remember, remember always, that all of us are descended from immigrants."

IMMIGRATION: THE STORIES
OF THE PEOPLE

The inscription on the Statue of Liberty reads:

> Give me your tired, your poor
> Your huddled masses yearning to breathe free,
> The wretched refuse of your teeming shore.
> Send these, the homeless, tempest-tossed, to me:
> I lift my lamp beside the golden door. (Emma Lazarus)

When I came to the United States for the first time it was very hard for me to cross the border. I spent two weeks in Tijuana trying to cross. I finally was allowed into the United States, got my resident card, and hope to get my citizenship soon. I have a job and am studying to get a better job to support my family. I still miss Mexico, but here is better. (Remigio)

My name is Tina Duong. I come from Vietnam. I came from a big house and my family lived together and owned a business. After 1975 we fled to Malaysia by boat. We lived in a refugee camp for two years where we were always hungry. We did not have enough rice or meat and vegetables. Two of my children died because we had no medicine. Finally, we were sponsored to come to the United States. We spent an additional six months in the Philippines to study English. Once in America we had more problems. I could not use the oven, turn on the faucet, and shower or vacuum the floor because I had never seen these things. I overcame the tough times and learned. I succeeded in life. (Tina)

My name is Linda Thong. I was born in Laos. My father died in the war. After the war I fled to Thailand on a boat so small it could barely hold the 55 people on it. We went for nine days with no food, was set upon by pirates who stole our jewelry and clothes and raped the women. I was lucky because my short hair and loose clothing made me look like a man. They took my daughter and threw her into the sea. I could not save her. We finally made it to Thailand. From there we came to the United States where we had no clothes or money and slept on the floor for three months. We found an apartment with one bedroom for nine people. My husband and I finally save $5,000 to start a small business. I thank God very very much for my family have freedom. (Linda)

My name is Long Vang and I was born in Laos. My father was shot by the Communists as I was forced to watch. I ran and joined people who lived in the mountains and fought for freedom. We fought one day and ate the next. My gun was my only friend. I was 12 years old. I left the mountains and found the Mekong River. I cut a tree and built a small boat just for me. The Thai soldiers found me and took me to a camp where I lived for five years. I never thought to come to America. I wanted to go back home. Finally I realized that I could never go home. I came to America. I have found a new home. (Long Vang)

I was born in Somalia. I was traumatized by the lack of food, draught, no water, and wars. I escaped to the United States and I still was scared. I could not find a job or a place to live. I stayed on the streets finding food in the garbage cans behind stores. Then someone took me in and helped me to live again. I am in school and struggling to learn English. I will make it. My life is changing. I will never go back. (Hihib)

Let's not close the doors to America. Unless you've had to flee your home because of civil war, or poverty, or because it is not safe where you live, you can't know what it is like. You would try to run away, too, if it meant a better life for your family. (Palestinian immigrant)

Immigrants remain distinct because of cultural differences and the circumstances under which they arrived here. Our newest immigrants, the Hmong, are viewed as a model. Considered backward hill people in their home territory, Minnesota's Hmong transplants have excelled at organizing, particularly on the political front. Two Hmong Minnesota legislators are younger than 35. The groups currently arriving from a Thailand refugee camp are stepping into a built-in support network. Many are refugees of war who are eager to learn, trusting, industrious, worried, unsettled, and hardworking people who need a place to heal. Because of their status as refugees and American allies during the Vietnam War, many are embraced with open arms.

However, for most Somalis, also legal refugees, the echo of the 1993 U.S. raid on Somalia, followed by the attacks of 9/11 and increased suspicion toward Islam, has made their reception less warm.

Hispanics from Mexico, Central America, and South America have the longest history of migration to the United States. In some areas, families can count back four or five generations to their immigrant ancestors. More recent Hispanic arrivals include many undocumented workers (known to many by the more negative term "illegal aliens").

The strength each of the immigrant groups brings to this country is their abiding loyalty to their ethnicity and culture. In turn, the fabric of American life has been enriched and strengthened by our immigrant population.

Chapter Two

A History of Multicultural America

That our songs are different is nowhere near as important as the fact that we have a song to sing.

—Frank Siccone

What happens when someone with the authority of a teacher describes our society and "you are not in it"? Such an experience can be disorienting, a moment of psychic disequilibrium, as if you looked in a mirror and saw nothing.

Through their narratives about their lives and circumstances, the people of America's diverse groups are able to see themselves and each other in our common past. They celebrate a society unique in the world because the world is a place where cultures crisscross.

Much of America's past has been riddled with racism. At the same time, culturally diverse students offer hope as they deconstruct and reinterpret the messages that are sent to them through the media, affirming the struggle for equality as a central theme in America's history.

At its conception, our nation was dedicated to the proposition of equality. What has given concreteness to this powerful national principle has been our coming together in the conception of the United States. "Stuck here" together, people of different backgrounds have attempted to get along with each other.

People harvesting
Work together unaware
Of social problems

wrote a Japanese immigrant describing a lesson learned by Mexican and Asian farm laborers in California (Reed, 1988, p. 497).

How do we see our prospects for working out America's cultural diversity crisis? Do we see it as through a clouded glass? The twisted images of racial hatred that riveted us in 1992 during the days of rage in Los Angeles still frame our future. Will we be able to connect ourselves? History, a look at our past, will help. Whatever happens, we can be certain that much of our society's future will be influenced by the choice of the mirror in which we choose to see ourselves. America does not belong to one race or one group. Americans have been constantly redefining their national identity from the moment of first contact in St. Augustine in 1565 and later on the Virginia shore. We must understand and appreciate our racial and cultural diversity. To do this we need to review the story of our coming together to create a new society in America. Can we forget the past and get on with the future? You'd have to be illiterate not to know that American Indians and blacks got a really bad deal historically. The Chinese, Japanese, Mexicans, and, yes, the Irish and Italians weren't met by the welcome wagon when they got off the boat, either. Everyone has had to fight for fair treatment, and the fighting is not over.

The story of the past can provide collective self-knowledge. Let us now take a walk through our culturally diverse past.

AFRICAN AMERICANS: A VIEW FROM THE CABINS

African Americans have been the central minority throughout our country's history. They were initially brought here on a slave ship in 1619. Actually, the first 20 Africans might not have been slaves; like most of the white laborers, they were probably indentured servants. How and when was it decided to institute a system of bonded black labor? What happened was conditioned by class conflicts within white society. Once established, slavery would have consequences for centuries to come. During the 19th century, the political storm almost destroyed the nation.

Since the Civil War and emancipation, race has continued to be promoted by some whites in relation to African Americans, segregation, civil rights, the underclass, and affirmative action. The struggle of African Americans has been a constant reminder of America's moral vision as a country committed to the principle of liberty.

Martin Luther King Jr. clearly understood this when he wrote from a jail cell, "We will reach the goal of freedom in Birmingham and all over the nation, because the goal of America is freedom. Abused and scorned through we may be, our destiny is tied up with America's destiny" (King, 1964, pp. 92–93).

Let us take a closer look at our African American history. What struck the Europeans most about Africans was their color. "These people are all black, and are called Negroes, without any apparel, saving before their privates," wrote an English traveler during his visit to Cape Verde in the 1560s. In the European mind, the color black was freighted with an array of negative images: deeply stained with dirt, foul, dark or deadly in purpose, malignant, sinister, wicked. The color white, on the other hand, signified purity, innocence, and goodness.

Scenario: After he had been captured he was marched to the seacoast. "The first object which saluted my eyes when I arrived was the sea, and a slave ship, which was riding at anchor, and waiting for its cargo. I was filled with astonishment, which soon became terror. Their complexions, differing so much from ours, their long hair, and the language they spoke confirmed my belief that I was in a world of evil spirits. As I looked around I saw a multitude of black people of every description, chained together, expressing horror and anguish. I was put down under the decks and the stench made me ill. I could not eat. I heard bitter cries night after night. I was beaten for no reason. When we landed I was told we were not to be eaten by our captors as we had believed, but were to work." (Sithoff, 1978)

Africans were degraded into a condition of servitude for life and even given the status of property. In 1661, the Virginia Assembly defined a slave as property, a part of an owner's estate.

Thomas Jefferson supported the broadening of landownership for he believed it provided the basis of social and political stability. Jefferson felt ambivalent toward slavery and recommended its gradual abolition. Slavery had to be abolished, Jefferson argued, but when freed, blacks would have to be removed from American society. This had to be done as soon as possible because slaves already comprised nearly half of Virginia's population.

But how could a million and a half slaves be expatriated? To send them

away all at once would not be "practicable." Jefferson suggested deport-
ing the future generation: black infants would be taken from their mothers
and trained for occupations until they reached the proper age for deporta-
tion. Jefferson suggested that slave children be shipped to the independent
black nation of Santo Domingo. He was confident the effects of this plan
would be "blessed." Needless to say, Jefferson's idea was widely challenged.

Jefferson believed in black intellectual inferiority. He believed in white
racial purity. White landowners reported that slavery enabled planters to
develop a disfranchised and unarmed black workforce. Slavery was to
remain. Driven by immediate economic interests and blinded by a short-
term horizon, the planters had not carefully thought through what they
were doing to black people as well as to American society and future generations.

Unlike Indians, blacks were not outside white society's "borders";
rather, they were within what James Madison called the "bosom" of the
republic, living in northern ghettos and on southern plantations. Freedom
in northern society was only a façade for the reality of caste. Blacks were
allowed to receive only minimum wages for menial jobs. Everywhere in
the North, blacks experienced discrimination and segregation. Transportation facilities were often segregated. In Philadelphia, blacks were allowed
to ride only on the front platforms of streetcars, and in New York City,
separate buses for blacks were used. Told that their presence in residential
districts would lower property values, blacks found themselves trapped in
squalid slums.

Blacks were restricted in their right to vote. They suffered from attacks
led by white workers. Victims of discrimination, segregation, and violence, blacks in the North encountered a powerful cluster of negative
racial images. Blacks were denounced as "immature," "insolent," and
"good for nothing."

While northern whites generally viewed blacks as childish and mentally deficient, they also saw them as threats to racial purity. This led some
states (Indiana and Illinois were the first) to prohibit interracial marriages.
Fear of interracial unions stirred demands for segregated schools. The
Indiana Senate agreed that the "Negro race" was inferior and that the
admission of Negro children into the public schools would bring the white
children down. The North, for the blacks, was not the Promised Land.

Meanwhile, in 1860, 4 million blacks were slaves, representing 35% of the total population of slave states. To manage this enslaved force, masters used various methods of discipline and control. Power had to be based on fear. Masters tried to brainwash their slaves into believing they were racially inferior and racially suited for bondage. The blacks, however, were ready to break for freedom.

The black women especially wanted to escape the confines of the plantation, for they had experienced bondage in different ways than men. Slave women were viewed as "breeders," and the laws allowed masters to separate slave children from their mothers and sell them.

As slaves, many women found that more than their labor and their children were appropriated: their bodies were regarded as property to be used to satisfy the erotic desires of their masters. Women were not only whipped and mutilated, they were also raped. Sexual exploitation of enslaved women was widespread in the South. The presence of a large mulatto population stood as vivid proof and a constant reminder of such sexual abuse.

As the Civil War raged around the African race, African Americans realized that deliverance from slavery was to come from the barrel of a gun. What blacks wanted most of all, more than education and voting rights, was economic power. The blacks viewed landownership as power. Their demand for land, they argued, was reasonable and just. They had already paid for the land through a life of tears and groans, under the lash and yoke of tyranny.

Though the Civil War led to the destruction of slavery, blacks in the South found themselves transformed from "property" to freedmen. No longer slaves, they became wage earners or sharecroppers, working the land of their former masters in exchange for part of the crop. Forced to buy goods from the plantation store, they were trapped in a vicious economic cycle, making barely enough money to pay off their debt. Most sharecroppers, in fact, were permanently in debt; the system wasn't designed to allow the debt ever to be repaid.

Signs of progress became evident in the rise of cities and the proliferation of factories. Blacks became an important source of industrial labor. Blacks were urged to get an education, not just "book learning" but a practical education. Industrial training was the path to economic independence and racial equality. Despite good intentions, by the end of the 19th century, the progress for blacks was distressingly slow. Racial borders had been reinforced by class and caste.

An exodus from the South was under way. The African American population in the large cities of the North and West reported a steady stream of new people from the southern states. From 1910 to 1920, the black population jumped from 5,000 to 40,800 in Detroit; 8,400 to 34,000 in Cleveland; 44,000 to 109,000 in Chicago; and 91,700 to 152,400 in New York City (Takaki, 1993).

All over the South, blacks found themselves swept up in the migration "fever." They were driven by particular pushes. After emancipation, most blacks had been forced to become sharecroppers or tenant farmers. Though they were free, many were in economic bondage. Their economic situation became dire as floods destroyed their farms and insects ravaged their cotton crops.

In the midst of this a new generation of blacks was coming of age. African Americans born after the Civil War were unwilling to stay on the plantations as servile laborers. The younger class was discontent and wanted to roam. Tired of the South, these young blacks wanted to escape racial violence. (For every lynching that took place, a score of blacks left for the cities.)

Free from the shadow of slavery, young blacks were able to imagine new possibilities in the North. By 1930, some 2 million blacks had migrated to the cities of the North and changed the course of history. This migration is probably, next to emancipation, the most noteworthy event that has ever happened to African Americans.

As the southern blacks traveled to the North, they gave their migration religious meaning. They spoke excitedly about the "flight out of Egypt"; they were "bound for the Promised Land" and "going into Canaan."

The black migration to the northern and western cities sparked an explosion of white resistance. The newspapers depicted the newcomers as shiftless and lazy. Determined to repel this invasion, hundreds of white residents formed Improvement Protective Clubs. The districts that are now white must remain white, these clubs declared. Meanwhile, the schools had become racial battlegrounds. The workplace became a terrain of competition and conflict. White gangs attacked blacks in the streets and in the parks.

African Americans began to fight back through black solidarity and ethnic enterprise. Black political and business leaders advised blacks to turn inward and develop their own communities. They were encouraged to establish their own banks, insurance companies, stores, and churches. Chicago was the "Black Metropolis" and New York City was the home of Harlem, "the Negro capital of the world." Harlem was the home of more than two-thirds of all blacks living in Manhattan, the largest colony of blacks outside Africa. Black folk culture was important. The "New Blacks" would become artists, poets, musicians, and workers.

The Great Depression destroyed much of what was built in the 1920s. Blacks fell into deeper poverty everywhere, in the South as well as the North. Their livelihoods crumbled along with the stock market. Cotton dropped from 18 cents per pound in 1929 to 6 cents in 1933. Blacks moving to cities in search of work encountered angry unemployed whites. By 1933 more than 50% of all blacks were unemployed (Wolters, 1970).

The New Deal seemed to offer little relief to blacks. Federal programs designed to provide a safety net for people in distress forced blacks to take a backseat. The Agricultural Adjustment Administration offered white farmers and workers higher rates of support than their black counterparts. The National Recovery Administration failed to protect black workers from discrimination in employment and wages. Black workers felt that their government had betrayed them.

Along came the politicians. Seeking to attract black votes, New Deal policy makers were beginning to address the needs of blacks. The Works Progress Administration mandated no discrimination on account of race, creed, or color. The massive migration of blacks to northern cities led to a national political realignment. Increasingly, they became an important force in the northern states that possessed a large number of electoral votes. In the 1936 presidential election, over three-fourths of northern blacks voted for Franklin Delano Roosevelt, who had been promoted among them as the second "Emancipator" (Sithoff, 1978, p. 76). Blacks were becoming major players in a newly emerging Democratic coalition.

World War II was the transition to the civil rights revolution. The defense of democracy abroad stirred demands for racial justice at home. With peace came new challenges against discrimination and inequality. The winds of democracy began sweeping through American political institutions, especially the courts. The grave wrong that blacks were seeking to have redressed was segregation. In the *Brown v. Board of Education*

(1954) decision, the U.S. Supreme Court declared that segregated schools were unconstitutional. Segregation was a denial of the equal protection of the law. The decision was hailed as a significant assault on the barriers of racial segregation and a powerful affirmation of America's principle of freedom.

However, integration remained largely a court ruling on paper while segregation persisted as a reality in society. A year after the *Brown* decision blacks shifted the focus of their struggle from the courts to the community. What would turn out to be a momentous stirring for racial justice began on December 1, 1955, when a 42-year-old black seamstress boarded a bus in Montgomery, Alabama. Tired from working all day at a department store, Rosa Parks sat down in the first seat behind the section reserved for whites. City law stipulated that the first four rows were reserved for whites, and that if whites filled up their section, blacks would have to move to make more room should that be needed. The bus became full. The driver ordered Parks to stand up so that a white man could sit down. She refused. Rosa Parks was arrested, which led to an explosive protest, the Montgomery bus boycott. Although blacks were dependent on the buses to get to and from work, thousands refused to ride them. They shared rides, rode in black-owned taxis, and walked. "My feets is tired," a woman said, "but my soul is rested." Another walker, an elderly woman, explained, "I'm not walking for myself. I'm walking for my children and my grandchildren." This dramatic protest ushered in the civil rights movement (Sithoff, 1981, pp. 41–42).

A young black minister found himself suddenly catapulted into the leadership of the struggle. Martin Luther King Jr. gave voice to black frustration. King fused together the Christian command to "love your enemies" and Mahatma Gandhi's tactic of nonviolence. After Montgomery came other actions. Sit-ins of black students at the Woolworth's lunch counter in Greensboro, North Carolina, in 1960 ushered in "freedom rides," acts of civil disobedience by blacks and whites to integrate interstate buses and bus terminals.

The nation watched as television cameras filmed freedom riders being yanked from the buses and brutally beaten by racist white mobs. The famous March on Washington at which King delivered the equally famous "I Have a Dream" speech took place in 1963.

The civil rights revolution, however, was unable to correct the structural economic foundations of racial inequality. While laws and court orders prohibited discrimination, they failed to abolish poverty among blacks. African Americans had won the right to sit at a lunch counter and order a hamburger, but many of them did not have the money to pay for their meal.

Next came the long hot summer of 1965. The firebombs of the Los Angeles neighborhood of Watts blasted the civil rights movement into a new phase. The limelight now shone on Malcolm X. Growing up in the ghettos of the North, he had pursued a life of drugs and crime. His high school had been the black ghetto of Roxbury in Boston and his college, the streets of Harlem. As a leader of the Black Muslims, Malcolm X advocated a separatist ideology and mocked King for his belief in integration as well as his strategy of nonviolence. Malcolm X advised blacks to use violence to defend their rights.

Between 1970 and 1980 there emerged what has been called a "black underclass." There was a persistence of intergenerational poverty, increasing unemployment, and the dramatic rise of black female–headed households. Families were being pushed onto welfare rolls. Survival was difficult. The need to educate black youth and prepare them to enter the workforce suddenly became an urgent issue during the 1990s. People needed to take off their rose-colored glasses and take a hard look at what they had been doing. "A riot," Martin Luther King asserted, "is the language of the unheard."

What happens when there are no dreams? American society has the opportunity to change. Let's shift our resources to promote economic expansion and alternative education programs that aid all students. Let's learn from our past.

ASIAN AMERICANS

Asian Americans have been here for over 150 years, before many European immigrant groups. But as "strangers" coming from a "different shore," they have been stereotyped as "heathen," exotic, and unassimilable. The Chinese arrived first, and what happened to them influenced the reception of the Japanese, Koreans, Filipinos, and Southeast Asian refugees like the Vietnamese and the Hmong. The 1882 Chinese Exclusion

Act was the first law that prohibited the entry of immigrants on the basis of nationality. This precedent later provided a basis for the restriction of European immigrant groups such as the Italians, Russians, Poles, and Greeks.

The Japanese painfully discovered that their accomplishments in America did not lead to acceptance. During World War II, unlike Italian Americans and German Americans, they were placed in internment camps. Two-thirds of the Japanese in those camps were U.S. citizens by birth (Takaki, 1993).

"How could I as a six-month-old child born in this country be declared by my own government to be an enemy alien?" asked Congressman Robert Matsui, in a speech in the House of Representatives on September 17, 1987 (Matsui, 1987, p. 105).

Today, Asian Americans are the fastest-growing ethnic group in America. They have also become the focus of much media attention as "the model minority" because of their academic and economic success. Two major Asian groups, the Chinese and the Japanese, are reflected in our historical past and will be reviewed in this section.

The Chinese: Strangers from a Pacific Shore
Searching for Gold Mountain

The war against Mexico reflected America's quest for expansion to the Pacific Coast. The movement toward the Pacific Coast became a part of America's destiny. As whites migrated westward they were destroying savagery. As civilization advanced, the "capitol" had replaced the "wigwam," Christians had replaced "savages," and white matrons had replaced "red squaws." The western wilderness came to life.

The annexation of California led not only to American expansion toward Asia but also to the migration of Asians to America. Policy makers in the mid-1800s proposed that Chinese laborers should be imported to build the transcontinental railroad as well as bring the fertile lands of California under cultivation. They believed that no people in all the East were so well adapted for clearing wild lands and raising every species of agricultural product as the Chinese.

Pioneers from Asia, Chinese merchants began to arrive in America. However, they came for their own reasons. Many sought sanctuary from adverse conditions in China caused by the British Opium Wars. Many Chinese were also fleeing from the turmoil of peasant rebellions against foreigners in China over possession of the fertile Yangtze Delta. Harsh economic conditions also drove Chinese migrants to seek survival in America. High taxes caused many peasant farmers to lose their lands. Floods during the 1850s intensified the suffering. Behind the emigrating spirit was the fear of starvation.

The migrants entering the United States were mostly men, planning to work away from home temporarily. They were illiterate or had very limited schooling, but they dreamed of new possibilities inspired by stories of "gold hills." To these hopeful migrants, America possessed an alluring boundlessness, promising not only gold but also opportunities for employment. In the port cities of China, circulars distributed by labor brokers announced that Americans wanted the Chinese to come and would make them welcome. They would receive enormous pay, large houses, food, and clothing. Chinese who returned to their villages with money in their pockets reinforced the excitement about emigration.

Contrary to the popular stereotype and myth, the Chinese migrants were not forced laborers who had been kidnapped or pressed into service by coercion and shipped to a foreign country. They came to America as free laborers who paid their own way.

Workers left China by the thousands. Three hundred and twenty-five migrants joined the Forty-Niners rushing to California to search for gold. A year later, 450 more Chinese arrived in California. They came in greatly increasing numbers: 2,716 in 1851 and 20,026 in 1852. By 1870 there were 63,000 Chinese in the United States. Most of them, 77%, were living in California. The remainder went elsewhere in the West as well as the Southwest, New England, and the South. By 1930, about 400,000 Chinese had made the Pacific crossing to America (Takaki, 1993).

Most of the Chinese worked in the California mines as independent prospectors or worked on the railroad. They were hired by the Central Pacific Railroad to help lay tracks for the transcontinental line leading east from Sacramento. The immigrant laborers were praised by company president Leland Stanford as quiet, peaceable, industrious, economical, and ready and apt to learn the railroad-building business. Stanford also said that the Chinese were nearly equal to white men in the amount of labor they performed and were much more reliable. The savings derived from the employment of Chinese rather than white workers were enormous.

After the Chinese workers were released by the Central Pacific Railroad in 1869, thousands of them went to San Francisco, where they formed an urban Chinese community. In 1860, 2,719 Chinese resided in San Francisco; ten years later the population soared to 12,022, a 343% increase. The Chinese worked in the city's four key industries: boot and shoe, woolens, cigar and tobacco, and sewing.

Meanwhile, in rural regions, the Chinese were helping to develop California's agriculture industry. They helped transform farming in California from wheat to fruit. The Chinese shared their agricultural knowledge with their white employers, teaching them how to plant, cultivate, and harvest orchard and garden crops. They constructed networks of irrigation canals and miles of dikes and ditches. They drained the swamps and transformed the marshes into agricultural havens.

Even though the Chinese were paid low wages, they became targets of white labor resentment, especially during hard times. White men and women who desired employment began quiet protests against vineyards and packing companies that employed Chinese in preference to whites. Their protests soon became violent as economic depression led to anti-Chinese riots by unemployed white workers. Chinese men were beaten and shot. Many were loaded onto trains and shipped out of town. This ethnic antagonism in the mines, factories, and fields forced thousands of Chinese into self-employment, especially in garment stores, restaurants, and laundries.

The Chinese laundryman was an American phenomenon. He did not learn his trade in China. There were no laundries in China (Chin, 1968). These laundrymen were taught by American women.

Why did Chinese men in America enter into this line of work? Unlike the retail or restaurant businesses, a laundry could be opened with a small capital outlay. The requirements were minimal: a stove, trough, drying room, sleeping apartment, and a sign. A Chinese laundryman did not need to speak much English to operate his business.

The Chinese were considered racially inferior. They found that racial qualities previously assigned to blacks had become Chinese characteristics. Like blacks, the Chinese were described as heathens, morally inferior, savage, childlike, and lustful. Chinese women—what few there were in the earlier days—were condemned as depraved and immoral because of their physical appearance—the fact that they wore makeup, similar to a geisha, and wore a dress with the leg slit. Like blacks, Chinese men were viewed as threats to white racial purity.

Originally, Chinese immigrants lived in a virtually womanless world. In 1852, of the 11,794 Chinese in California, only 7 were women. Eighteen years later, of the 63,199 Chinese in the United States, 4,566 were female, a ratio of 14 to 1 (Takaki, 1993).

Chinese tradition and culture limited migration for women. All classes of Chinese women were regarded as inferior to men and were expected to remain at home. Women were also left behind because it would have been too expensive for them to accompany their husbands, who thought they would be gone only temporarily. Finally, harsh conditions and racism in America discouraged women from joining their husbands.

As the years went by, Chinese families gradually formed as men began to leave mining and railroad construction and enter more stable pursuits like farming and shopkeeping. During the early decades of Chinese immigration, most of the Chinese women came alone, often forcibly transported to America as prostitutes. These women worked in the mining outposts, railroad camps, agricultural villages, and in the Chinatowns of Sacramento, Marysville, and San Francisco. Virtual slaves, many of the prostitutes became opium addicts, seeking a drug-induced psychic sanctuary from their daily abuse and degradation. Disease was a constant threat; syphilis and gonorrhea were widespread. Life was dangerous and sometimes short. Occasionally prostitutes were beaten to death by their customers or pimps, and others committed suicide by taking an overdose of drugs or drowning themselves in San Francisco Bay (Yung, 1946). Chinese prostitutes decreased significantly in numbers after 1870 as many became self-sufficient or married.

Though they generally considered themselves sojourners, the Chinese showed signs of settling down from the very beginning. During the 1850s Chinatown in San Francisco was already a bustling colony of 33 general merchandise stores, 15 apothecaries, 5 restaurants, 5 herb shops, 3 boardinghouses, 5 butcher shops, and 3 tailor shops (Chin, 1968).

The immigrants also built Chinatowns in rural towns like Sacramento, Marysville, and Stockton, where these business communities served the needs of Chinese miners and farmers. They built altars to honor their gods and celebrated traditional holidays. Gradually, over the years, as the Chinese built their businesses and developed personal and social ties to their new communities, they came to feel detached from their homeland and their families in China.

In America the Chinese found their lives circumscribed in new and different ways. As strangers from a different shore, they had been denied equality of opportunity and were separated from their homeland by the laws of exclusion. "They called us 'Chink,'" complained an old laundryman, cursing the "white demons." "They think we no good." Though they could not become citizens, the Chinese felt they had earned the right to claim their adopted country (Lai, 1924).

The Japanese: Pacific Crossings, Seeking the Land of Many Trees

During the 1890s, American society witnessed not only the massacre at Wounded Knee, South Dakota, and the end of the frontier but also the arrival of a new group of immigrants. The Japanese went east to America, pushed here by circumstances in their homeland. Japanese farmers suffered severe economic hardships during the 1880s. Thousands of farmers lost their lands and hunger stalked many parts of Japan. Searching for a way out of this terrible plight, impoverished farmers were seized by an emigration *natsu*, or fever. To prospective Japanese migrants, "money grew on trees" in America (Kazuo, 1973, p. 15).

Initially most of the migrants from Japan were men, but what became striking about the Japanese immigration was its eventual inclusion of a significant number of women. By 1920, women represented 46% of the Japanese population in Hawaii and 35% in California (Takaki, 1993).

Why did proportionately more women emigrate from Japan than China? Unlike China, Japan was ruled by a strong central government that was able to regulate emigration. Japanese women were allowed to emigrate to the United States as family members. Over 60,000 women came as "picture brides." The picture bride system was based on the established custom of arranged marriage. In situations involving distance, the bride and groom would exchange photographs before the initial meeting (Wilson & Hosokawa, 1980).

Japanese women were also more receptive to the idea of traveling overseas than Chinese women. Japanese girls were educated alongside boys, and English was adopted as a major subject in middle school. Japanese women were pulled to Hawaii and to the U.S. mainland where they were needed as workers alongside their husbands.

A huge supply of labor was needed in the cane fields of Hawaii. Field work was punishing and brutal. Yet the Japanese stayed on. As planters now employed men with families, cottages were authorized for married laborers. The work camps were transformed into ethnic communities. The Japanese immigrants also enjoyed their own foods and shared memories of their distant homeland.

Gradually, over the years, Japanese immigrant workers found themselves establishing families in the new land. The immigrants were planting new roots through their children. These parents wanted their children educated. But the planters did not want the children of immigrant workers to have opportunities. They needed the second generation as plantation laborers. In their view, these children should not be educated beyond sixth or seventh grade, and their education should be vocational training.

Many schools, however, were not preparing these children to be plantation laborers. The children were learning about freedom and equality, reciting the Gettysburg Address, and reading the Declaration of Independence—about democracy or at least the theory of democracy.

Seeing their parents suffer from drudgery, low wages, and discrimination, many second-generation Japanese Americans did not want to be tracked into plantation labor. Education, they believed, was the key to employment, opportunity, and freedom from plantation work. The immigrant parents believed that their children were entitled to educational advantages.

On the mainland, the Japanese faced a fundamentally different situation: they were a racial minority, only 2% of the California population in 1920 (Takaki, 1993). They felt scorned by white society and became the target of hostile and violent white workers. Denied access to employment in the industrial labor market, many Japanese entered entrepreneurial activity. Thousands became successful farmers.

As early as 1910, Japanese farmers produced 70% of California's strawberries. By 1940, they grew 95% of the fresh snap beans, 67% of the fresh tomatoes, 95% of the celery, 44% of the onions, and 40% of the fresh green peas. In 1900, California's Japanese farmers owned or leased

29 farms totaling 4,698 acres. Within five years, the acreage had jumped to 61,858 acres and by 1910 increased again to 194,742 acres. By 1920, Japanese farmers owned 458,056 acres of land (Kazuo, 1973).

The workday was long and demanding. Stooped over rows of plants, husbands and wives worked side-by-side, their hands in constant motion. Women had double duty, fieldwork and housework.

These pioneer men and women felt a certain boundlessness, driven by their dreams of making the land yield a rich harvest. Over the years, they converted marginal lands (marshes in the San Joaquin Valley, dusty dry lands in the Sacramento Valley, and desert lands in the Imperial Valley) into lush and profitable agricultural fields and orchards.

Many Japanese immigrants believed that their success would help them become accepted into American society. This strategy of acceptance failed to recognize the depth of racial exclusionism. Their very success provoked a backlash and the creation of new borders. California and many other states enacted legislation to exclude Japanese immigrants from owning and leasing land.

The Issei, the first generation, feared they would have no future in their adopted land except through their children, the Nisei, the second generation. Through the Nisei, parents hoped, the Japanese would someday find tolerance in America. English-speaking and educated in American schools, the second generation would be ambassadors for the first generation. They would teach white Americans about the culture of Japan and the hopes and dreams of the immigrant generation. They would be the bridge to the larger society. Education would give the second-generation access to employment opportunities denied to the immigrants.

But citizenship and education did not immunize the Nisei against racial discrimination. Japanese children were often attacked by white boys. They experienced widespread housing discrimination and were denied employment. The Nisei were trapped in an ethnic labor market.

Deep in their hearts, many Nisei did not wish to be completely assimilated to become wholly American. They felt they were a complex combination of the two cultures and should be allowed to embrace their two lands. Everything they had learned at school had taken root, and they felt they were Americans. Nevertheless, many second-generation Japanese did not want to reject the culture of their parents, which had also become a part of them. Their hope to be both Japanese and American was violently shattered on a December morning in 1941.

Shortly after Japan's attack on Pearl Harbor, the federal government forcibly interned 110,000 Japanese Americans, most of them citizens by birth. Their constitutional rights of due process had been denied solely because of their race. They were considered disloyal and judged to be an internal military security threat.

Many young Japanese Americans were determined to create a better future for themselves as well as for their parents, and they believed that one way to accomplish this was to serve in the American armed forces. By defending their country, they would be able to demonstrate their loyalty as well as claim their American birthright. They served as interpreters and translators on the Pacific front. Others participated in military campaigns in Northern Africa, Italy, and Europe.

In 1946, President Harry Truman welcomed home Japanese American soldiers, saying, "You fought for the free nations of the world. You fought not only the enemy, you fought prejudice, and you won" (Tanaka, 1982, p. 89).

World War II was the most important historic event of our times, and for the first time not only Japanese but also Chinese felt they could make it in American society. The war abroad required reform at home, and many of the exclusion laws were repealed. After over 100 years in America, the Asian immigrants who had helped build America were truly at home.

CHICANOS: FOREIGNERS
IN THEIR NATIVE LAND

Chicanos are the largest group among the Hispanic population, which is projected to outnumber African Americans within the next few years. This diverse group has been in the United States for a long time, initially incorporated by the war against Mexico. The treaty had moved the border between the two countries, and the people of occupied Mexico suddenly found themselves foreigners in their native land.

The Chicano past is an integral part of America's westward expansion, its "manifest destiny." But while the early Chicanos were a colonized people, most of the people today have immigrant roots. Many began the trek to El Norte (the North) in the early 20th century. They came step by step, walking, waiting, and working, as if they were feeling their way up a ladder.

The Chicano experience has been unique, for most of the people have lived close to their homeland, a proximity that has helped reinforce the preservation of their language, identity, and culture. The migration to El Norte has continued to the present. Los Angeles has more people of Mexican origin than any other city in the world except Mexico City. A mostly mestizo people of Indian as well as African and Spanish ancestries, Chicanos currently are the largest minority group in the Southwest, where they have been visibly transforming culture and society.

It all began with the attempt to wrest California from Mexico. American westward expansion was reaching the Pacific, and Americans wanted California's natural resources: its forests, grazing land, and harbors. By the 1840s Americans were entering a new world, driven there by dreams of wealth and landownership. Determined to transform the territory into their own image, American foreigners were coming in groups. Many brought their families and saw themselves as Americans, not future Mexicans. The Mexicans residing in the area felt threatened by the hordes of white settlers flooding into their lands.

The key American objective of the Mexican-American War was the annexation of California. This territory was an important source of raw material for the market revolution. It exported cattle hides to New England where boots and shoes were manufactured. California was also the site of strategic harbors. Sperm whale oil was a crucial fuel and lubricant in the economy, and the American whaling industry was sending its ships to the Pacific Ocean. The ports of California were needed for repairs and supplies. Moreover, policymakers wanted to promote trade with the Pacific Rim.

The war itself would begin more than a thousand miles away from the east coast, in Texas. Americans had crossed the Mexican border and settled in a territory known as Texas. Many were slaveholders from the South in search of new lands for cotton cultivation. President John Quincy Adams had tried to purchase Texas in 1826 but Mexico refused to sell.

The Mexicans saw Americans from the North take possession of eastern Texas without the permission of Mexican authorities. In 1830 further American immigration was prohibited. Americans in Texas were furious at the new restrictions. They defied the abolition of slavery and continued to cross the border as illegal aliens. By 1835 there were 20,000 Americans in Texas, greatly outnumbering the 4,000 Mexicans. Tensions were escalating. Stephen Austin urged his countrymen to "Americanize" Texas and bring the territory under the flag of the United States. Viewing the conflict as one between a "mongrel Spanish-Indian and Negro race" and "civilization and the Anglo-American race," Austin declared that violence was inevitable: "War is our only recourse" (DeLeon, 1983, p. 33).

The war came in 1836, when some Americans in Texas began an armed insurrection against Mexican authority. The center for the rebellion for independence was San Antonio, where a mission had been converted into a fort that would become the stuff of American legend. Barricading themselves in the Alamo, 175 Texas rebels initiated hostilities in a struggle for what would be called the Lone Star Republic. The Mexican government declared the action illegal and sent troops to suppress the rebellion. Surrounded by Mexican soldiers, the rebels refused to surrender. Led by General Antonio Lopez de Santa Ana, the Mexican soldiers stormed the Alamo and killed most of the rebels.

Rallying around the cry "Remember the Alamo," Sam Houston organized a counterattack. Houston's troops surprised Santa Ana's forces at San Jacinto. According to historian Rudolfo Acuna, Houston's soldiers "clubbed and stabbed" Mexican soldiers seeking to surrender, "some on their knees." The slaughter became "methodical" as "the Texan riflemen knelt and poured a steady fire into the jostling ranks. After the battle, two Americans and 630 Mexicans lay dead" (Acuna, 1981, pp. 6–8).

Houston forced Santa Ana to cede Texas. Mexico broke off diplomatic relations. A brutal, unrestrained military campaign took place. It all ended in 1848 under the Treaty of Guadalupe Hidalgo. The Rio Grande became the Texas border and the Southwest Territories (California, New Mexico, Nevada, and parts of Colorado, Arizona, and Utah) became part of the United States. This was America's manifest destiny. The doctrine of manifest destiny embraced a belief in American Anglo-Saxon superiority, the expansion of Jefferson's homogeneous republic and Franklin's America of "the lovely white" (Weinberg, 1963, p. 102).

Mexicans viewed the conquest of their land very differently. Suddenly they were thrown among those who were strangers to their language, customs, laws, and habits. The border had been moved and thousands of

Mexicans found themselves inside the United States. In the years that followed, a dynamic Mexican-American identity came about. This identity showed a proud attachment to the culture south of the border as well as a fierce determination to claim rights as American citizens.

In growing numbers during the early 20th century, Mexican migrants began to cross their northern border. Like the Japanese immigrants who were arriving about the same time, many Mexicans came with extravagant hopes. Those who remained in Mexico welcomed their brothers and friends returning from the United States with shoes and good clothing, and cash in their pockets. Immigration fever swept through the Mexican villages. If one family left, 20 more followed. They fled Mexico to escape starvation and poverty.

Unlike the immigrants from Asia and Europe, Mexicans could enter and leave without passports whenever they wished. Entry was easy. Many simply walked across the shallow Rio Grande. Driven north by economic desperation, they were painfully separated from their homeland. Rural people in Mexico, many of them became urban industrial workers in America. They were the primary manual workforce in the construction industry.

The urban Chicano workforce included women. Employed in garment factories, food-processing plants, and canneries, many women were members of a family wage economy, pooling resources to put food on the table. Other Chicanas worked as servants, waitresses, cooks, and maids. They were usually assigned to the worst jobs and received the lowest wages. Even where Mexicans and Anglos did the same work, they received different wages. In the Los Angeles garment factories, Chicana seamstresses were paid only $3 a day, compared to $5 a day for their Anglo counterparts.

Most Chicanos worked in agriculture. Farmwork was seasonal and migratory, and Mexicans followed the crops. They moved from California to Ohio, Indiana, Minnesota, Iowa, the Dakotas, and Michigan. Conditions in migrant labor camps were squalid and degrading. Education was nonexistent. Mexicans were excluded socially, kept at a distance from Anglo society. They were isolated by the borders of racial segregation. Their world was one of Anglo over Mexican. Racial etiquette defined proper demeanor and behavior for Mexicans. They were expected to assume a deferential body posture and a respectful tone of voice. They were permitted to shop in the Anglo business section of town only on Saturdays. They could patronize Anglo cafés, but only at the counter and carryout service. Mexicans who were well dressed for a night out at a restaurant were told they needed to go to a special area designated "For Colored People."

In the mornings Mexican parents sent their children to segregated schools. Many educators felt that there would be a revolution in the community if Mexicans wanted to attend white schools. The predominant attitude among whites was, "Let the Mexican have as good an education but let him know he is not as good as the white man. God did not intend him to be or he would have made him white." Furthermore, an Anglo rancher angrily declared, "A damned greaser is not fit to sit by the side of a white girl" (Montejano, 1987, p. 226).

In the segregated schools, Mexican children were trained to become obedient workers. Educated Mexicans were hard to handle. Americans felt that they would become more desirable citizens if they stopped their education about the seventh grade. Consequently, the curriculum for Mexican students emphasized domestic science and manual training.

Fortunately, some educators saw that Mexican children were capable of learning. These same educators tried to instill pride in being Mexican. Experiences like these were exceptional because Mexican children were not usually encouraged to develop self-esteem.

During the 1960s, as more and more Mexicans migrated to El Norte and began attending American schools, they were increasingly viewed as threatening Anglo racial and cultural homogeneity. Mexicans were not only entering the country in great numbers, but they were also increasing rapidly because of their birthrate. (The average American family had three children, Mexican laborers averaged between nine and ten children to the family.) Mexican immigration seemed to threaten not only the genetic make-up of Anglo America but also its cultural identity.

Americans demanded the preservation of the nation's genetic purity by including Mexico in the national origins quota system. The demand for Mexican exclusion resonated among Anglo workers. Viewing Mexicans as a competitive labor force, they demanded the closing of the border.

For most Mexicans, the border was only an imaginary line, one that could be crossed and recrossed at will. Unlike the migrants from Europe, Africa, and Asia, they came from a country touching the United States.

Standing on the border, migrants had difficulty knowing where one country began and the other ended. Mexicans had been in the Southwest long before the Anglos, and they would emigrate despite repatriation programs. In El Norte, there were jobs and also communities.

Over the years, Mexicans had been creating a Mexican American world in the barrios of El Norte. By the 1970s, in their own communities they did not feel like aliens in a foreign land as they did whenever they crossed the railroad tracks and ventured uptown into the Anglo world. Though their neighborhood was a slum, a concentration of shacks and dilapidated houses, without sidewalks or even paved streets, the barrio was home to its residents. The people were all compatriots. They had come from different places in Mexico (Chihuahua, Sonora, Jalisco, and Durango) and had been here for different lengths of time. Together they formed "the Colonia Mexicana."

In El Norte, Mexicans were recreating a Mexican community and culture. They celebrated national holidays like September 16, Mexican Independence Day. The celebration stirred all the residents in the barrio to give them the feeling that they were still Mexicans.

The religion of the Mexicans was a uniquely Mexican version of Catholicism, a blending of a faith brought from the Old World and beliefs that had been in the New World for thousands of years before Columbus. For the Mexicans, God was deeply personal, caring for each of them through the saints.

In the 1970s, what bound the people together was not only ethnicity but also class. Mexicans were all poor. Beds and meals were provided for the newcomers if they had no money. In the barrio, people helped each other. Survival depended on solidarity and mutual assistance.

AMERICAN INDIANS:
A TEMPEST IN THE WILDERNESS

American Indians offer a critical contrast, for theirs was not an immigration experience. The Wampanoags were on the shore as the first English strangers arrived in what would be called New England. The encounters between American Indians and whites not only shaped the course of race relations but also influenced the very culture and identity of the general society.

President Andrew Jackson, the architect of Indian removal, believed that removal was necessary in order to transform America. Frederick Jackson Turner identified the frontier as our transforming crucible. The American Indian has had a different view. "The white man," Luther Standing Bear of the Sioux explained, "does not understand the Indian for the reason that he does not understand America." He went on to say, "The man from Europe is still a foreigner and an alien. He still hates the man who questioned his path across the continent" (Standing Bear, 1973, p. 307). American Indians questioned what Jackson and Turner trumpeted as "progress."

The American Indian believed the frontier had a different significance. Their story has been one of resistance. As Vine Deloria declared, "Custer died for your sins" (Deloria, 1969, p. 1).

American Indians were considered a tempest in the wilderness. Here is their story:

> *Scenario: From the shore, the small band of Indians saw the floating island pulled by billowy clouds and the landing of strangers. Never before had they seen such people. The newcomers looked like animals, monsters, hairy and pale skinned, their eyes the color of the sea, and their hair the color of the sun. In their hands the monsters carried shiny, sharp sticks that looked like long, vicious claws. Their foreign speech sounded like gabble. Confused and frightened, the Indians quickly hid beneath their skin-colored boats, hoping to look like three mounds on the beach. They could hear footsteps approaching. Suddenly their boats were violently overturned. All but one of the Indians were captured. Paddling away frantically, the lone survivor looked back and saw red stains darkening the beach.*

In their first encounter with Europeans, the Indians tried to relate the strangers to what was familiar in their world. The European colonizers, however, established a two-tiered social structure. The new world order was to be one of European over Indian. The Europeans claimed that they had a God-given responsibility to "inhabit and reform so barbarous a nation and to educate the savages." The Indians seemed to lack everything the Europeans identified as civilized: Christianity, cities, an alphabet and literature, linen clothing, and swords.

When the Indians brought food and rescued the starving strangers, the Europeans repaid them by trying to extort further food supplies by attacking the Indians and destroying their homes and villages. Soon the Europeans wanted more than just part of the Indian territory. Their need for land was suddenly intensified by a new development, the cultivation of tobacco as an export crop.

The Europeans possessed tremendous power to define the places and peoples they were conquering. Indians personified the Devil and everything the Europeans feared: the body, sexuality, laziness, sin, and the loss of self-control (Standing Bear, 1973). The ideology of "savagery" was born. Thomas Jefferson advocated the removal and even the destruction of hostile Indians. In his view, Indians were to be civilized or exterminated. To civilize meant to take Indians from their hunting way of life and convert them into farmers. The Indian must also adopt the culture of the white man. The land was not to be allowed to "lie waste." Citizens of the new land were to subdue the land and advance their frontier westward.

Andrew Jackson made this happen. His fortunes, both economic and political, were tied to what happened to the Indians. Jackson led American troops against the Indians and conquered the cream of the country for the expansion of the Republic. Jackson then justified the removal of the Indians by saying that efforts to civilize them had failed. Whites purchased some lands and expropriated others, thrusting the Indians farther into the wilderness. This land-allotment program became the primary strategy for taking territory away from the Indians.

A greater threat emerged, the railroad. The "highways to the Pacific" must not be obstructed. Behind the railroad were powerful corporate interests, deliberately planning the white settlement of the West and the extension of the market. Railroad companies saw the tribes as obstacles.

The Indians viewed the railroad very differently. They watched the iron horse transport white hunters to the plains, transforming the prairies into buffalo killing fields. They found carcasses littering and rotting along the railroad tracks, a trail of death for the buffalo, a main source of life for the Indian tribes.

The very identity and existence of the Indian had depended on the boundlessness of their sky and earth. But now railroad tracks cut across their land like long gashes, and fences enclosed their grasslands where buffalo once roamed freely. In the areas of the country outside the Great

Plains, the forces restricting and marginalizing the Indians were quite different. Farming and the sheer increase in the white population caused them to become a racial minority in lands they had occupied for thousands of years.

The love for the land and for their traditional ways had inspired resistance to the white westward expansion, especially after the Europeans failed to honor the very treaties established to protect the Indians. Treaties were broken and the reservation system was removed. The government began managing the affairs and welfare of the Indians. Since industrial progress had cut the Indians off from their traditional means of livelihood, Indians were given temporary support to help make the necessary adjustment for entering civilization. To accomplish this, Indians were placed on reservations. This left the rest of the West open for white settlement.

In addition, to advance and civilize the Indian, white reformers argued that the tribal system had to be destroyed. Living in tribes perpetuated idleness, frivolity, and debauchery. The key to civilizing Indians was to convert them into industrial landowners (Takaki, 1993). Allotment was allegedly designed to make Indians more independent and self-reliant. Allotment was unsuccessful so whites turned to assimilation and finally tribal recognition. Indians on reservations were finally allowed to establish local self-government.

The education of Indians played a big part in remaking Indian culture. Indian education sprang from the misguided notion that assimilated Indians would be happy Indians. In fact, the goal of the government and the religious community was that they would not be Indians at all. The belief that Indian education should consist of courses in the mechanical and domestic areas persisted well into the 1900s. Strong undertones of racism colored reports that identified Indians as being "good with their hands" or possessing "natural" artistic abilities.

Education of Indians followed a misguided and corrupt pattern. From the beginning, the intent of the U.S. government was to remake Indians in the cultural image of white people. Only European education was considered. All of Indian life—culture, social and political systems, norms, and religion—was disregarded. Civilize the Indian through European education was the norm. Dr. Lyman Abbott stated in his paper *Education for the Indian*, written in 1888, that schools are less expensive than war and it costs less to educate an Indian than it does to shoot him (Abbott, 1888).

In a blatant transgression of the separation of church and state, Congress handed over the job of educating Indians to Christian religious groups. This policy, having no regulation or monitoring, resulted in widespread corruption and extreme cruelty to children and produced generations of children forced into long separations from their families. The goal of the mission boarding schools was to change the identity of Indian children into that of the dominant culture. Terms like "dirty Indians" and "little savages" were used in the classrooms. The schools were like prisons, filled with human rights violations against defenseless young children. Compulsory education of Indian children in these schools was designed to obliterate their identity, their culture, and their existence as a sovereign people.

The conditions were unacceptable. The school buildings were old and were at risk of fires. The dormitories were crowded and the sanitary conditions were below standard. Serious malnutrition occurred because of lack of milk, fresh fruits, and vegetables. Children had their hair cut and their clothing taken away and replaced by European fashions, and they were forbidden to speak their own native language. Discipline was restrictive rather than developmental. Many students spent 10 to 13 years at the school without ever going home. Needless to say, the mission boarding school concept has caused alienation between American Indians and traditional American education that still exists today.

Changes continue to take place with American Indian tribes. By 1980 more than half of the total Indian population no longer lived on reservations. Instead they resided in such cities as New York, San Francisco, Seattle, Tulsa, Minneapolis–St. Paul, Chicago, and Los Angeles. American Indians are now integrating into our modern urban society. Conditions on the reservation have made it impossible to live above the poverty level. This is not forced assimilation, this is survival.

CULTURAL AMERICA:
THE INTEGRATION OF MANY

By looking at these groups (African Americans, Asian Americans, Chicanos, and American Indians), as well as our newer immigrants (Southeast Asian, Arab Americans, and newly arrived African immigrants), from a multicultural perspective, we can comparatively analyze their experiences in order to develop an understanding of their similarities and differences. Race has been a social construct that has historically set apart culturally diverse people from European white Americans.

American Indians were already here, while African Americans were forcibly transported to America, and Mexicans were initially enclosed by America's expanding border. The other groups came here as immigrants. America was, to them, a new world where they could do things they had thought were beyond their capabilities. These immigrants made bold and dangerous crossings, pushed by political events and economic hardships and fueled by their own dreams for a better life. "To America!" became the cry.

The signs of America's ethnic diversity are discerned across the continent: Ellis Island, Angel Island, Chinatown, Harlem, the Lower East Side. There are places with Spanish names like Los Angeles and San Antonio and Indian names like Massachusetts and Iowa. Much of what is familiar in America's cultural landscape actually has ethnic origins. The Bing cherry was developed by an early Chinese immigrant named Ah Bing. American Indians were cultivating corn, tomatoes, and tobacco long before the arrival of Columbus. One proposed etymology of the term *okay* says that it is derived from the Choctaw word *oke*, meaning "it is so." There is evidence indicating that the name *Yankee* came from Indian terms for the English, from *Cankke* in Cherokee and *Yankiois* in Delaware. Jazz and blues, as well as rock and roll, have African American origins. Miners learned mining techniques from the Mexicans, and American cowboys acquired herding skills from Mexican vaqueros.

All ethnic groups have contributed to the building of the American economy. They worked in the South's cotton fields, New England's textile mills, Hawaii's cane fields, New York's garment factories, California's orchards, Washington's salmon canneries, and Arizona's copper mines. They even built the railroads. Their stories are worthy. Through their stories, the people who have lived America's history can help all of us understand that Americans originated from many shores.

The telling of stories liberates. The remembering is also for the children. All children should know where they come from in order to know better who they are. Seeking to know how they fit in America, many young people have become listeners. They are eager to learn about the hardships and humiliations experienced by their ancestors. They want to hear their stories, unwilling to remain ignorant or ashamed of their identity or past.

America's continuing allure has also been as a place for a fresh economic start. Recent newcomers have been pushed by grim economic conditions at home. Most of today's immigrants come from Southeast Asia, Latin America, Africa, and the Arab States. The overall educational level is well below the average of their homelands. The need to educate culturally diverse youth and prepare them to enter the workforce has become an urgent issue. The day-to-day living conditions with which many of America's urban poor must contend is a tale of economic injustice.

America is moving toward a multiethnic future in which Asians, Hispanics, Caribbean Islanders, Arabs, Africans, and other immigrant groups compose a diverse and changing social mosaic. We need to take off the rose-colored glasses and realize that racial antagonisms exist and are being fueled by a declining economy and growing unemployment. Asian Americans have been bashed for the invasion of Japanese cars and electronics. Hispanics have been accused of taking jobs away from "real Americans." Blacks have been attacked for their dependency on welfare.

Let's look for new prospects for change and progress. Advocate for economic change. "Let America be American again," sang the poet Langston Hughes. "Let America be the dream the dreamers dreamed." Americans represent the races and cultures of the world. America has been settled by the people of all nations.

Who are we? America's dilemma has been our resistance to ourselves, our denial of our immensely diverse selves. To get along with each other requires self-recognition as well as self-acceptance. As Americans, we originally came from many different shores, and our diversity remains at the center of the making of America. Our stories contain the memories of different communities. Together they inscribe a larger narrative.

Such awareness of this narrative must come from a "re-visioned history" (Yamada, 1983, p. 40). The revolution from within must ultimately be grounded in "unlearning" much of what we have been told about America's past and substituting a more inclusive and accurate history of all the peoples of America. "To finally recognize our own invisibility," declared Mitsuye Yamada, "is to finally be on the path towards visibility" (Yamada, 1983, p. 40).

By viewing ourselves in a mirror that reflects reality, we can see our past undistorted and no longer have to peer into our future as through a glass darkly. America has been settled by "the people of all nations," Herman Melville observed over a century ago. "All nations may claim her for their own. You cannot spill a drop of American blood without spilling the blood of the whole world" (Melville, 1849, p. 169). America's dilemma has always been our resistance to ourselves, our denial of our immensely varied selves. But we have nothing to fear but our fear of our own diversity. "We can get along," Rodney King reassured us during an agonizing moment of racial hate and violence (King, 1992, p. 6). To get along with each other, however, requires self-recognition as well as self-acceptance.

Black Elk of the Sioux saw "in a sacred manner the shapes of all things in the spirit, and the shape of all shapes as they must live together like one being." And he saw that the "Sacred hoop" of the people was "one of many hoops that made one circle, wide as daylight and as starlight, and in the center grew one mighty flowering tree to shelter all the children of one mother and one father" (Black Elk, 1988, p. 43). Today what we need to do is to stop denying our wholeness as members of humanity as well as one nation.

Throughout our past of oppressions and struggles for equality, Americans of different races and ethnicities have been singing their strong melodious songs. These songs ring out from the textile mills of Massachusetts, the cotton fields of Mississippi, on the Indian reservations of South Dakota, the railroad tracks high in the Sierras of California, in the garment factories of New York's Lower East Side, the cane fields of Hawaii, the truck farms of the Southwest, and a thousand other places across the country. As we hear America singing, we find ourselves invited to bring our rich cultural diversity on deck, to accept ourselves. "Of every hue and caste am I," sang Walt Whitman. "I resist anything better than my own diversity" (Whitman, 1958, p. 38).

Chapter Three

Multicultural Education: Curriculum, Issues, and Perspectives

A vision without action is but a dream; action without vision is a waste of time; but vision with action can change our lives.

—M. Ignacio Tinajero

Each year, the United States becomes more ethnically and linguistically diverse. Over 90% of our recent immigrants come from non-English-speaking countries. However, while the number of culturally diverse students has grown exponentially across the United States, their level of achievement has lagged significantly behind that of their language-majority peers. One congressionally mandated study reported that culturally diverse students received lower grades, are judged by their teachers to have lower academic abilities, and score below their classmates on standardized tests of reading and mathematics (Moss & Puma, 1995). Furthermore, these students have high dropout rates and are often placed in lower-ability groups. These findings reflect growing evidence that most schools are not meeting the challenge of educating culturally diverse students successfully.

Culturally diverse learners in schools today are not alike. Many enter U.S. schools with a wide range of language proficiency (in their native language as well as in English) and of subject matter knowledge. We find diversity in their educational backgrounds, their expectations of schooling, their socioeconomic status, their age on arrival, and their personal experiences while coming to and living in the United States. All these factors impinge on the type of instructional experiences the students should receive in order to succeed in school.

At one end of the spectrum among immigrant students we find students who have strong economic backgrounds. Some are above equivalent grade levels in school curricula (math and science). They are literate in their native language and may have started learning a second language.

At the other end of the spectrum, some immigrant students arrive at our school doors with very limited formal education, perhaps owing to war in their native countries or the remote, rural location of their homes. These students are not literate in their native language and have not had educational experiences such as sitting at desks all day, changing teachers for each subject, or taking tests. These students have significant gaps in their educational backgrounds, lack knowledge in subject areas, and often need time to become accustomed to school routines and expectations.

We also have students who have grown up in the United States but speak a language other than English at home. At one end of the range of students in this group are those children who are literate in their home language, such as Hmong, Spanish, Arabic, or Somali, and just need to add English; or they may be caught in a state of semiliteracy that is hard to escape.

Given the variability in these students' backgrounds, they often need different pathways to academic success. To meet this challenge we need to shift our curricula, materials, instructional practices, and assessment methods.

The 21st century has arrived, and it is essential that the nation's schools help future citizens acquire the knowledge, values, and skills needed to participate in the forging of a democratic society that fosters the common good. Educators must enable groups on the margins to participate fully in the making and perpetuation of a moral and civic community that promotes the nation's democratic ideals.

The United States is sharply divided along racial, gender, and social-class lines. These divisions are caused by political, social, and economic factors that prevent many culturally diverse segments of society from fully participating in our nation's development. The goal of inclusion has been an elusive one.

Multicultural education can transform the schools in ways that promote educational equality and can play an important role in helping the nation's schools to promote national unity. Multicultural curriculum must reflect the experiences, struggles, and visions of all groups, thus fostering the common good.

The workforce demands, the demographic changes in the nation's population, the widening gap between the rich and the poor, and the global challenges we face all make multicultural education essential. Students must be able to compete in a service- and knowledge-oriented economy. However, if significant educational reforms are not successfully implemented, there will be a mismatch between the knowledge and skills demanded by the workforce and the knowledge and skills of a large proportion of American workers, many of them immigrants with culturally diverse backgrounds.

Approaches to school reform that do not include important aspects of multicultural education will not be successful because the learning styles and motivational characteristics of students from diverse cultural groups often differ in significant ways from those institutionalized within the schools. Not only will culturally diverse students make up the majority of the students, they will also be increasingly poor. The gap between the affluent members of U.S. society and the poor continues to widen. More students are living in low-income, single-parent families.

Multicultural education will help all students to acquire the academic skills needed to function in a culturally diverse society. Multicultural education is an education for life in our democratic society. It helps students transcend their cultural boundaries and acquire the knowledge, attitudes, and skills to engage in public discourse with people who differ from themselves. Race, gender, and class interact to influence student behavior.

Multicultural education is an idea, an educational reform movement, and a process whose major goal is to change the structure of schools so that students who are members of diverse racial, ethnic, and cultural groups will have an equal chance to achieve academically in school. Each major variable in the school—its culture, power relationships, the curriculum and materials, and the attitudes and beliefs of the staff—should be changed in ways that will allow the school to promote educational equality for culturally diverse students.

To transform the schools, educators must be knowledgeable about the influence of particular groups on student behavior. I have observed that in the early grades girls and boys achieve equally in math and science. However, the achievement scores of girls fall considerably behind those of boys as children progress through the grades. Culturally diverse girls are less likely than boys to participate in class discussions. They are more likely to be silent in the classroom. On the other hand, boys are more likely to be disciplined than are girls, even when their behavior does not differ from that of the girls. Males of color, especially African American males, experience a highly disproportionate rate of disciplinary actions and suspensions in school.

In early grades, the academic achievement of students of color (African American, Hispanic, and American Indian) is close to parity with the achievement of white mainstream students. However, the longer these students remain in school, the more their achievement lags behind that of whites.

Can a reform movement stressing multicultural education change achievement rates? Educational equality is an ideal human beings work toward but never fully attain. Racism, sexism, and discrimination will exist to some extent no matter how hard we work to eliminate these problems.

Multicultural education must be ongoing, not something we "do." I asked a colleague, a school principal, what efforts his district was taking to implement multicultural education, and he told me that his district had "done" multicultural education last year and this year the reform was to improve students' reading scores. My colleague not only misunderstood the nature and scope of multicultural education, but he also did not seem to understand that it could help increase the students' reading scores. A major goal of multicultural education is to improve students' academic achievement.

A BRIEF HISTORY OF
MULTICULTURAL EDUCATION

Multicultural education has a brief but rich history. It is linked directly to African American scholarship of the late 19th and early 20th centuries. One of the earliest and most urgent calls for multicultural education came from Carter G. Woodson in his 1933 book, *The Miseducation of the Negro*. The concerns expressed by Woodson (equity, funding, curriculum, and teachers) more than 70 years ago are still relevant today.

The struggle for educational opportunity reached a climax in the 1950s. During this time, the United States witnessed an event that changed the power and focus of education, *Brown v. Board of Education*, 1954. *Brown* represents a legal and moral imperative grounded in the principle of equality, the principle that all children should receive an education on equal terms.

Multicultural education really came to the forefront in the 1960s. It grew out of the ferment of the civil rights movement. The 1960s ushered in compensatory educational programs designed to redress inequities in learning opportunities for economically disadvantaged students, particularly minority students. Such programs as Head Start and Chapter I had the expressed goal of closing the educational gap (or gulf) between the economically disadvantaged and advantaged children, between poverty and plenty. The ultimate goal was to ensure the educational success of all students regardless of their racial and socioeconomic status by equipping them with the skills necessary to compete in the educational arena.

During this decade, African Americans embarked on a quest for their rights that was unprecedented in the United States. A major goal of the civil rights movement was to eliminate discrimination in public accommodations, housing, employment, and education.

The apparent success of the civil rights movement, plus growing rage and a liberal national atmosphere as well as the consequences of the civil rights movement had a significant influence on educational institutions. First African Americans and then other groups demanded that the schools reform curricula so that they would reflect the groups' experiences, histories, cultures, and perspective. Ethnic groups also demanded that the schools hire more black and brown teachers and administrators so that their children would have more successful role models. Ethnic groups also pushed for community control of schools in their neighborhoods and for the revision of textbooks to make them reflect the diversity of America.

The mid-1960s also experienced the War on Poverty and Great Society programs, which represented dramatic calls to reform education on the equality principle. The Great Society programs were justified by a theory of education as an "investment in human capital." In 1964, Congress officially enacted the Civil Rights Act. Title VI prohibits discrimination on the basis of race, color, and national origins in federally assisted programs.

The first responses of schools and educators to the ethnic movement of the 1960s were hurried. Courses and programs were developed without the thought and careful planning needed to make them educationally sound or to institutionalize them within the educational system. Holidays and other special days, ethnic celebrations, and courses that focused on one ethnic group were the dominant characteristics of school reforms related to cultural diversity during the 1960s and early 1970s.

By the late 1970s, the United States witnessed a groundswell of opposition to the equality principle. As laws were passed to protect the rights of minority and economically challenged students, backlash mounted. Opponents demanded a greater deference to the individual rights of the majority.

However, reform was under way. It was during these three decades that culturally diverse students took greater ownership of their destiny and were energized by a sense of empowerment. This sense of self-efficacy was ignited by such leaders as Martin Luther King Jr., Malcolm X, Cesar Chavez, and Russell Means and by groups such as the National Association for the Advancement of Colored People (NAACP), the Black Panthers, and the American Indian Movement. They sought structural changes in education and employment. Because of these people and groups, education has been elevated from a public benefit to a significant right.

Multicultural education emerged from the diverse courses, programs, and practices that the schools devised to respond to the demands, needs, and aspirations of the various groups. It is not simply one identifiable course or program. Educators use the term to describe a wide variety of programs and practices. Overall, multicultural education is an effort designed to increase educational equity for a broad range of cultural, ethnic, and economic groups. The challenge to multicultural educators, in both theory and practice, is to increase equity for a particular victimized group without further limiting the opportunities of another.

WHAT EXACTLY DOES CULTURE MEAN?

The term *culture* is often used, misused, and abused. One definition says that culture is values, beliefs, attitudes, and norms unique to a group bound by race, gender, location, religion, or social class. Others define culture as the consciousness of a community with its own unique customs, rituals, communication style, coping patterns, social organization, and child-rearing attitudes and patterns. Culture is also defined as the aggregation of beliefs, attitudes, habits, values, and patterns that form a view of reality. These patterns function as a filter through which a group or an individual views and responds to the environment. Learning styles are experienced in terms of acting, feeling, and being.

Garcia (1994) defines culture as a group's program for survival in, and adaptation to, its environment. The cultural program consists of knowledge, concepts, and values shared by group members through systems of communication. Culture also consists of the shared beliefs, symbols, and interpretation within a human group. The United States, like other nation-states, has a shared set of values, ideations, and symbols that constitute the core or overarching culture. Culture is shared to some extent by all the diverse cultural and ethnic groups that make up the nation-state. It is very difficult to identify and describe the overarching culture in the United States because it is such a diverse and unique nation.

When trying to identify the distinguishing characteristics of U.S. culture, one should realize that the political institutions within the United States, which reflect some of the nation's core values, were heavily influenced by both the British and the American Indians, especially those related to making group decisions, such as in the League of the Iroquois.

A key component of the U.S. core culture is the idea, expressed in the Declaration of Independence, that "all men are created equal, that they are endowed by their Creator with certain inalienable rights, that among these are life, liberty, and the pursuit of happiness." When this idea was expressed by the founding fathers in 1776, it was considered radical. A common belief in the 18th century was that human beings were not born with equal rights and others, such as kings, had divine rights given by God. When considering the idea that "all men are created equal" is a key component of U.S. culture, one should remember to distinguish between a nation's ideals and its actual practices, as well as between the meaning of the idea when it was expressed in 1776 and its meaning today. When the nation's founding fathers expressed this idea, their conception of men was limited to white males who owned property. White women and all

African Americans and Indians were not included in their notion of people who were equal or who had "certain inalienable rights."

Although the idea of equality expressed by the founding fathers had a very limited meaning at the time, it has proven to be a powerful and important idea in the quest for human rights in America. Throughout the nation's history since 1776, victimized and excluded groups such as women, African Americans, Indians, and other cultural and ethnic groups have used this cogent idea to justify and defend the extension of human rights to them and to end institutional discrimination such as racism, sexism, and discrimination against people with disabilities.

Two other important ideas in the culture of the United States are individualism and individual social mobility. In the U.S. core culture, individual success is more important than commitment to family, community, and nation. An individual is expected to experience success by his or her sole efforts. This strong individualism in U.S. culture contrasts sharply with the group values and group commitment found in Asian nations as well as among African Americans, American Indians, and Hispanic Americans who have not experienced high levels of cultural assimilation into the mainstream culture.

Schools in the United States are highly individualistic in their learning and teaching styles, evaluation procedures, and norms. Students from more group-oriented cultures experience problems in the highly individualistic learning environment of the school. Teachers can enhance the learning opportunities by using cooperative teaching strategies that have been developed and tested by Cohen (1994) and Slavin (1995).

A major goal of multicultural education is to change teaching and learning approaches so that students from diverse cultural groups will have equal opportunities to learn in our schools. When individuals encounter cultural patterns that are different in new situations, difficulties may arise. A new situation may include being placed in a school program where teachers and school personnel may not understand the students' cultural styles and orientations. The less cultural congruence between the home and school, the more difficult the cultural transition and the more negative will be students' educational outcomes.

Major changes need to be made in the ways that educational programs are conceptualized, organized, and taught. Individuals learn the values, symbols, and other components of their culture from their cultural group.

Therefore, knowledge about the group to which a student belongs provides important clues to and explanations for the student's behavior.

We are teaching children who are growing up in a country of unparalleled diversity. A critical examination of both the nation and the world is essential if we are to prepare students to live in a multicultural, pluralistic society. When we view the world through myopic lenses, it is difficult to see the richness of differences and diversity. We must determine who the people in these diverse non-Western cultures are and what we as educators know about these groups to promote effective educational opportunities for them.

In a sense, everything in education relates to culture, which is in us and all around us. It is personal, familial, communal, institutional, and societal. Culture is the product of human creativity in action. Schools can support or hinder the culture of their students. Teaching about the cultural practices of others without stereotyping or misinterpreting them and teaching about one's own cultural practices should be the aim of multicultural education. Direct connections between the daily lives of students outside the classroom and the content of instruction in history, social studies, and literature can make curriculum come alive. Voices and identities also come alive.

Schools remain a focal point of debate. What should we teach? How do we prepare students for life? How do we prepare teachers for the diversity among students? How do we address domestic social problems such as drug and alcohol abuse, teen pregnancy, and gang involvement? These issues cross cultures.

Schools have experienced tremendous growth in ethnic and racial diversity. Public debate about what diversity means has become prolific. Ask yourself what you really know about cultural diversity as it applies to classroom life and the overall school community. If you know the learning styles and strengths of your culturally diverse students, you can build on these strengths to help your students learn much more effectively. Build bridges for the students to help them acquire the knowledge and cognitive and social skills they need to survive in their new environment. Address individual differences as well as similarities to promote tolerance and acceptance. Focus on curriculum that promotes diversity (e.g., African American history, Hispanic literature, American Indian wisdom, and Asian music and dance).

Multicultural education strives to reduce prejudice and discrimination, to work toward equal opportunity and social justice for all groups, and to effect equitable distribution of power. Learn what is important to the group. For example, teachers who wish to teach about famous American Indians should ask different tribal members whom they would like to see celebrated. Don't assume it is Pocahontas, Sacajawea, or Sitting Bull. African Americans are becoming increasingly concerned because the black athlete or entertainer is often held up as the hero for the group, instead of African Americans who have done well in other areas of life, such as science, literature, or politics.

In this approach, instruction starts with the student's capability for learning. The teacher draws upon students' learning styles, ways of thinking, and knowledge about the world. Cooperative learning should be fostered. Equal attention is given to a variety of cultural groups regardless of whether specific groups are represented in the school's student population. The multicultural approach advocates total school reform to reflect diversity.

APPROACHES TO MULTICULTURAL
CURRICULUM REFORM

The United States is made up of many different racial, ethnic, religious, and cultural groups. In many school curricula, textbooks, and other instructional materials, these groups are given scant attention. The focus is on white Anglo-Saxon Protestant groups. The dominant cultural group in U.S. society is often called "mainstream America." A curriculum that focuses on mainstream Americans and largely ignores the experiences, cultures, and histories of other ethnic, racial, and cultural groups has negative consequences for both sides. A mainstream curriculum is one major way in which racism is reinforced and perpetuated in the schools and society at large.

A mainstream curriculum has negative consequences for mainstream students because it reinforces their false sense of superiority, gives them a misleading conception of their relationship with other racial and ethnic groups, and denies them the opportunity to benefit from the knowledge, perspectives, and frames of reference that can be gained from studying and experiencing other cultures. A mainstream curriculum also denies white students the opportunity to view their own culture from the perspectives of others. When students view their own culture from the point of view of another culture, they are able to understand their own culture more fully, see how it is unique and distinct from other cultures, and understand better how it relates to and interacts with other cultures.

A mainstream curriculum negatively influences culturally diverse students because it marginalizes their experiences and cultures and does not reflect their hopes, dreams, and perspectives. Students learn best and are more highly motivated when school curriculum reflects their own cultures, experiences, and perspectives. Many culturally diverse students are alienated in the schools in part because they experience cultural conflict and discontinuities that result from differences between their school and community.

The schools can help culturally diverse students mediate between their home and school cultures by implementing a curriculum that reflects all cultures. Schools can make effective use of community values when teaching writing, language arts, science, and mathematics. Many events, themes, concepts, and issues are still viewed from a white European perspective. Take, for example, events such as the European explorations in the Americas. When viewed from a Eurocentric perspective, the Americas are perceived as having been "discovered" by explorers like Columbus and Cortez. American Indians were discovered by the Europeans and their lands rightly owned by the Europeans who claimed and settled them.

Look at the development of American music. In many cases, music and dance art forms became important and significant only when they were recognized or legitimized by white critics and artists. The music of African American musicians such as Chuck Berry and Little Richard was not viewed as significant by white society until white singers like Rod Stewart and the Beatles publicly acknowledged that their own music had been deeply influenced by these African American musicians. It often takes white artists to legitimize ethnic cultural forms and innovations created by Asian Americans, African Americans, Latinos, and Indians.

The content and structure of textbooks also affects how multicultural education is approached. Teachers may not have the in-depth knowledge about ethnic cultures and experiences needed to integrate ethnic content, experiences, and points of view into the curriculum. Even though several significant changes have been made in textbooks in recent years, the content about ethnic groups is usually presented from mainstream perspectives and criteria and rarely incorporate information about ethnic groups throughout the text in a consistent integrated way. Information about ethnic groups is usually discussed in special units, topics, and chapter sections in the textbooks. Teachers therefore approach the teaching of ethnic content in a fragmented fashion.

I have found that most schools take one of four approaches to integrating multicultural content. The following approaches have evolved since the 1960s.

Contributions Approach

This approach to integration (level 1) is the most frequently used approach. It is characterized by the insertion of ethnic heroes/heroines and discrete cultural artifacts into the curriculum. Thus, individuals such as Crispus Attucks, Benjamin Bannaker, Sacajawea, Booker T. Washington, and Cesar Chavez are added to the curriculum. They are discussed when mainstream American heroes/heroines such as Patrick Henry, George Washington, Thomas Jefferson, Betsy Ross, and Eleanor Roosevelt are studied in the core curriculum. Discrete cultural elements such as the foods, dance, music, and artifacts of ethnic groups are studied, but little attention is given to their meaning and importance within ethnic communities. The mainstream curriculum remains unchanged in its basic structure, goals, and salient characteristics.

Individuals who challenged the dominant society's ideologies, values, and conceptions and advocated radical social, political, and economic reform are seldom included in the contributions approach. Thus, Booker T. Washington is more likely to be chosen for study than is W. E. B. Du Bois, and Sacajawea is more likely to be chosen than is Geronimo.

The holidays approach is a variant of the contributions approach. Ethnic content is limited to special days, weeks, and months related to ethnic events and celebrations. Cinco de Mayo, Martin Luther King Jr.'s birthday, and American Indian month are examples that come to mind.

The contributions approach provides teachers with a way to integrate ethnic content into the curriculum quickly, giving some recognition to ethnic contributions to U.S. society. It is the easiest approach for teachers to use. However, using heroes/heroines tends to gloss over the issues and concepts related to victimization and oppression of ethnic groups and their struggles against racism and for power. The end result is often the trivialization of ethnic cultures.

Additive Approach

Level 2 is the additive approach. Content, concepts, themes, and perspectives are added to the curriculum without changing its basic structure, purpose, and characteristics. It is simply accomplished by the addition of a book, a unit, or a course to the curriculum without making any substantial changes. Content is selected using mainstream Eurocentric criteria. The content, materials, and issues that are added to the curriculum are added as appendages instead of being integral parts of a unit of instruction. Adding ethnic content to the curriculum in a sporadic and segmented way can result in trouble for the teacher (students may lack background; the additions may create community controversy, student confusion, and adverse parental reaction).

Transformation Approach

The transformation approach (level 3) differs from levels 1 and 2 because the fundamental goals, structure, and perspectives of the curriculum are changed to enable students to view concepts, issues, events, and themes from the perspectives of culturally diverse groups. This infusion extends students' understanding of the nature, development, and complexity of U.S. society.

When subjects such as music, dance, and literature are studied, the teachers acquaint students with the ways these ethnic art forms have greatly enriched and influenced the nation's artistic and literary traditions. African musicians such as Bessie Smith, W. C. Handy, and Leontyne Price have influenced the development of U.S. music. Writers such as Langston Hughes, Toni Morrison, N. Scott Momaday, Carlos Bulosan, Maxine Hong-Kingston, Rudolfo Anaya, and Piri Thomas have not only significantly influenced the development of American literature but have also provided unique and revealing perspectives on U.S. society and culture.

When studying U.S. history, language, music, arts, science, and mathematics, the emphasis is not be placed on the ways that various ethnic and cultural groups have contributed to mainstream society and culture. The emphasis is on how the common U.S. culture and society emerged from a complex synthesis and interaction of the diverse cultural elements that originated within the various cultural, racial, ethnic, and religious groups that make up U.S. society.

Social Action Approach

The social action approach (level 4) includes all the elements of the transformation approach but adds components that require students to make decisions on important social problems and take actions to help solve them. Major goals of instruction in this approach are to educate students for social awareness and social change and to teach them decision-making skills. To empower students to help them acquire political efficacy, the school must help them become reflective social critics and skilled participants in social change.

Political education in the United States has traditionally fostered political passivity rather than political action. A major goal of the social action approach is to help students·acquire the knowledge, values, and skills they need to participate in social change so that victimized and excluded ethnic and racial groups can become full participants in U.S. society so that the nation will move closer to attaining its democratic ideals.

I think it is important to note that contact with ethnic groups does not necessarily lead to more positive racial and ethnic attitudes. Rather, the conditions under which the contact occurs and the quality of the interaction in the contact situation are the important variables.

MULTICULTURAL TEACHING

Multicultural understandings are fundamental to the education of all children, not only children from culturally diverse backgrounds. Multicultural education is an integral part of the curriculum, not a separate course, a special unit of study in February, or a series of discrete activities added to a prescribed curriculum. A climate must be created in which students can dare to question, to take risks, and to learn from each other. This approach prepares students for a world in which learning is neither limited to information presented within the covers of a textbook nor confined within the school walls.

Guidelines for Teaching Multicultural Content

The 14 guidelines that follow are designed to help teachers better integrate content about culturally diverse groups into the school curriculum and to teach effectively in multicultural environments. These guidelines have been followed in successful, innovative schools across the nation.

1. *As a teacher, you are an extremely important variable in teaching cultural content.* When you encounter racist content in materials or observe racism in the behavior of your students, you must be able to utilize the necessary knowledge, attitudes, and skills to teach lessons about the experiences of culturally diverse groups in the United States.
2. *Knowledge about culturally diverse groups is needed to teach cultural content effectively in your classroom.*
3. *Be especially sensitive to your own racial attitudes, behavior, and the statements you make in the classroom.*
4. *Make sure your classroom conveys positive images of all groups.*
5. *Be sensitive to the racial attitudes of your students and do not accept the belief that "kids do not see colors."* Even very young children are aware of racial differences.
6. *Choose your teaching materials carefully.* Some materials contain blatant stereotypes of ethnic groups.
7. *Use trade books, films, videotapes, and recordings to supplement the textbook treatment of groups and to present the ethnic perspective.* Show experiences of what it is like to be a person of color in the United States.
8. *Get in touch with your own cultural heritage and share it with your students.*
9. *Be sensitive to the possibly controversial nature of the curriculum you are required to use, and develop clear objectives to enhance student knowledge.*

10. *Be sensitive to the developmental levels of your students when you select concepts, content, and activities related to cultural groups.* Learning activities for children in kindergarten and the primary grades should be specific and concrete (concepts of similarities and differences, prejudice, and discrimination). As students progress through the grades, introduce more complex learning activities. If you teach in a racially and culturally integrated classroom or school, you should keep the culture of your students first.

11. *View all students as winners. Believe all students can be successful and help them succeed.*

12. *Keep in mind that most culturally diverse parents are very interested in their child's education even though the parents may be alienated from the school.* Do not equate education with schooling. Many parents have mixed feelings about the schools. Try to gain parental support and make parents partners in the education of their children.

13. *Use cooperative learning techniques and group work to promote racial integration in the classroom.*

14. *Make sure school plays, pageants, cheerleading squads, dance teams, school publications, and other formal and informal groups are racially integrated.* Make sure culturally diverse groups have equal status in school performances and presentations. In a multiracial school, if all leading roles are filled by white students, a mixed message is sent.

Planning the Multicultural Curriculum

Curriculum should help students develop the ability to make reflective personal and public decisions. It should be conceptual, interdisciplinary, and based on higher levels of knowledge. The focus should be on helping students master key concepts that highlight major themes in the experiences of ethnic and cultural groups in the United States.

All students need to master certain concepts—race, racism, prejudice, and discrimination—if they are to gain a full understanding of American society and history. We must keep in mind that racism remains a major problem in society today. There are five key concepts related to ethnic groups:

1. *Conflict exists among different generations and subgroups within ethnic groups.* These conflicts are evident in values, goals, and methods of protest.
2. *Cultural diversity is exhibited in a wide range among and within various ethnic groups.* Group identification is influenced by such factors as skin color, social class, and personal experiences.
3. *Values differ from those of mainstream Americans despite cultural assimilation.*
4. *Social protest occurs in movements that have emerged to develop pride, shape new identities, gain political power, and shatter stereotypes.* The intensity, scope, and type of movements have varied widely from group to group and have been influenced by the unique histories, values, cultures, and lifestyles of ethnic groups.
5. *Assimilation is evident.* As ethnic groups become more assimilated, they abandon certain elements of their traditional cultures. Later generations often reclaim aspects of their cultural heritage.

The Components of an Effective Multicultural Curriculum

The effective multicultural curriculum must be conceptual (it must include a wide range of ethnic groups), interdisciplinary, comparative, decision making, and social-action focused. It is also a process of transformation.

When identifying concepts for a curriculum, we need a balanced approach. People of color should not be depicted as only victims. They should be depicted as people who helped shape their own destiny, who built ethnic institutions, and who played major roles in attaining their civil rights. It is necessary to teach such concepts as prejudice, discrimination, and racism. It is also essential to teach such concepts as protest, empowerment, and interracial cooperation in order to portray a full and accurate view of the experiences of culturally diverse groups in the United States.

Criteria for Selecting Interdisciplinary Concepts

Within the various academic fields and disciplines are a wide range of concepts from which you might select when planning the multicultural curriculum. What criteria should you use when selecting concepts to organize lessons?

- *Consider whether the concept will help explain some significant aspect of the history, culture, and contemporary experiences of the culturally diverse population in U.S. society.* Culture is a more powerful concept than language because it can be used to organize and teach more information.
- *Concepts should be interdisciplinary, capable of encompassing facts, generalizations, and examples from several disciplines and areas.* For example, during the civil rights movement of the 1960s, African Americans expressed protest not only in politics but also in their literature, songs, dances, art, and language. Thus, students need to examine social protest in these forms of communication to fully understand black protest in the 1960s.
- *Pay attention to the developmental level of your students.* Young children can understand discrimination more easily than they can understand institutionalized racism, in part because almost every child of color has been the victim of some kind of discrimination.
- *Focus on concepts that can be taught using concrete examples, such as similarities and differences.* Open-ended stories and role-playing situations can make concepts real and meaningful.
- *Look at the students' previous experiences.*
- *Study the differences that exist within culturally diverse groups.*

Overall, a sound multicultural curriculum should help *all* students, from both majority and minority groups, break out of their cultural and ethnic enclaves and learn that there are many ways to live and survive. Just because an individual has a different lifestyle does not mean he or she is inferior or superior. Schools should help students learn how to live with people who speak a different language/dialect, eat different foods, and value things that others do not value. In most societies, the social significance of race is much more important than the presumed physical differences among groups. It is the values and related lifestyles that constitute their essence, not chow mein, basket weaving, sombreros, or soul food.

When planning a multicultural unit, you should first decide which key concepts you will use to organize the unit. These concepts should be higher-level ones that are capable of encompassing a wide range of data and information. The concepts chosen should also be interdisciplinary (capable of encompassing facts, generalizations, and examples from several disciplines and content areas).

After you have identified organizing concepts, choose key generalizations related to each of the concepts. Use universal generalizations that apply to all cultures, times, and people, as well as intermediate-level generalizations that are limited in their application to a particular nation, subculture, or time period. The following is an example:

Key Concept: Cultural Assimilation

Universal Generalization: Whenever a minority ethnic group comes into contact with the dominant culture, it is usually expected to acquire the culture and values of the dominant culture.

Intermediate-Level Generalization: In the United States, ethnic minority groups are expected to acquire the culture and values of the mainstream American culture.

After the key and intermediate-level generalizations have been identified, you should decide which ethnic groups will be included in the unit. It is neither possible nor desirable to include every U.S. ethnic group within a particular unit or curriculum.

After the ethnic groups to be included in the unit have been identified, you should then identify low-level generalizations—low-level statements that explain how the experiences of specific groups are related to the key concepts.

When the low-level generalizations for each ethnic group have been identified, the teacher is then ready to write the strategies and identify the materials for teaching. To formulate the key generalizations in the unit, the students are then given opportunities to compare and contrast the experiences of different ethnic groups. Students cannot learn by studying only one group.

Multicultural units should have clearly stated objectives so that the teacher can effectively evaluate instruction and student learning. These lessons have two major kinds of objectives, cognitive (related to mastery of knowledge) and affective (related to student attitudes and values).

The next step is to write the objectives in clear, concise terms. Also consider the fact that many students have negative, confused, conflicting feelings and attitudes toward racial and ethnic groups. Whenever possible, use multimedia resources such as tapes, films, videotapes, photographs, and books/magazines. Also remember that every community has resources you can use to enrich the multicultural curriculum. The range extends from community organizations to colleges and universities.

The final step is evaluating outcomes. You can use paper/pencil tests, open-ended stories, and even decision-making responses. Always remember that the teacher is the most important variable in the multicultural curriculum. His or her attitudes toward ethnic content and ethnic cultures are critical. The teacher must clarify in his/her mind any attitudes toward people of color before attempting to teach ethnic lessons.

A teacher who is sensitive and knowledgeable regardless of his or her ethnic or racial group can teach any subject effectively. However, it is important for students to be exposed to the points of view and perceptions of members of the various ethnic groups. This can be done by selecting sensitive and powerful teaching materials written by ethnic authors, using powerful videotapes such as *Eyes on the Prize: America's Civil Rights Years* and *How the West was Lost*, and using various types of community resources. Sensitive and knowledgeable teachers who approach teaching with integrity and openness can defend their right to teach ethnic content to any individual or group.

The need for teachers to be intellectually competent before they embark on teaching ethnic content cannot be overemphasized. This may involve unlearning of facts and interpretations we learned in school and much new learning. It involves a personal transformation in both attitudes and conceptual understanding.

More humanistic views of other cultures are imperative within our increasingly interdependent and ethnically polarized world. Humanistic views of other groups and cultures may help to create the kind of social and ethnic harmony that our society must have to survive and prosper in the future.

Multicultural Counseling

Schools seldom offer multicultural counseling, which is necessary to help children develop an understanding of themselves and their role in society.

Racial identity becomes a central focus for students and educators. Previously used techniques, strategies, and interventions were inadequate for culturally diverse learners. The trend today cautions counselors against imposing their culturally laden goals, values, and practices on clients from diverse backgrounds.

Multicultural counselors must address the following central issues:

- *Address early on the special issues that plague immigrant students.*
- *Look at underachievement.* It is an unfortunate reality that too many culturally diverse students have dismal educational outcomes (poor test scores, high dropout rates, high truancy rates, and high suspension rates). Underachievement can be reversed if addressed early and consistently.
- *Observe academic self-concept.* A person's self-concept is one of the most important variables in an individual's life. The perceptions students have about their ability to fit in socially, satisfy the expectations of parents and teachers, and perform academic tasks in the prescribed manner determine success in school.
- *Observe social self-concept.* One of our basic needs is the desire to belong and to feel loved. There is also a need to bond with others who share similar concerns and interests.
- *Address social injustices and discrimination.* Prejudice is a prevalent and persistent problem in schools and society. Many students experience racism on a daily basis, a problem students bring into the classroom. Persistent racism conquers the spirit.

Discover racial identity. By age 3 or 4, children know their race, and by the time they enter school the implications of racial group membership and status become even more evident.

TEACHER ISSUES

The best camera in the world will not produce the best pictures if the photographer lacks formal training in photography. Likewise, the best education cannot be provided if school personnel lack preparation for a culturally diverse curriculum.

The scarcity of racially and culturally diverse teachers is a major and persistent issue in education nationally. Projections show the representation of culturally diverse students is decreasing in our teacher training courses. In essence, we need more teachers of color in our classrooms, and we need educators who are culturally competent. Teachers must be prepared to be culturally aware and instructively effective.

Teachers of color do much more than teach content. They also personify content. Teachers of color stand as models for what it is like to be an educated person. If we want students to believe that they themselves might one day become scientists, writers, or mathematicians, or that they might be mentors, guides, and educated people, then students need to see diverse examples of such people, including at least one who looks like they look.

Multicultural Competencies Needed by School Personnel

Without the support of all school personnel, multicultural education cannot become a reality. Increased diversity among school personnel, modifications in curriculum and instruction, and philosophical changes can be implemented more effectively when school personnel are trained to be more culturally aware and competent.

Culturally competent educators seek greater self-awareness and understanding regarding their biases, assumptions, and stereotypes. This self-awareness comes from understanding one's own cultural values and norms and in understanding that individuals are a product of their culture.

Culturally competent educators seek to understand the worldviews (values and norms) of culturally diverse students without negative judgments. Educators do not need to adopt these views but should respect them as different and legitimate rather than as inferior or otherwise substandard. We must move from the stage of tolerance for cultural differences to a point where educators truly embrace culturally diverse differences.

We are teaching in a nation of unparalleled diversity. Through self-understanding, educators become more informed of how attitudes and prejudices affect teaching and learning. Just as with children, our sense of self-worth influences our work. Our self-awareness influences the way we relate to children. Our personal histories reflect biases about how other people live, work, and play.

Culturally competent educators attempt to increase multicultural awareness and understanding among *all* students. Socially responsive teachers/
educators are activists who seek positive changes on behalf of culturally
diverse students. As advocates, we seek equity in all areas of the educational process. Inequities in materials, instruments, policy, and so on are
being addressed.

Culturally competent educators attempt to make education relevant,
appropriate, and sensitive to students' diverse needs. They create a learning environment aimed at achieving pride, equity, power, wealth, and cultural continuity. Teachers go beyond the subject matter and encourage
students to value achievement and understand the personal value, the collective power, and the political importance of academic success. Teachers
engage all students in reflections about life's realities. Teachers must integrate the realities of students' lives, experiences, and cultures into the
classroom, while validating and affirming students' identities.

It is my belief that teacher preparation programs must develop future
teachers who have knowledge and understanding of the following:

- Human difference
- Social, cognitive, emotional, and environmental factors that affect
  child development
- A variety of assessment methods
- Current research on cultural diversity
- What it means to be a change agent in social, cultural, political, and
  economic environments
- Variation in teacher and student learning styles
- Multicultural curriculum and instruction
- Learning environment
- Personal exposure and experience with diversity
- Influence the family, school, and peers have on students relative to
  achievement needs of the students

Becoming a competent educator is a lifelong process. Educators must
continue to seek experiences that help to refine their skills and abilities to
work with culturally diverse students. Professional development becomes
a critical factor for teacher growth.

Teachers must be well informed and possess knowledge that is accurate and up-to-date. Next comes a well-planned delivery system. The teacher is the key to success or failure of any program, so what you do in your classroom is critical. You must be aware of the climate of the classroom, the way you treat students, and how you handle student behavior, evaluation, individual needs, and parental issues. Above all, respect your students and their families.

Avoid the following pitfalls:

- *Trivializing.* Don't organize lessons and activities only around holidays and food.
- *Tokenism.* Don't display one black doll or Hmong doll amid several white dolls or one multicultural book among many others.
- *Disconnecting cultural diversity from daily classroom life.* Avoid teaching one unit related to cultural diversity and never addressing the topic again.
- *Stereotyping.* Don't present people of color always in the context of past history or always as poor or uneducated.
- *Misrepresenting American ethnic groups.* Avoid using only books about Mexico, Japan, or African countries to teach about contemporary cultural groups.

Focus on your students. Understand individual student strengths, challenges, learning styles, and interests. Observe your students and listen to them to determine a learning strategy and then do problem solving. Determine the overall levels of student performance. Adopt the philosophy that as long as we are learning, we are growing. As long as we are growing, we are moving closer to our human potential.

The most important and most effective way to determine a student's need is to listen to that student. Culturally diverse students notice immediately that most of their education focuses on the successes, contributions, accomplishments, and histories of white Americans. Students also observed that if any other group was the center of attention, it was African Americans. Black students contended that classes consistently focused on the same black heroes (Harriet Tubman and Martin Luther King Jr.) while ignoring contemporary role models (Colin Powell, Barbara Clark, and Jesse Jackson), controversial persons (Malcolm X, W. E. B. Du Bois, and Reverend Al Sharpton), and events (slave revolts and the Watts riots). Students went on to say that these superficial learning experiences occurred primarily during February, Black History Month.

The students also said that school is much more interesting, engaging, motivating, and relevant when they learn about their own culture and the culture of others. In essence, students' comments tell us they *want* and *need* more multicultural education. Students do not want to dwell in the past at the expense of the present and future.

Here are some student perceptions:

I get more interested in school when we learn about other people. I want to know what a White teacher has to say about my people. Is it good or bad? I often confront my teachers and this gets me into trouble for asking questions. (9th grade, female)

You get tired of learning about the same White people and the same things. I want to broaden my horizons and learn about people in other countries. The White people are just trying to advance Whites and leave us behind. (8th grade, male)

I like to watch the expressions of white students when they hear that black people are successful. I love seeing their faces because they are shocked! We are not bad people. (10th grade, male)

It is important to learn about your culture and heritage, then you can understand yourself better. (11th grade, female)

Seriously, there are twelve months in a year. They chose February, the shortest month, to teach blacks about themselves. Black people get one month, Indians get one month, and White people get the rest. You can't fit our history into only 28 days. (9th grade, male)

There should be an equal amount of attention given to all groups. We have all contributed to society, theories, innovations, inventions, and such. Stop treating us like dirt! (7th grade, male)

Racially and culturally diverse students learn early that their communication styles are significantly different from those espoused in school. Because communication styles and learning styles differ, students require an approach to curriculum and instruction that accommodates individual differences. Multiple approaches, models, and strategies (concrete and abstract, whole-to-part and part-to-whole, visual and auditory, hands-on) that reflect the diversity of the students will help them to acquire knowledge.

We must build on students' strengths. Teaching is not telling. It is active engagement by the learner that constructs meaning. When we reflect on ourselves, our strengths and weaknesses, and all the other factors that have contributed to our personality, life experience, and beliefs, we learn to see others for who they are and to appreciate how they are both similar to and different from ourselves. These differences then become more a subject of interest and less a direct threat to us.

Students are eager to teach and learn from other students. Therefore, we must structure multiple opportunities for students to test their ideas against others through talk and small-group work. Students learn, not by smoothly and steadily accumulating knowledge, but by taking small steps and giant leaps, often in unexpected directions. We can't know how much our students are capable of grasping unless we listen to them. All students, no matter what their ethnicity, language, or family background, have the potential to succeed in school.

As students learn about themselves, they prepare to learn about each other. They develop empathy and see the world from another's point of view. Students need to reflect on who they are and what forces have influenced them. As educators, we must offer them the opportunity to succeed by bringing their own background into the classroom. We can celebrate birthdays, prepare a "me" collage that reveals facts about their lives, discuss how we differ and are similar, encourage free writing in a journal, and reflect on color.

Names are one of the most salient features of ourselves, representing our individual identity as well as our connection with family and heritage. Names also have a great deal of influence on our expectations of others. Studies show that teachers consistently grade students with "normal" names (Susan, Anne, Robert, Bill, and John) higher than they do children with unusual names (Gao, Sundown, Von, Shabria, Kamari, and Antaneisa). Talk about names and what they mean. Explore one name in many languages. One such illustration is the name John, which can be found in a variety of languages (John is Yohanna in Arabic, Iban in Basque, Juan in Spanish, Sean in Irish, Giovanni in Italian, Ivan in Russian, etc.).

Another area where ethnic diversity has been much appreciated is food. Food habits and the preparation of traditional dishes are central to the identity of a culture, and they linger long after other cultural characteristics are lost. Because sharing food is such a positive experience, food is also a subject that breaks down barriers between members of different cultures. Students are curious to find out what the other students in the classroom eat everyday and what the differences and similarities are. Collect recipes and create a class recipe book. Talk about food prejudices. Discover which foods are acceptable for eating and which are not. For example, many people in the United States turn up their noses at foods that are delicacies in other countries (snails and frog's legs). Likewise, people in some other countries think the American custom of eating corn on the cob is disgusting because, to them, that food is fit only for pigs.

Social Status

One type of minority status has a significant impact on learning and educational outcomes. Voluntary minorities such as Asian Americans moved to the United States because of their desire for greater economic and political independence, as well as greater overall opportunities. They came in search of the American dream. Involuntary minorities such as African Americans were brought to the United States against their will. Voluntary minorities accept biculturalism and perceive that "playing the game by the rules" will yield long-term gains, employment, upward mobility, and the realization of the American dream. With these beliefs, voluntary minorities are able to cross cultural boundaries.

Picture three babies born at the same time to parents of different social class backgrounds. The first baby is born into a wealthy, well-educated business or professional family. The second is born into a middle-class family in which parents attended college and have middle-class managerial jobs. The third is born into a poor family in which neither parent finished high school or has a steady job. Will these children receive the same education? Although the United States is based on the promise of equal opportunity for all, the educational experiences of these three children are likely to be quite different.

Education in the United States is not a single uniform system that is available to every child in the same way. Children of different social classes are likely to attend different types of schools, to receive different types of instruction, to study different curricula, and to leave school at different rates and times. As a result, when children end their education, they differ more than when they entered. Overall, social class inequality is greater in the United States than in any other industrial or postindustrial society in the world. Germany, Japan, Italy, France, England, Sweden, Switzerland, and the Netherlands all have considerably less social class inequality than the United States. Moreover, income inequality has increased in the United States during the last 20 years, which has increased inequality among children as well. At the same time, the United States has a historical belief in opportunity for all in the dominant group, regardless of their social origins. What is wrong with this picture?

At upper- and upper-middle-class high schools, the grounds are spacious and well kept, the computer laboratory and language and athletic facilities are extensive. Classes are small, nearly every student studies a college preparatory curriculum, and considerable homework is assigned.

Private and parochial facilities are generally relatively small and students study a rigorous academic program and do even more homework than do their public school peers.

Urban schools are usually quite large, and they are part of an even larger school system that is invariably highly bureaucratic. These schools offer varied courses of study, including academic, vocational, and general-curriculum tracks. Most culturally diverse students attend urban schools. These schools spend considerable time explaining to the general public, politicians, and school officials why African American children do less well in school than white children, and why lower-class students do less well than middle- and upper-middle-class children. Schools attended by children of different social classes also vary in terms of how much work they expect of their students.

Social class background affects where students go to school and what happens once they are there. As a result, lower-class and culturally diverse children are less likely to be exposed to valued curricula, are taught less of whatever curriculum they study, and are expected to do less work in and out of the classroom.

Teachers, educators, and connected parents and community members made these recommendations for action:

- Work politically to increase the educational resources available to all children.
- Work to reduce economic inequalities in society.
- Work to build economically and racially integrated communities.
- Work to support prenatal care for all pregnant women. (This could reduce or eliminate one-third of all learning disabilities.)
- Work to support Head Start programs.
- Use testing procedures for diagnosing learning disabilities.
- Work on finding what abilities students do have.
- Support efforts to get rid of tracking.
- Expect and demand a lot from students in the way of thought, effort, and assignment completion.
- Teach students content and subject matter.
- Help students understand how relevant and useful education is in their lives.

Despite its desirability, to date, the goal of achieving educational equality for culturally diverse students has been elusive and unattainable. Reasons for this are complicated. Some are associated with how educational equality is conceived. Others are located in the indicators used to determine the educational attainment of students from different ethnic groups and whether these indicators are culturally sensitive enough to be valid measures of academic performance of culturally diverse students. Still other reasons have to do with the quality and opportunities and experiences students from different ethnic groups receive in the educational process. Education must be reformed to move us closer toward achieving the goal of equality in learning.

Educational equality in the United States is popularly understood to mean the physical access of culturally diverse students (African American, Latino, Asian, Arab, and American Indian) to the same schools and instructional programs as middle-class European American students. The prevailing assumption is that when these groups become students in our nation's schools, equal educational opportunity is achieved. Little attention has been given to the quality of the curriculum content and instructional processes as key factors in formulas for educational equity.

Many Americans believe that desegregation has resolved the issue of educational inequality. They argue that federal and state laws now prohibit educational discrimination on the basis of race, color, creed, gender, nationality, and social class. For these people, the persisting discrepancies between the academic achievement of culturally diverse students and European Americans are not a result of differences in educational opportunities at all. Rather, these problems are matters of personal abilities, aspirations, and responsibilities. Students of color and poverty do not achieve as well in school as their middle-class white counterparts because of individual deficiencies, not because of discrepancies in available opportunities.

Equating sameness of opportunity with educational equality ignores the more fundamental issue of quality of learning opportunity and how this has to be understood and acted on within the context of ethnic and cultural diversity. It also fails to acknowledge the fact that treating different individuals identically is inherently discriminatory. Their differences demand variability in treatment so that each can have the best chance to perform at maximum capacity. Thus, equality of educational opportunities should be understood to mean parity, equity, and comparability of treatment based on the diagnosed needs of culturally diverse students.

Despite legal mandates prohibiting them, educational inequalities continue to prevail at crisis levels today. This inequality becomes clearer when we look at the problems American Indians, African Americans, Mexican Americans, and Puerto Ricans have in the classroom. The situation is not quite as serious for Asian Americans on some standardized test measures of academic achievement, school attendance, and graduation rates.

Many elementary and secondary schools in the United States continue to be racially segregated. Students of color now constitute the majority population in at least 49 of the nation's 100 largest school districts, and this distribution is increasing yearly. The percentages of students of color range from a low of 58.3% in Pittsburgh, to 96.6% in Washington, D.C. In 31 of these districts, the percentage is 75 or higher (U.S. Department of Education, 2000). Yet the ethnicity of teachers, administrators, and policy makers in these districts is the reverse; European Americans far outnumber educators of color in school leadership and instructional positions (U.S. Department of Education, 2000).

Traditionally, urban schools have had less money, fewer resources, poorer facilities, larger numbers of inexperienced teachers, greater management problems, and higher turnover rates among teachers, administrators, and students. Moreover, too few systematic and sustained high-quality teacher education and leadership development programs exist to prepare educators to work effectively with urban students.

Levels of educational attainment for culturally diverse students, as measured by such factors as high school graduation, daily attendance records, persistence rates, and levels of academic proficiency, are increasing for successive generations. However, dropout rates for African Americans, Latinos, and American Indians continue to be higher than the national average.

Another school attendance factor that contributes to educational inequality is school delay, defined as the discrepancy between the educational level reached by students and the normal level corresponding to their age. African Americans, Latinos, and American Indians repeat grades more often and generally take longer to complete school. These delays may indicate a cumulative process that ultimately results in the child leaving school permanently. Even for students who remain in school, the likelihood of the greater number of them receiving educational equality is dubious. The academic achievement levels of many culturally diverse students (except some Asian Americans) are significantly lower than the national average. The overall academic achievement profiles of culturally diverse students send mixed messages. Small gains have been made in math and science but not in reading and writing.

Dropout rates, limited English proficiency, discipline problems, and various special education needs are high and growing among some Asian students, particularly those who are recent immigrants to the United States. When entering school, many Vietnamese, Hmong, and Cambodian students are placed in classes below grade level (Miller-Lachmann & Taylor, 1995). The social stigma and isolation associated with this placement increase their dropout rates. Many do not feel positive about their physical features and stature, have psychological problems because of what they experienced in their home country, and suffer ethnic identity conflicts.

Achievement patterns may be a direct result of curriculum differentiations that exist in schools. Another possibility is that all students are not receiving the best quality of education possible. The pattern of differential educational achievement among ethnic groups is firmly established by grade 4 and it prevails thereafter. These patterns give credence to the contention that the longer African Americans, Latinos, and American Indians remain in school, the further they fall behind academically. As to the mix, the system of teaching routinely used to organize students for instruction is probably the most effective means of denying educational equality. Because African Americans, Latinos, American Indians, and our newest Southeast Asians are overrepresented in lower-track curricular programs, they are continuously and systematically denied equal access to the substance of quality education.

When the background of the teacher differs greatly from that of the students, a setting results that is alien and tension-producing for the student, the teacher, or both. The fact is that unfriendly, tension-filled, and culturally incompatible classroom climates can reduce the potential for educational equality for students who function in those classrooms. It is the educational system that needs to be changed and restructured, not the culturally diverse child. I would suggest that the existence of equal access to educational opportunities is contingent on comparability in culturally relevant learning experiences, instead of treating all students identically.

Teachers are often guilty of the color-blind perspective, which sees racial and ethnic group membership as irrelevant to the ways individuals are treated. They believe that all children, regardless of their backgrounds, should be given the assurance that they have a fair chance to compete with others as they make their way in American society. Children should be seen as individuals and not as members of ethnic groups. Interviews with teachers (white and those of color) suggested that many see schools as institutions that can help impart middle-class values and modes of behavior to culturally diverse and lower-class students so they can break out of the cycle of poverty and become middle-class persons themselves.

A black administrator said that she does not address group differences in her school when she is dealing with children. "I don't care if they are black, white, brown, green or yellow, they must follow the school rules and remember they are no longer in their communities. They are here. School values are what is important. They simply have to get used to it.

Until we can counsel them into the right types of behavior we will continue to have problems" (anonymous quote).

For some teachers and administrators, acknowledging that one was aware of another's race was viewed as a sign of prejudice. When I said to a white male teacher that I had noticed only one white girl in his class of 18, he responded, "Well, just a minute. Let me check." After looking at his class roster in his grade book, he said, "You know, you are right. I never noticed that before."

Many teachers also asserted that their students rarely noticed race. However, interviews with those same students made it clear that they are very conscious of their race or the race of other students. When I asked one young woman who her friends were, she responded, "Well, Stacey and Lou and Amy, even though she is white."

Student awareness of cultural diversity is also illustrated by an observation of a seventh-grade classroom. Henry, a white male student, came up to me (a white female observer) and said, "You know, it just isn't fair the way they set up this class. There are 15 black kids, and 6 American Indians, and only 4 white kids. I can't learn here." When asked why, he said that the kids picked on him and copied his work. "It just isn't fair," he repeated. In this case, the teacher refused to recognize and deal with the existence of cultural intergroup tensions.

PARENT/FAMILY INVOLVEMENT

In today's society, what the school teaches as well as who and how the school teaches can create tensions between parents and schools. To alleviate these tensions, parents, educators, and communities must work together. Parents must become involved.

Student diversity mirrors parent and community diversity. Parent involvement challenges teachers. Parents are from different racial and ethnic groups, single parents, low-income parents, and parents who do not speak English. The increase in the number of grandparents who are providing primary care to their grandchildren is another example of parent diversity.

One of the most significant social changes in the United States in the last 30 years is the increase in the percentage of children living with one parent. Many of these parents are also living in poverty or are homeless. However, these parents are strong supporters of education. They see education as a means to a better life for their children.

Many teachers are ambivalent about parent and community involvement in education. Even though teachers often say they want to involve parents, many are suspicious of parents and are uncertain what parents expect from them. Some feel parents disrupt their routine. Others do not think they have the time or skill to work with parents.

However, teachers are the key ingredient in parent-community involvement. They play multiple roles, including facilitator, communicator, and resource developer. Attitude is important. Parents of all groups are supportive if they believe that teachers like their children and want their children to succeed. Teachers can increase parent involvement in the classroom by establishing two-way communication, creating a positive climate for involvement, learning about the communities represented in the school, developing learning resources for parents, and allowing parents to play many roles, depending on their interests, skills, and talents.

CONCLUSION

The accelerating demographic and economic changes within our society, the deepening racial divide, and the elusive quest for equality and justice make multicultural education imperative in the 21st century. The gap between the rich and the poor has widened, visible signs of racial crisis have become stark, and the rate of increase of low-income and culturally diverse youth within the nation's schools has continued to outpace the growth rate of whites.

Yet the American dream is alive, and our nation continues to make gradual steps toward its realization. The significant numbers of immigrants that settle in this nation each year are testimony to the vitality of the American dream. The continuing growth of multicultural education courses is also evidence that educators are committed to actualizing the nation's democratic principles.

One goal of multicultural education is to help students develop decision-making skills so that they can become effective change agents in contemporary society. The students learn to view events, concepts, issues, and problems from diverse cultural and ethnic perspectives.

Additional goals of multicultural education include:

- Increasing students' sense of self-worth and belief that they have a chance for a successful future
- Making sure all students have equity, an equal opportunity to learn
- Encouraging the development of positive cultural attitudes
- Promoting empowerment to help students become self-directed, independent, and interdependent learners
- Empowering administrators to become stronger advocates for students
- Promoting inter- and intragroup harmony by providing knowledge, skills, and a classroom environment that prepares students to live and work with members of their own cultural group and members of other groups
- Providing instruction that includes opportunities for students to work together, learn from each other, and rely on each other

When teaching from a multicultural perspective, educators challenge assumptions and stereotypes; they examine curriculum from a broader point of view and in a proactive manner. They educate students for the real world by increasing students' understanding of diversity, race, and culture, for the less we know about another group, the more we make up. In addition, cultural continuity is promoted between the home and school. The students' culture is used to transcend social barriers and empower group identity.

The following are strategies that will help meet the above goals:

- Use social and cooperative learning.
- Vary teaching styles to accommodate learning styles.
- Use appropriate assessment instruments and practices.
- Promote student-centered classrooms.
- Discuss social issues.
- Set high teacher expectations.
- Share multiple perspectives.
- Involve parents and families.

- Develop bilingual education programs.
- Hire culturally diverse staff.
- Teach conflict-resolution strategies.
- Teach critical thinking and problem solving.
- Teachers need to be role models and adopt the role of mentor.
- Modify the curriculum as necessary so that individual needs are met based on ethnicity and culture.
- Prevent and reverse underachievement.
- Make supportive services available to help students adjust psychologically and socially.
- Train teachers to work effectively with their students and thus provide a culturally relevant and appropriate education.

In other words, proponents of a rich, culturally diverse curriculum must ensure that higher-order thinking and problem-solving skills are promoted. Educated citizens are able to apply, analyze, synthesize, and evaluate. They are able to recognize and solve problems. These skills are essential for academic success. More importantly, these skills are essential for success in life. One parent summed it up when she stated, "We must feel good about who we are before we can feel good about others."

Americans have always held tightly to the idea that ethnic cultures would melt or vanish. A strong assimilationist idea has dominated American society since early in our history. The American assimilationist idea envisions a society in which ethnicity and race are not important identities. This idea is symbolized by the melting pot concept. Even though the strong assimilationist idea in American society contributed greatly to the making of one nation out of disparate ethnic and immigrant groups, it has not eradicated ethnic and cultural differences and is not likely to do so in the future.

Diversity is a challenge and an opportunity. When groups with different cultures and values interact within a society, ethnocentrism, racism, and religious bigotry, as well as other forms of institutionalized rejection and hostility, occur. Cultural diversity is also an opportunity. It can enrich a society by providing novel ways to view events and situations, solve problems, and look at our relationship with the environment. (Traditional Indian cultures in North America viewed the earth as sacred and had deep reverence for all living creatures.) The challenge to schools is to try to shape a modernized, national culture that has selected aspects of traditional culture coexisting in some kind of delicate balance with a modernized society. As educators, we must help students develop cross-cultural competency, which consists of the abilities, attitudes, and knowledge the students need to function effectively within American society, within their own ethnic subsocieties, and within and across different ethnic cultures.

The total school curriculum should be transformed. All students, regardless of their race, ethnicity, or social class, should study about ethnic conflict in America. Curriculum should enable students to derive valid generalizations and theories about the characteristics of ethnic groups and to learn how they are similar and different, in both their past and present experiences. It is also essential to reconceptualize how we view American history and society in the school curriculum. We should view American history, literature, art, music, and culture from diverse perspectives rather than primarily or exclusively from the point of view of mainstream historians, writers, and artists.

Both insider and outsider perspectives should be studied. People who have experienced a historical event or social phenomenon, such as racial discrimination, refugee camps, or internment, often view and express the event differently than do people who have watched it from a distance. World events, issues, and concepts should also be studied from diverse cultural perspectives.

The current curriculum is not preparing most students to function successfully within the culturally diverse world of the future. Many students grow up in middle-class schools. Their world is very different from the world society in which they will be required to function in the future. The white race is a world minority. At least two out of three people in the world live in poor and developing nations in regions such as Africa, Asia, and Latin America. Yet, the one out of three people in the world who live in the developed Western nations consume most of the earth's resources and exercise most of the world's political and economic power. The world is sharply divided between the few who are rich and well-fed in the Western developed nations, who are predominantly white, and the many who are poor and hungry in Third World countries who are people of color. These sharp divisions also exist within nations. Experience has taught us that culturally diverse groups can work cooperatively only when they function in equal status (have a decent standard of living and access to political and economic power).

It has become increasingly obvious that the way we live affects people in other countries and that what they do affects us here in America. From the clearing of the rain forests in the Amazon to an oil spill in Alaska, human actions can upset the earth's elaborately balanced ecological system. The overthrow of apartheid in South Africa and the dismemberment of the Soviet Union had consequences for people in many other countries. The events of 9/11 alerted many groups in the United States to the effects of terrorism. More than ever before, students need to know about their peers in other countries.

Through looking carefully at conditions around them, students can develop an understanding of what it means to respect their heritage, to understand social forces of discrimination and prejudice, and yet to be free to live as citizens of the global world.

Americans must be prepared to live in a more closely interactive, interdependent world society. At the same time we must remember that even though we are all members of a society, each one of us remains a unique individual and each of us was born into a special culture.

The outcomes for students are clear and concise if a multicultural curriculum is effectively taught. Students will be able to

- Identify a strong sense of their own self-esteem and accept the right of all others to similar feelings of self-esteem.
- Describe their own culture.
- Identify culturally diverse groups represented in our pluralistic society.
- Discuss the history of immigration to the United States and how thinking about immigrants evolved over the years.
- Identify needs and concerns universal to people of all cultures (family, love, health).
- Compare cultural variations (food preparation, dance).
- Read and discuss literature by and about members of diverse cultures.
- Share folklore from different cultures.
- Discuss age- and gender-related concerns.

- Identify examples of stereotyped thinking and prejudice in real life and in literature.
- Participate in community and school affairs as informed, empathetic young citizens.
- Continue to learn about cultural diversity as part of lifelong learning.

As John Dewey wrote in 1902, "Education enables individuals to come to full possession of all their powers." The aim of all good teaching should be to assist each student in reaching his or her fullest potential. As stated earlier in the book, multicultural education is a philosophy, goal, and process. It is a philosophy based on the fundamental belief that all people must be accorded respect, regardless of age, race, ethnicity, socio-economic status, religion, or physical or mental ability. It is predicated on the belief that all people have intrinsic worth. Thus, multicultural education seeks to affirm individual differences and human diversity through the elimination of prejudices, biases, and stereotypes based on sociodemographic variables. When an education is multicultural, it permeates all aspects of schooling. It is comprehensive, penetrating, and integrating rather than narrow, supplementary, restrictive, and assimilating.

Multiculturalism succeeds best in a society that has many different ethnic groups and a political system that promotes freedom of expression and awareness and understanding of cultural differences. Ethnic groups bring variety and richness to a society by introducing their own ideas and customs.

As a process, multicultural education helps students to develop competencies relative to perceiving, evaluating, and doing. The focus is on students' understanding and learning to negotiate differences across cultures. As a process, multicultural education emphasizes that individuals can learn to become pluralistic in their thoughts, behaviors, and affect. Similarly, individuals do not have to reject their cultural identity to function effectively in diverse settings.

In a classroom today, to teach with excellence, one needs to affirm the students' diversity. Pay attention to students' identities to help them achieve. Acknowledge the importance of African American men to American life to hold the attention of Lester and Ralph. Acknowledge the prior learning of Mai-ka and Chi to help them learn English. Become familiar with each student's learning style to teach effectively. Pay attention to personal and social needs to help students perceive school as a positive experience. Address prejudice and stereotypes.

Children are connected with their own cultural context. As a classroom teacher, you must understand why families immigrated and the pressures the children experienced. Realize that the future of the United States depends on its diverse children. What kind of adults will they become? Will they become clear and critical thinkers? Will they have a sense of social justice and care for others?

How will you approach excellence and equity in your classroom? We can guarantee that students will have their identities shaped by their culture. All will respond in one way or another to people who differ from themselves. All will grow up in a society that is still racist and classist. You are the only one who can guarantee what you will do about that.

True Americans value fairness and honesty when it comes to cultural diversity. Skin color does not matter. We must continue to advocate for change. As Mohandas Gandhi once said, "You must become the change you want to see in this world."

Chapter Four

Language Diversity and Education

Language is a shared and sharing part of culture that cares little about formal classifications and much about vitality and connection, for culture itself perishes in purity or isolation.

—Carlos Fuentes

Language diversity has a strong influence on the content and process of educational practices for both culturally diverse language students and majority students in the United States. Language, as a system of communication linking sound, written or visual symbols, and meaning, is an indispensable bridge for sharing knowledge, skills, values, and attitudes within and across cultures.

Language is a powerful and transformative part of culture. As with culture, language is learned, it is shared, and it evolves and changes over time. Language is a forceful instrument for giving individuals, groups, institutions, and cultures their identity. Through language we communicate our values, attitudes, skills, and aspirations as bearers of culture and as makers of future culture.

"Can't we all get along?" asked Rodney King, following a race riot in Los Angeles that started because of miscommunication, because of not understanding another's communication process. Involved in a chase and brutally beaten by white police officers, this black American spoke plaintively after days of chaos resulting from the ensuing initial trial and the acquittal of these officers, which triggered widespread protest and destruction. King's question is still being addressed in classrooms across the country. Language diversity among cultures may contribute to racial violence and abuse of human rights, which continue to appear in all areas of the country today, threatening everyone's chance to live a full life. "Getting along" has never been a simple matter. It clearly demands the concerted efforts of all of us. Learning to get along with culturally diverse people requires commitment and communication.

During the first half of the 20th century, the national aim was to assimilate all immigrants into the American culture as quickly as possible. Newcomers were expected to forget their native languages and to learn to speak and write English, the accepted language of the nation, the language of business and society. Metaphorically, the United States was seen as a huge cauldron, a melting pot, into which all diverse immigrants were dumped until their differences melted away and they became much alike.

However, the melting pot metaphor has become inappropriate as we recognize the presence of cultural diversity as a strength, not a weakness. Therefore, we see this country now as a tossed salad, where languages are accepted and various groups contribute to the national multiculture while mainstreaming their distinct identity. Another metaphor is the image of a quilt of many cultures and many histories, stitched together to create a beautiful and useful object. As a result, individuals can be proud of their ethnic heritage and language instead of ashamed of their differences. This stance directly affects the school community and language development and how it is presented.

Teachers need to understand the complexity of our population and how this diversity has evolved. The history of our pluralistic population begins with the heterogeneous American Indian civilizations and their languages that flourished here before the explorers from Europe encountered them on the North American continent. On the East Coast, immigrants in the early years came from various European countries: England, France, Germany, and Spain. At the same time, exploration was taking place on the West Coast as Russian hunters ventured east into the vast territory known as Alaska and south to California. Cortez and other explorers moved through Mexico into the Southwest.

People came with many different goals: freedom of religion, challenge of exploration, and hope for wealth. Thousands were brought forcibly from Africa as slaves. Twentieth-century immigrants include Vietnamese, Hmong, Haitians, Ethiopians, and Mexicans. The history of the United States clearly identifies the polyethnic roots of a wide and fascinating variety of people.

Through multicultural education we seek to promote equity and excellence across such variables as race, ethnicity, nationality, social class, and language background. It is vital for educators to understand the function language can play in either helping or inhibiting the educational success of students.

Given the strong connection between language and identity it seems very important for educators to think carefully about how they respond to a child's use of his or her native language at school. Often schools work hard to strip away the child's native language, asking parents to speak only English to their children at home, punishing children with detention for using their native language at school, or even holding back education until children have mastered English.

Margarita, a high school student from Puerto Rico, said, "In school there were stereotypes about the bilingual students, big time. Since they don't speak 'the' language (English) they don't belong here." While fluency in English is a necessary educational goal, the child's fluency in his or her native tongue need not be undermined to achieve it.

There is increasing evidence that the level of proficiency in one's native language has a direct influence on the development of proficiency in the second language. Contrary to common belief, it makes sense to use students' native language to reinforce their acquisition of English. Research suggests it takes five to seven years, on average, to develop the level of English proficiency needed to succeed academically in school (National Association for Bilingual Education, n.d.).

The attempted destruction of an oppressed people's native language has been an issue for American Indians. In fact, Indian education as carried out by the U.S. government in the 19th and 20th centuries served as the model for early Americanization efforts in Puerto Rico. The physical and cultural dislocation visited upon American Indians still has major implications for the identity development of Indian youth today.

LANGUAGE VARIETY IN THE UNITED STATES

As a language laboratory, the United States is truly remarkable. Of the scores of American Indian languages existing prior to European contact, 175 have survived the overwhelming assimilative powers of the English language. The successive waves of immigrants to the United States have also made the nation linguistically rich. Today the nation's language assets range from such languages as Navajo, still spoken in the same communities in which it was spoken hundreds of years ago, to Hmong, spoken by refugees from the highlands of Laos, Thailand, and Cambodia. Others include Gullah, a creole of English and West African origin spoken from the Carolinas to northern Florida; Louisiana French creole, a blend of French and African vocabulary; and Hawaiian creole, a blend of English, Hawaiian, Japanese, Chinese, Portuguese, and Ilocano. Hawaiian creole plays a key role in the lives of many Hawaiian children both socially and academically.

Black English is also a unique American language that evolved during the 20th century and spread throughout the United States. Black English reflects influence from British and American English, as well as English-based pidgin from 16th-century West Africa. As with any type of language use, there is great speech variation among speakers of black English. Because of African Americans' historical status as an oppressed minority, whites have tended to perceive black English as a mass of random errors committed by blacks trying to speak English.

Multiple negation is perhaps one of the most stigmatized aspects of black English when speakers enter the formal school system. Yet there is no logical basis for such stigmatization. Acceptance or nonacceptance of the double negative as a socially correct form is essentially a historical accident. According to Penelope O'Malley, an ebonics scholar, multiple negation was an integral part of the English language up to the time of Shakespeare. Latin is credited for having influenced the single negation in English. Romance languages such as Spanish, French, and Italian use the double negative as part of their standard speech patterns.

Experts in language acquisition are now beginning to realize that children who are not using standard English are certainly not language deficient. If anything, these children reflect a high level of creativity and spontaneity with language behavior, which is highly desirable for cognitive development (National Association for Bilingual Education, n.d.).

Gullah, Louisiana French creole, Hawaiian creole, and black English have much in common. They are rule-governed and they are legitimate linguistic expressions, just as standard English is. They are a link to our past, and they have a birthright to exist and be accepted. Yet they are not given much recognition in the larger society. They are viewed by many as aberrant and inferior language varieties. Our goal should be to build on and add to what is already present in the lives of students. Creative bridges using the early socialization patterns of the home language and culture can be useful in motivating students to learn.

Now that we have surveyed a few nonstandard language varieties found in the United States, we can move on by looking at the backgrounds of students from non-English-speaking communities.

As a result of shifting demographics, the United States is currently experiencing an increase in the number of English-language learners in the schools. Since the passage of the 1968 Title VII Bilingual Education Act and the landmark U.S. Supreme Court Decision *Lau v. Nichols*, which provided a legal basis for equitable treatment of students from non-English-speaking backgrounds in U.S. schools, educational policy for non-English-language communities has put linguistic culturally diverse students in the national spotlight.

Non-English-background students in America's schools come from an astounding variety of backgrounds. For example, many foreign-born children come to the schools speaking only the language of their home country. Their families may be voluntary immigrants or involuntarily uprooted refugees, such as the Hmong. They may reside in the United States legally or as undocumented immigrants. There are also U.S.-born language-diverse students. This group includes speakers of American Indian languages.

Upon entering school, all of these students may fall anywhere on a broad continuum of language status. The child may be entirely monolingual in the non-English language, bilingual in the home language and English, or dominant in English, with only a few fragmentary skills in the ancestral language.

The diversity of languages in the United States is truly amazing. In remote Anchorage, Alaska, students speaking more than 100 different languages from virtually every region of the world have been identified in the local school district's bilingual educational program. The Los Angeles School District, whose identified culturally diverse students speak at least 80 different languages, offers bilingual instruction in Spanish, Cantonese, Vietnamese, Korean, Filipino, and Armenian. With its large diverse language population, California has become the Ellis Island of the new century (Los Angeles School District, 2004).

Overall, between 1990 and 2000, the demographic trend showed that the American Indian population (including Eskimo and Aleut) grew by 37.9%, Asian and Pacific Islanders by 107.8%, Hispanic Americans by 53%, and "Others" by 45.1% (National Association for Bilingual Education, n.d., p. 1). Increased immigration from both Latin America and Asia and high fertility rates within these populations are some of the major factors contributing to this demographic shift.

The upswing in immigration has resulted in large numbers of school entrants whose first language is not English. The problem for schools now becomes who is eligible for bilingual services and how long they are to be served. There are still a disproportionate number of English language learners who do not achieve well academically. Despite the research-based knowledge we have gained over the past 30 years about how individuals learn their first and second languages and how assimilative forces work with immigrants, there is still a wide gap between theory and practice. There continues to be strong resistance to bilingual instruction by many in educational circles despite the evidence indicating that English language learners who develop a strong sociocultural, linguistic, and cognitive base in their primary language tend to transfer those attitudes and skills to the other languages and culture.

ADDRESSING LANGUAGE
NEEDS IN THE CLASSROOM

The basis for debate surrounding the education of culturally diverse language students has to do with the kind of citizens we want in our society. Should the school curriculum affirm cultural and linguistic pluralism, or should schools pursue a conservative agenda of assimilating non-English-speakers into mainstream U.S. society by subtracting their ancestral cultures and languages?

These questions raise some pointed and difficult issues regarding the nature and extent of cultural and linguistic pluralism in the United States. Rather than thinking in either/or terms of pluralism or assimilation, we need to view U.S. society as a dynamic and complex cultural and linguistic organism, one that is constantly undergoing evolution according to the nature of circumstances. It is not acceptable to blame the students' genetic, environmental, cultural, or linguistic background for lack of academic success in the English-dominated classroom. Programs and practices can be implemented to redress some of the past inequities experienced by both English-background students who come to our schools speaking stigmatized nonstandard versions of English and students whose primary language is not English. Given our current political climate, however, implementation of such programs can resemble paddling a canoe against a powerful and recurring tide with strong, cold winds buffeting it from all sides.

A good place to start in designing quality programs for language-diverse students is by examining teaching and learning classroom climates. Should students be trained to be bidialectical, that is, to be able to switch from their home language to standard English according to the situation? According to the Southwest Center for Educational Equity and Language Diversity, students learn better if they are able to switch from home language to English. Other educators view bidialecticalism as a waste of educational effort, suggesting students discard their home language and replace it with standard English. This is the focus of a study conducted by Sondra Thiederman. Yet most linguists keep reminding us that suppressing their language is confusing and detrimental to the academic and social well-being of students. Teachers should not judge children's language abilities by their schoolyard grammar. Poor academic performance could be the result of the school's reaction and approach to the child. For those students who come from totally non-English-speaking backgrounds, an active, hands-on teaching style rather than a lecture style is needed, with frequent checking for understanding.

School achievement in language skills is influenced significantly by one's learning style, hence, what contributes to school failure in language acquisition is not only *what* is taught, but also *how* it is taught and learned. Learning styles are a developmentally imposed set of personal characteristics that make the same teaching method effective for some students and ineffective for others. In other words, students are products of family and community settings that predispose them to patterns of behavior that are more or less functional in school settings. Learning styles are significantly influenced by culturally induced cognitive styles related to communicating, interacting, perceiving, and acquiring knowledge, often in their home language.

A large number of white students, fluent in English, prefer formal learning classroom designs, less structure in learning materials, and auditory modes of presentation. They are reflective, tactile, kinesthetic, independent learners who are responsible for their own language skills, learning, persistent, motivated, and task-oriented. Culturally diverse students tend to be holistic, rational, and visual learners. They learn best in social and cooperative settings, are socially oriented, and prefer tactile and kinesthetic learning and teaching experiences. Culturally diverse students do not fail in school because of learning style and language diversity, but because schools fail to accommodate these differences.

Concepts, knowledge base, and thinking skills should be developed in the home language through bilingual instruction, which includes an English as a Second Language (ESL) component. Social communicative skills, which are acquired fairly rapidly, are not sufficient for academic success. Schools must continue to provide support for students to achieve cognitive-academic language proficiency in English. The ESL teacher strives to enable the English-language learner to develop phonology, morphology, syntax, and vocabulary primarily through real communicative activities rather than through such approaches as lecture and drills.

With respect to cultural knowledge, effective ESL teachers do not necessarily need to speak the first languages of their students, but they do need to have as broad an understanding as possible of the history, folklore, traditions, values, attitudes, and current sociocultural situation of the cultural groups with which they work. This knowledge helps the teacher to understand behavior of ESL students as they adjust to life in the United States. Equally important, it shows the students and their parents that the teacher values the family's cultural background and recognizes that students do not come as blank tablets, but rather as unique individuals with a rich background.

There is also a need for continued development and maintenance of social and cultural bridges between the student's home life and school life. An awareness of how language is used in the home community will enable educators to be sensitive to school environments that are different. Efforts to equalize the social and linguistic status of white and culturally diverse students within the school setting will help to produce positive results for all students in the classroom and, ultimately, in society.

Language diversity is a powerful ingredient of multiculturalism and enriches the lives of those who use languages other than English. It also enriches the lives of monolingual English speakers as they live, study, and work with people of non-English-language backgrounds.

For English-language learners to succeed, they must master not only English vocabulary and grammar but also the way English is used in core content classes. They must be able to read and understand expository prose (material in textbooks), write persuasively, argue points of view, and take notes. They must also articulate their thinking skills in English.

Children from culturally diverse backgrounds may struggle with comprehending a text or concept presented in class because their schemata do not match those of the culture for which the text was written. In the United States, most school reading material, such as content-area texts, relies on the assumption that students' prior knowledge is knowledge that is common to all children. Many culturally diverse students immigrate from other countries and bring an array of experiences that are quite different from those of the mainstream culture in America, and many have gaps in their education. Even for students born in the United States, culture has strong effects on reading comprehension. We must remember that students who are learning English as an additional language are the fastest-growing segment of the school-age population in the United States.

MAKING ALL STUDENTS FEEL INCLUDED

All students come to school as members of specific cultural groups. Along with their native language, they have learned a particular way of being in the world; they were socialized into their culture. They also came to school carrying their parents' hopes for the future.

From family and community members children unconsciously absorb standards of behavior, attitudes toward authority, patterns of speaking, and spiritual values. When culturally diverse children enter school, they are exposed to another set of values and expectations called "school culture." In school, for example, students are expected to work independently and often competitively. They are asked to show off in front of others or to expose their imperfect reading. Rewards are given for speed and uniformity. How can we provide a bridge between students' home culture and school? How can we keep students from feeling excluded? Today's culturally diverse classrooms require teaching that incorporates and responds to the many cultural influences affecting students' ability to learn.

Educators must become culturally responsive teachers. Learn about your own cultural background and strive to understand why we make the judgments we do in order to accept how other cultures reach different conclusions. Learn about your students. They may have a language you can't understand, practice a religious philosophy contrary to yours, and have made life-or-death choices that you hope never to face. Finally, share (do not force) your own culture, your customs, and beliefs with your students. By doing so you model respect for others and demonstrate that culture is important in everyone's life. Get acquainted, build a community, and break down prejudice and stereotypes.

Students bring unquestioned stereotypes and expectations to the classroom that they have picked up from their own family, the media, and their experiences outside of school. We must bring these out into the open and examine them through discussion. Students already know about bias and unfair approaches to life. As educators we can help our students learn how to generalize from their individual experiences with prejudice to a positive approach to diversity.

Students are individuals, and they bring their language diversity with them to school. Their cultural background affects what they do. Because culture is usually invisible, it is often difficult to recognize its effects. As educators we can't resolve all the social issues that beset our students' lives, but we can make a difference through effective teaching. Student-centered teaching involves students in partnership as everyone brings something to the classroom.

One of our primary tasks as educators is to prepare students to live in the larger world. Because we cannot know exactly what they will face, we try to give them the adaptability and self-confidence to make their way under any circumstances. Because we are all part of a community, we cannot separate the interests of some people from the interests of the rest, the success of some students from the success of all. Every one of us has a stake in the task of educating our children for the future. Language and communication lead the way.

Many of our students live in urban settings. They are familiar with violence, poverty, and the increasing breakdown of traditional support systems. Focus attention on the nature of their community, the language, and the factors that influence its condition.

As we look at the variety of groups in the United States, we can see that the assimilationist model is an illusion. Immigrants from different countries were glad to achieve greater freedom and economic opportunities, but they never lost awareness of their distinct heritage. For many, schooling has been a double-edged sword. It has provided the necessary access to prestige, knowledge, and skills, yet at the same time it has acted as a mechanism to reduce the uniqueness of local identities and traditional cultures. Today as we shift our perspectives to look at diversity as an asset, schools can welcome many languages and many cultures that were not acknowledged before.

We must eliminate bias in our language curriculum. We must provide mirrors and windows that are not distorted or broken. School personnel must carefully and consistently examine materials and resources. A historian's view of the past is influenced by his or her language, culture, personal bias, available data and the times in which he or she lives and writes. Language involves presenting interpretations and points of view.

Also, remember, throughout human society, history has been written by the victors and not by the vanquished. Students study histories of American Indians and African Americans that were written by mainstream historians who had little empathy or understanding of the language or cultures of those whom they are writing about. In Colonial America, male Anglo-Saxon Protestants with property controlled most social, political, economic, and military institutions. Our founding fathers had a deep suspicion of and contempt for individuals who were culturally and racially different and did not speak English. They perpetuated stereotypes and myths about excluded groups to justify their oppression.

Key biases to look for in regard to language are:

- Negative representations: Using language to represent certain groups in an unflattering or demeaning manner. (Indians are savages, Mexican Americans are lazy, African Americans are on welfare, and gang members are black, Indian, or Asian.)

- Overgeneralizations: Black families are headed by women; Hispanic families have several children; drugs, violence and crime, poverty, and homelessness are restricted to culturally diverse groups.
- Stereotyping: Asians are studious, African Americans are athletic, Hispanics are lazy.
- Omissions: The reading materials omit certain groups altogether or underrepresent them.
- Superficial and insignificant changes: To diversify materials, some authors and publishers simply darken pictures of whites without changing the content; thus pictures of diverse groups may be unrealistic.
- Superior/inferior positions: Materials place culturally diverse groups in low-level or subservient roles/jobs; whites are in supervisory, prestigious, professional positions.
- Ethnocentrism: Materials present the white perspective and the English language exclusively.
- Minimization: Materials gloss over, ignore, or trivialize the contributions, histories, and strengths of culturally diverse groups, glossing over issues like slavery, language discrimination, and other injustices.
- Classism: Materials present and show preference for middle-class European standards and values (e.g., success means having a college degree) and the English language.

As educators, we must look at these biases carefully and then ask five questions when addressing language curriculum and instruction:

- Does the language used in materials, lessons, and strategies promote educational equity?
- Does the language used in curriculum and instruction promote intergroup harmony?
- Does the language used in curriculum and instruction help increase students' knowledge regarding various groups, including their own?
- Are windows (focus on others) and mirrors (focus on self and own group) provided so learning is relevant, engaging, and empowering?

- Does the language used in curriculum and instruction help to correct distortions about culturally diverse groups?

To reduce or eliminate language bias, the following strategies are recommended:

- *Deal with prejudice head-on.* Have students examine television programs, movies, magazines, and textbooks for prejudice, bias, and stereotyping.
- *Deal with stereotypes.* Replace teaching about tepees, igloos, etc. with discussions of real, current problems and issues (reservation poverty, Alaskan land claims).
- *Deal with power.* The ethnic experience within the United States cannot be understood without considering the role that the struggle for power among competing ethnic groups has played in shaping American history.
- *Build a sense of community.* Provide opportunities for student dialogue, use a partner system (buddy, liaison, tutor, mentor, interpreter) to facilitate learning inside and outside the classroom.
- *Increase self-understanding.* Incorporate self-esteem, self-concept, and racial/cultural identity building as part of the affective curriculum.
- *Increase empathy.* Help students to see history and current events through the eyes of the "oppressed."

EXPLORING LANGUAGE
AND LINGUISTIC DIVERSITY

Language changes are normal. Remember as you present the English language to students that so-called standard English is the product of influences from many different people and languages. The English that exists today bears the imprint of factory workers as well as scientists, children playing in the streets, and English professors. It contains the particular speech patterns of people from different cultural backgrounds.

The increasing number of students in the classroom who speak languages other than English is an area of great concern and controversy today. All educators need to know how to teach this population effectively. Unfortunately, the labels usually associated with these students, such as ESL (English as a second language), LEP (limited English proficiency), and NES (non-English-speaking), focus our attention on what they cannot do, leading to language deficiency models and remedial instruction. In addition, many people confuse an inability to express oneself fluently in English with an inability to think clearly, so that students needing assistance only with English language skills are denied access to the full academic content of their grade level. An alternative approach is to view the students' native language as an asset, both in helping them learn a new language and also as a benefit to all students. New instructional strategies, such as sheltered English, in which teachers modify their delivery of lesson content to make new information more comprehensible, serve to make all students feel included.

In school, students learn language, they learn *about* language, and they learn *through* language. As educators we must acknowledge the critical role that language plays in teaching and learning. Language is the heart of the students' identity. We have the responsibility to bring language into the classroom in a way that acknowledges its importance in knowing who we are and what the world is all about. We do this by reflecting on our own language, its history and variety, and by exploring other examples of languages and their uses. As we reflect we must include families. A Ghanaian proverb states, "The ruin of a nation begins in the homes of its people." How true this statement is.

Thousands of articles and hundreds of books, reports, and programs have focused on families and education and a significant percentage of these publications focus on family involvement and its impact on student achievement. One theme threads through these works: families play a central and critical role in their child's education and language development.

Many significant and troubling issues face culturally diverse families. They are more likely to live in poverty, to be headed by single-parent mothers, and to have parents with lower educational levels than white students. Single-parent status is often associated with poverty, role strain, and the need to meet survival or subsistence needs.

Strategies must therefore be tailored to meet the individual needs of culturally diverse families. In essence, there is a critical need to promote literacy among culturally diverse families. There is also a need to promote racial pride, for far too many families wrestle with poor racial identities.

Family involvement has been defined and described in many ways. For example, family involvement that impacts achievement can be minimal (fundraising, field trips) or substantive (volunteering in classrooms, participating on decision-making committees). Further, family involvement can take place in school settings or at home (monitoring homework, setting times for studying). Family involvement ranges from superficial to substantive, from temporary to permanent.

Family involvement and partnerships between home and school help to improve student outcomes, including grades, test scores, attendance, and classroom behavior. Certainly, role strain and economic problems serve as barriers to culturally diverse family involvement. Just as important, but seldom addressed, is the reality that many (perhaps most) families do not know how to be involved. Thus, family education programs are essential if family involvement is to increase and if families are to truly impact their children's academic achievement.

One suggestion is to involve families in literacy initiatives. Schools can create literature and literacy workshops for families. These workshops should help families understand and choose multicultural books, to ask higher-level-thinking questions, and to develop problem-solving skills. Schools can also survey students and families about their favorite books, invite families to visit the classroom to watch teachers model effective teaching with literature, have books displayed in a showcase near the office and/or classrooms, and make books accessible to families through a lending library.

If parents are to be truly involved in their children's education, they (like educators) must have knowledge, strategies, and skills for helping their children. Teachers acquire these in formal educational settings, while families seldom receive formal training in rearing and educating their children. Families must know how to choose high-quality literature containing multicultural themes and concepts. Literature needs to be accurate and realistic and help increase the child's self-awareness and understanding of self and others. Dozens of topics can be addressed when families read together: self-understanding, self-pride, social skills, relationships, and realistic family expectations.

Overall, family education programs can give families a sense of empowerment to share in the ownership of their children's education, achievement, and school outcomes. This is a shared responsibility between school and home. Both partners must promote, nurture, and sustain students' achievement.

INFUSING MULTICULTURAL EDUCATION INTO READING AND LANGUAGE ARTS PROGRAMS

"As children and young people learn their language, they learn to think," stated James Squire, in a speech given at the Central California Council of Teachers of English Conference in San Francisco in 1982. Language and literacy are foundational to learning across the curriculum. Oral language enables even very young children to express their thinking, which can later be expressed in writing.

Because we live in a multicultural world, multicultural education should be an integral part of instruction. Multicultural education extends to any area of study. Every teacher chooses consciously or unconsciously to allow multicultural education either to exist only as the "hidden curriculum" that children absorb or to enhance explicit learning experiences designed to combat cultural misunderstanding.

We must provide a language arts curriculum that will provide us with a knowledge base from which to begin planning a multicultural-based language arts program. This program should include promotion/development of listening, speaking, thinking, reading, and writing.

Let the following assumptions guide your lessons:

- *A strong-thinking language base is necessary for success in reading and writing.* Thinking and language permeate all learning.
- *Reading and writing cannot be taught in isolation.* Integrating the language arts reinforces learning efficiently and effectively.
- *Beginning readers need to learn basic phonics information but reinforce this learning through reading and writing whole language.*
- *Children learn through frequency of practice.*
- *Literature must be an integral part of instruction across the curriculum.*

- *Both author and audience work together to construct meaning.*
- *Reading, writing, and thinking abilities grow uniquely for each individual.*

While oral language provides the foundation for all learning, we must also realize that what we read is writing, an expression of a person's thinking. Literature offers an outstanding way of promoting multicultural understanding. Selected novels present people of different cultures experiencing emotions and solving the problems they face. We can then develop empathetic feelings for all people.

Multicultural concepts, language, and attitudes must be infused into learning activities across the curriculum over time if students are to feel the full effect. The following are areas you may choose to develop using a language base:

- *Art.* Art reveals historical development and plays a major role in human development.
- *Music.* Music is a part of every culture. Students should experience a variety of musical themes (blues, jazz, bluegrass, classical, new age, country, pop, and music of a specific culture). Music is a universal language all can share.
- *Physical education and health.* Around the world eyes watch the performance of the Olympic contestants who represent their countries proudly. All share their emotions as the national anthem is played for the gold medalist. Physical performance, the power and the grace, is a universal language we all understand.
- *Mathematics.* The use of numbers and mathematical concepts represents yet another universal language that we share around the globe.
- *Science.* Literary selections frequently provide science backgrounds, for science appears in both fiction and nonfiction.
- *Social studies.* The study of geography provides a sense of place, where we are in relation to others, and how we fit into the huge global village. History can help us realize that not all problems have solutions, teach us to accept compromise, and show that democracy is a way of living.

We need to make sure all students learn about other cultures as well as their own. To do this we must develop multicultural understanding in students that requires more instructional attention than presenting a unit on African Americans in February or a unit on Mexico in September. Students must be constantly involved in exploring and discussing the similarities and differences among human beings.

Listen to one another. Listening is perhaps the greatest gift we can offer one another. Listening and learning are closely linked. If we do not listen well, we do not learn well. Learning then becomes a consequence of thinking about what we have heard or read or seen. Judgment shuts down thinking, whether it is praise or rejection.

Therefore, be present, be open, listen without judgment and with empathy, seek understanding, view learning as mutual, honor the individual, and honor the process.

Chapter Five

American Indian Students: The Invisible Minority

Education is your most powerful weapon. With education you are the White man's equal, without education you are his victim.

—Chief Plenty Coups (Crow Tribe)

The first people in America were the Indians. They built their wigwams where the homes, schools, factories, and stores of modern cities now rise. They hunted deer or buffalo over land where today massive farms exist. Their hunters, warriors, and traders used paths now followed by roads and railroads. Indian words dot America's map. Place names such as Massachusetts, Mississippi, Ohio, Chicago, and Pontiac, Michigan, originated from American Indian languages. Twenty-seven states and large numbers of towns, cities, rivers, and lakes bear names from the languages of the first Americans.

Indian farmers were the first to grow corn, potatoes, tomatoes, peanuts, pineapple, cranberries, chocolate, popcorn, and beans and the first to make maple sugar and grits. They found uses for such plants and trees as rubber, tobacco, and the cinchona tree (for quinine).

Words borrowed in English show how much the first settlers owed the American Indian (*chetmunk* became chipmunk, *moos* became moose, *aposoun* became opossum, *paccan* became pecan, etc.). Other gifts from the American Indian include knowledge of the best trails and ways of traveling across the country by canoe and snowshoe. Indians also invented hammocks, fry bread, sports and games (hide-and-seek, follow-the-leader, crack-the-whip, blindman's bluff, baggataway, and ice hockey). American Indians also contributed their distinctive styles of weaving, beadwork, masks, folklore, poetry, pottery, and painting.

The Indians had lived in America for many centuries before the white man first came from Europe. When Christopher Columbus arrived on American shores, in San Salvador in 1492, he called the native people *Indios* (Spanish for Indians) because he thought he had reached India. From that first encounter began the demise of the American Indian.

EARLY LIFE IN THE AMERICAS

When European explorers arrived in the Western Hemisphere in 1492, it was populated by many different cultures and groups that became collectively known as "Indians" to Europeans. This misnaming of the aboriginal people of the Americas by the Europeans foreshadowed the misunderstanding, distrust, and hostility that later developed between the two groups.

The early history of American Indians is still somewhat a mystery to scientists and archeologists who are still trying to unravel their early history. Although the word *Indian* often conjures a stereotypic image in the popular mind, Indian people are quite diverse, both physically and culturally. Their skin color, height, hair texture, and facial features vary greatly. How Indians survived also varied widely. Some groups obtained food by fishing and hunting, others through agriculture. Political institutions also were quite diverse. Highly sophisticated confederations were common among the northeastern tribes, such as the League of the Iroquois, and in the southeast, the Creek Confederacy. California tribes had no formal political institutions but were organized into small family units headed by men who had group responsibilities but little authority over others. Warring and raiding were important aspects of the Apache culture, but the Hopi were "the peaceful ones." Social class had little meaning among the southwest tribes, but it was extremely important in the northwest Pacific Coast cultures. Food, hunting, home-style clothing, tools, and religious ceremonies also varied greatly among and within various American Indian cultural groups.

SIMILARITIES IN INDIAN CULTURE

Although American Indian cultures are highly diverse, they are similar in many ways. Indian cultures were and still are based on a deep spirituality, which greatly influences all aspects of life. They see themselves living in harmony with all beings on earth. Traditional Indian culture sees an interdependent relationship between all living things. Just as one seeks harmony with one's human family, so should a person try to be in harmony with nature, rather than dominant over it. "The earth was created by the assistance of the sun, and it should be left as it was. . . . The earth and myself are of one mind," said Chief Joseph of the Nez Perce. They view the universe as a harmonious whole, with every object and being having a sacred life. American Indians have a deep respect and reverence for the earth and for all other living things. People must not harm the earth because it is sacred. White man's agriculture defiled Mother Earth. White men plowed up the ground, cut down trees, and killed everything.

The Indian conception of the earth and their relationship to the land differed greatly from that of the Europeans and was a source of conflict among the cultures. The Europeans regarded the earth as a commodity that could be broken into parts and owned by individuals. To the American Indian, the earth was sacred and consequently could never be owned by human beings.

Indian people had a deep respect for the rights and dignity of the individual. Decisions were based on group consensus. There were few hierarchical positions. Respect was earned by becoming outstanding warriors, being able to communicate with the spirits, or learning to perform some other service the community needed and valued. Another shared cultural value between Indian groups included extended family and kinship obligations. Group needs are more important than individual needs. Communal sharing with the less fortunate was expected.

Because of their feudalistic background, the Europeans looked for kings among the Indians and assumed the Indian chiefs had absolute authority over their tribes. The Europeans made treaties with the chiefs and assumed they were binding. They did not understand that the chief's authority was usually limited by the tribal council. This cultural conflict between the Europeans and Indian groups haunted their relationships for centuries.

EARLY CONTACT WITH EUROPEANS

The Indians' earliest contacts with the Europeans were usually friendly and generally involved trade. In exchange for furs, the Indians acquired rum, guns, gunpowder, horses, tools, and other goods. Tribes that wanted European goods but had depleted the supply of fur-producing animals began to invade the territories of other tribes to obtain furs for trade.

From 1540 to 1790 no one power was dominant in the Indian territory that had been invaded by the Europeans. Once the British colonies were formed, struggles for power began between the British and the Indians, and this deeply influenced Indian policy. Deep factionalism within the tribes occurred. The League of the Iroquois was eventually destroyed by the European wars.

Next came removal. Once an Indian tribe had signed a treaty, the whites schemed to remove them from their land. The Indian people either had to relocate or be exterminated. The federal government legitimized Indian removal with the Removal Act of 1830. Many of the Eastern tribes were forced to settle in territories occupied by the Plains Indians. More fighting among the tribes resulted. The California gold rush of 1849 hastened the defeat of the Western tribes by the government.

Indians had been conquered by the late 1880s, and vigorous efforts to eradicate the cultures, values, and ways of life were already under way. Reservation life was forced upon the tribes, which were governed by agents who ruled the Indians with an iron hand and stifled all their efforts at self-initiative.

After the Indians had been thoroughly subjugated and placed on reservations, white authorities began efforts to "civilize" them, which meant to make Indians as much like whites as possible from dress to language. The goal became to assimilate the Indians quickly into the mainstream society. No attempt was made to give Indians a choice or to encourage them to retain their culture. The children were given white people's education. Children were sent to boarding schools far away from home reservations so that the authority of their parents would be undermined.

The schools were a dismal failure. When children returned home, they were unable to function well in their ethnic cultures or within the mainstream society. What the schools tried to teach had no relevance to life on the reservations. The schools also failed to teach Indian children the white culture owing to the poor quality of teachers and curricula. Though the U.S. government's practice of removing children from their home environment was reversed in the 1930s, by then several generations of Indian children had lost their traditional cultural values and ways.

The boarding school concept has caused alienation between American Indians and traditional American education. Traditionally, American Indian children were hands-on learners who received their education from every member of the tribe. The children were often considered "slow" by their white teachers because they did not catch on quickly with this new "book in hand" style of learning. Laura Wittstock-Waterman, an Indian educator, stated that parent apathy and lack of involvement in their children's education is a direct result of these negative boarding school experiences, creating a cycle that continues even today.

During World War II many Indians left the reservation to seek employment in the war industries of the larger cities. This start of Indian urban migration coincided with the federal government's efforts to remove the Indians from the reservations and to end its responsibility for the Indian tribes. Many Indians were taken from their homes and relocated in urban areas in a manner that brought back memories of the earlier forced removal to reservations. Unprepared for urban life, many were devastated by this upheaval. Alcoholism, suicide, and homicide increased to epidemic proportions and continue to be the leading causes of death among Indians (U.S. Census Bureau, 1999).

When white explorers and settlers encountered the native population in North America, they tended to see Indians as simple primitives, a view that was used to justify paternalistic treatment and genocide. This stereotype was succeeded by that of the Noble Savage, a romanticized image of a lost tradition. Such stereotypes fix American Indians in the past, making it difficult for young American Indians to develop a cultural identity suitable for the 21st century.

American Indians have been reduced to cardboard figures, all wearing headdresses and saying "how." Many of our young Indian students cope by hiding behind Latino or black ancestry rather than risking humiliation and embarrassment. Life outside the reservation brings economic opportunities but cultural starvation.

Stereotyping continues despite what we try to say and do to alleviate it. Popular images about American Indians and Eskimos are widespread. Older Western movies shown on television contribute greatly to this stereotypic image. Textbooks still call the Americas the "New World" and imply, if not state, that Columbus "discovered" America. The implication is that American civilization did not exist until the Europeans first arrived in the late 15th century. They consequently in effect deny the existence of the American Indian cultures and civilization that had existed in the Americas for centuries before the Europeans arrived.

A major goal of our curriculum content should be to help students view the development of the Americas and of U.S. society in particular from the point of view of American Indians. For example, the movement of European Americans from the eastern to the western part of the United States was not, from the Indian point of view, a westward movement. The Lakota Sioux did not consider their homeland the West but rather that their land was the center of the universe. Students need to understand that the "western movement" had very different meanings for the migrating European Americans and for the Indians whose homelands were being invaded. Such a belief does little to promote racial and cultural pride among American Indian students, and it has the potential for promoting misguided notions of superiority or supremacy among other students. Students are misinformed (at best) and miseducated (at worst) by whose story (white or Indian) is told. By helping students view concepts, events, and issues from diverse cultural and ethnic perspectives, we can help them become critical thinkers and more compassionate citizens.

WHAT DO WE MEAN WHEN WE SAY "INDIAN"?

It is conservatively estimated that prior to 1492 there were 3 to 5 million indigenous people in America. Following the disastrous contact with Europeans, the populations were greatly reduced, and by 1850 there were only about 250,000 Indians left in North America. Now there are almost 2 million American Indians and Alaska Natives living in the continental United States. They represent more than 500 different cultural communities federally defined as sovereign entities with which the United States has a government-to-government relationship. Only the Cherokee, the Navajo, the Chippewa, and the Sioux have more than 100,000 members. In addition there are an estimated 250 native groups that are not recognized by the U.S. government.

The first Americans (American Indians and Native Hawaiians) are the nation's smallest racial groups, representing approximately 1% of the

U.S. population (U.S. Census Bureau, 1999). Although once referred to as the "vanishing Americans" these groups have increased steadily since the 1940 census.

Most American Indians live in Oklahoma, California, Arizona, and New Mexico. Census data from 1999 indicate that 65% live in urban areas and 25% live on reservations. Approximately 10% are scattered in rural areas (U.S. Census Bureau, 1999). Poverty runs rampant among many American Indian populations.

Each of the American Indian cultural communities has its own language, customs, religion, economy, historical circumstances, and environment. They range from the very traditional, whose members speak their indigenous language at home, to the mostly acculturated, whose members speak English as their first language. Most Indians identify with their particular ancestral community first and as American Indians second.

K. Tsianena Lowawaima, a professor of American Indian studies, says that a member of the Cherokee Nation living in Tahlequah, Oklahoma, is different from an English-speaking, powwow-dancing Lakota Sioux born and raised on the Pine Ridge reservation in South Dakota, who is different from a Hopi fluent in Hopi, English, Navajo, and Spanish who lives on her reservation and supports her family by selling "traditional" pottery in Santa Fe and Scottsdale galleries. The idea of being generically "Indian" really was a figment of the European imagination.

From the beginning of their encounters with Europeans in the 1500s, Indian values were at odds with the individualistic and capitalistic orientation of white settlers. Throughout the centuries U.S. government leaders were convinced that changing Indian cultural values was the key to "civilizing" Indians and acquiring Indian-controlled lands.

An elder in the Minneapolis Indian community summed it up as she told me in an interview at her home in 2004:

> For 500 years my people have been told in so many ways that we are no good, we are savages, we are not civilized, not Christian and must change our ways. My grandfather gave up his tribal religion and customs. He adopted Christianity. He and my grandmother and the other people on the reservation did their best to give up the old ways, become farmers, quit hunting, go to church, and be "good Indians, civilized Indians." They cried when the government took away their children and sent them off to board-

ing school. Some of the children never came home. Some came home to be buried. My grandparents cried again because their children grew up learning alien ways, forgetting their language and customs in schools far too far away to visit.

My parents married soon after they came home from the boarding school. They came from different tribes. They left the reservation encouraged by the U.S. government and the boarding school system to find jobs in the "real world." The promised jobs never materialized and, stuck between two worlds, the white world and the Indian, my father drank and beat my mother. My mother worked at menial jobs to support us. I was never parented because my parents, raised in government boarding schools, had nothing to give me. They had lost their culture and language. They had never been parented themselves. Boarding school nurturing was having their mouths washed out with soap for talking Indian and receiving beatings for failing to follow directions.

So this is my legacy and the legacy of many Indians, both reservation and urban. We are survivors of multigenerational loss and only through acknowledging our losses will we ever be able to heal. (Charlotte Little Eagle, White Earth Reservation)

The legacy of loss is accompanied by a legacy of resistance. As they had in the past, Indians resisted the termination policy, a policy toward American Indians during the 1950s and 1960s in which conservative congressmen led by Utah senator Arthur Watkins sought to emancipate the Indians by terminating federal ties to Indian communities and withdrawing federal support for tribal governments. The policy ended in the 1960s following the election of John F. Kennedy. The civil rights era included American Indian demands for greater self-determination and the development of the American Indian Movement. In response to Indian activism the federal government promoted Indian-controlled schools, protected Indian religious freedom, and preserved the traditional Indian languages.

Michael Vasquez reflected on the future of Indians in the United States during a conversation we had in July 2004:

The major issue we face today boils down to survival, how to live in the modern world. We must remain Indians and this is the challenge. Our languages are being lost at a tremendous rate; poverty is rampant, as is alcoholism. But still we remain. The traditional world is intact.

It is a matter of identity. It is thinking about who I am. I grew up on Indian reservations, then I left the Indian world and entered the white world. But I am still Indian. People enter the white world but they keep an idea of themselves as Indians. That is the trick.

That is the trick, remaining anchored in a positive sense of one's cultural identity in the face of racism. The use of schools as instruments of forced assimilation was education at its worst. What would it look like at its best? How can we affirm the identities of American Indian students in our schools? That is the question to be considered next.

Before we look at cultural values and plan strategies and programs to break down cultural barriers we need to consider two additional indigenous groups, Native Hawaiians and the Inuit/Eskimos.

NATIVE HAWAIIANS

The experiences of Native Hawaiians parallel those of other indigenous peoples whose cultures and traditional lifestyles were drastically altered by European contact. In 1778, Captain James Cook's expedition landed on the islands that he named the Sandwich Islands, now called the State of Hawaii. There, Cook found nearly 300,000 people living in relative isolation. Since that time, Hawaiian history has been fraught with benevolent paternalism by Europeans and Americans to the detriment of Native Hawaiians. Their story is one of broken promises and exploitation by foreigners that, in some ways, is similar to the plight of American Indians.

Until foreigners started coming to Hawaii, Native Hawaiians did not have a word for *race*. There were two groups, Hawaiians and strangers—*kanakas* and *haoles*. As whites became more prevalent on the islands, the Hawaiian people were forced to deal with an alien white economic, social, and legal system that they did not understand.

In the early subsistence economy of Hawaii, the survival of Hawaiians depended on a communal effort to reap the maximum benefits from the islands' scarce resources. The Hawaiians were an agricultural and fishing people governed by powerful chiefs.

There were two Hawaiian customs that would lead to inevitable conflict with haoles in the future. One was a system of sharing and bartering, in which products were exchanged from one island to another. The Hawaiians did not use currency, and therefore the accumulation of wealth in a market economy as we know it was unknown. The other custom was the notion that the land belonged to the gods, and thus belonged to everyone and could not be owned by individuals.

The propensity of Hawaiians to share helped to seal their demise. Besides providing provisions for ships, Hawaiians were quite willing to share their women. The venereal diseases introduced by the European and American sailors found little natural resistance among the Hawaiians and, along with measles, cholera, and alcoholism, took a deadly toll. By 1840, only 100,000 Hawaiians remained.

Several groups entered the Hawaiian scene. Missionaries arrived from New England. Their goal was to Christianize the natives. As whaling in the Pacific began to decline, the Hawaiian economy shifted to plantation agriculture. Planters began importing field labor from China, Japan, Portugal, Korea, and Puerto Rico. The strategy was to keep any one nationality of laborers from becoming too numerous, and thus to thwart any type of labor organization. The nature of the sugar and pineapple plantations required a large concentration of land and capital, as well as a disciplined work force.

Annexation began in the 1890s as the United States saw value in the islands as a source of economic gain. Once Hawaii became a territory of the United States, its political and economic affairs were managed by forces on the mainland or by the island elites responding to powerful people on the mainland.

The opening of the Panama Canal made it much easier for Hawaiian products to reach markets on the East Coast of the United States. The plantation economy continued to flourish. After World War II, political leaders in Hawaii began to seriously discuss seeking statehood. It was argued that becoming a state would guarantee the large U.S. market for Hawaiian products.

Present-day Hawaii is a mixture of peoples with varied backgrounds. There are sizable communities of Chinese Americans and Japanese Americans. There is also a sizable number of Koreans who work in the restaurant and hotel businesses. They had come originally to work on the pineapple and sugar cane estates. Filipinos and Portuguese also came as agricultural workers. There are also a few thousand African Americans as well as the still powerful haoles (whites). Upward mobility by Asian Americans in Hawaii contrasts sharply with their status as primarily agricultural workers one or two generations ago. Hawaiians are very heterogeneous, which makes it difficult to classify them. Many have varied backgrounds, including Korean, Chinese, Japanese, and African ancestry.

As with all diverse groups, Hawaiians have many cultural values and norms that can be used to create an educational framework. The spirit of *Aloha Aina* (love for the land) persists. Hawaiian values were never lost and the traditional value of *ohana* is a cooperative system of social relationships found within an extended family. This value of ohana is sometimes counterproductive to Hawaiian children attending school where cooperation on academic work may be perceived as "cheating." Also, Hawaiian children do not particularly relish the peer competition engendered in many school situations, and consequently they often do not respond well to competitive tasks. School personnel need to become familiar with such Hawaiian values as strong family relations, respect for and love of nature, creativity, and expressiveness.

The average Native Hawaiians fall far below their white counterparts in economic prosperity. They generally live in facilities that are substandard. They comprise a disproportionately high percentage of school dropouts and police arrests.

Native Hawaiians have not adapted to the competitive nature of the dominant society. They are oriented toward affiliation rather than competition. Friendship and family harmony are prized and are not to be traded for economic status. The reluctance to compete is one way to retain ethnic identity in a society that rewards competition. Hawaiian schoolchildren seem to achieve much better when they are evaluated collectively rather than individually.

INUIT/ESKIMO

Inuit/Eskimo are a people who live in and near the Arctic. Their homeland stretches from the northeastern tip of Russia across Alaska and northern Canada to Greenland. *Inuit* refers to the people formerly called Eskimos, a term from American Indian languages that may have meant *eater of raw*

fish or *netter of snowshoes*. Many natives consider the term Eskimo insulting and prefer the name Inuit, which means *the people* or *real people*.

Inuit culture developed more than 1,000 years ago in what is now
Alaska and Siberia. The Inuit have always lived by the sea, which has
provided much of their food. As the Inuit moved eastward, they modified
their way of life to suit the Arctic environment they encountered. They
caught fish, hunted seals and walruses, and went after whales. They also
hunted caribou, musk oxen, and polar bears. They used the skins of these
animals to make clothes and tents. They crafted tools and weapons from
the animal bones, teeth, and horns. In the summer they traveled by boat,
in the winter on sleds pulled by dogs. Most Inuit lived in tents in the summer and sod houses in the winter. They built snow houses as temporary
shelters when hunting in the winter.

The Inuit way of life began to change in the 1800s. At that time, European whalers and traders began arriving in the Arctic in large numbers.
The Inuit eventually adopted many aspects of European culture and permanently altered their traditional way of life.

Today there are more than 100,000 Inuit in Russia, Alaska, Canada, and
Greenland. Most live in small settlements scattered along the Arctic coast.
They have retained a considerable knowledge of their ancient culture. The
traditional way of life has ended. The kayak has given way to the motor-
boat, and the snowmobile has replaced the dog team.

Many Inuit suffer from unemployment and other issues like alcoholism
and drug abuse. In addition, industrial and nuclear pollution are poisoning
their traditional homelands and food sources.

Inuit education tries to honor the past and create a future for their children. While Inuit parents were being moved from igloos to houses in the
1950s, their children were being assimilated into a European white educational system. In the worst cases, the children were taken from their families, harshly disciplined, and stripped of their culture. Only over the past
20 years have the Inuit been permitted to speak out about how their children are educated. After so many years of feeling marginalized by formal
European education, the Inuit today are a people trying to correct the
damage.

Many schools were built entirely for the Inuit, where even preschool
children live in residence. These preschool children get an introduction to
the classroom. When they do start school, a white teacher who knows

nothing about their heritage and culture will teach in a language they have never heard. This is one of the problems being addressed by the Inuit today.

In schools in the large cities where there is a mix of white and Inuit students there are difficulties. Inuit students are not flourishing in school. Parents feel more education in their native Inuktitut language and a culturally relevant curriculum would help. White parents, however, do not want their children "losing out" because of lagging Inuit students. An argument focuses on the difference between education and schooling.

In addition, a horrifying trend is developing: suicide among young teenagers. In 2003, in one small village in northern Alaska, eight young men killed themselves in the one year. Parents are shuddering at the thought that their teenage sons and daughters feel so isolated and hopeless that they would take their own lives. They wonder just how much the school system plays a part in this scenario.

If the Inuit could establish more control over educational policy and curriculum, Inuit culture and language could be thriving in schools. But it is not. On many playgrounds the children only speak English. Their native language is becoming a relic of the past Inuit culture just as it is in American Indian tribes.

CULTURAL VALUES

In general, American Indians from different tribes, Native Hawaiians, and the Inuit people share some common values. Particularly important is the collective identity, that is, one's belonging to the tribe. I have noticed that their values also include idealism, nonaggressiveness, and nonmaterialism. Remember, what is valued and respected in one culture is not necessarily valued in another.

Traditional American Indian, Native Hawaiian, and Inuit cultural values include:

- Traditional identity: approximately 550 tribes in the United States (versus white individual identity)
- Social and familial cooperation (versus white competition)

- Nonaggressiveness, avoidance of conflict, noninterference (versus white aggressiveness)
- Horizontal decision making, group consensus
- Nonmaterialism/respect for nature and humans' place within (versus white materialism where things and possessions are highly valued)
- Group life is primary; collective orientation
- Respect for elders, experts, and those with spiritual powers
- Spirituality, religion is a way of life (versus white religion, which is just one more institution)
- Maternalism (versus white paternalism)
- Introversion; avoidance of ridicule or criticism of others if possible
- Idealism (versus white realism)
- Accepts "what is"; holistic approach to life
- Emphasis on responsibility for family and tribal community
- Search for harmony, privacy, maintenance of traditions (versus white preference for progress, change)
- Observation of others' behavior; emphasis on how others behave and not on what they say
- Incorporation of supportive nonfamily or other helpers into family network
- Bilingualism; native languages still used and taught in many communities (versus white monolingualism)
- Use of nonverbal communication, gestures, expressions, body language (versus white verbal expressions)
- Belief in interconnectedness of all things, living and nonliving
- Emphasis on preserving a natural balance, in both nature and life
- Self-sufficient at an earlier age than other ethnic groups
- Living in the here and now, time is flexible, actions are controlled and influenced by cultural traditions rather than linear time systems (versus white future orientation, time is rigid)
- Oral history, songs and dances, ceremonial activities, and reservation communities are all important aspects of American Indian, Native Hawaiian, and Inuit life.

LEARNING STYLES

We think, learn, and create in different ways. The development of our potential is affected by the match between what we learn and how we learn with our particular intelligences. Education for Indian children should empower them to believe in their unique view of the world, including its cultural underpinnings.

American Indian students need real experiences both inside and outside the classroom, through which they can identify personal and cooperative interests, abilities, and talents. Learning styles are important.

Native learning styles include:

- Oral traditions give value to creating stories, poems, and recalling legends; good at storytelling
- Value cooperation, not competition; work well and communicate effectively in groups
- Learn holistically, beginning with an overview or "big picture" and moving to particulars
- Trial-and-error learning by private (not public) experiences
- Have well-developed visual/spatial abilities, highly visual learners
- Value life experiences in traditional learning
- Value design and create symbols to communicate; often exhibit visual artistic talent
- Intuitive ability valued and well developed
- Seek harmony in nature and life; are good mediators
- Excellent memory, long attention span, deductive thinkers
- High use of nonverbal communication
- Accept responsibility and discipline of leadership

In meeting the needs of American Indian, Native Hawaiian, and Inuit children, teachers should decrease competition via cooperative/ collaborative teaching methods and groupings as well as modifying instructional styles. These students benefit from increased use of visual aids, increased opportunity for storytelling, increased use of multisensory approaches to instruction, more open-ended or divergent assignments, and increased use of culturally relevant and affirming materials.

Teachers need to be aware that among American Indian, Native Hawaiian, and Inuit students, there is a tendency toward the following:

- *A global or holistic style of organizing information.* They first develop an understanding of the whole concept. Classrooms are dominated by analytic or linear thinkers who process the pieces first and then bring them together. This is contrary to the Indian learning style.

- *A visual style of mentally representing information in thinking (as opposed to verbal).*
- *A preference for a more reflective style in processing information.* Many Indian students learn by observing the tasks they are to perform. This is referred to as the watch-then-do approach.
- *A preference for a collaborative approach to task completion.* Parents encourage their children to collaborate with others to accomplish tasks and solve problems. In most classrooms students are expected to complete much of their work individually.

When I make an assignment, my American Indian students are reluctant to finish quickly or to correct other peers' papers (still a common practice in many schools). White students jump to the task. Indian students appear to need time to think about things before they take action on their assignment. It is almost like they have to make sure they can do it before they try. Often they seem to just not care about doing their assignments.

An elder once told me that Indians tend to ridicule the person who performs clumsily. An individual should not attempt an action unless he or she knows how to do it. If he or she does not know, then the individual must watch until the task is understood. In European and American cultures the opposite attitude is generally the case: "Give a man credit for trying." "The way to learn is to attempt to do so." Most Indian children observe an activity repeatedly before attempting any kind of public performance. Learning through public mistakes is not a method that Indians value.

Many Indian groups use the visual approach as a method by which to come to know and understand the world. My students also need to see the whole picture. Most classrooms tend to introduce new concepts and give all instructions verbally, which is in direct conflict with the encouragement of visual strengths.

I have also noticed that when I ask a question, my Indian students will not respond. There is dead silence. When I make a comment without questioning, they are more likely to join in the discussion.

Indian students want to blend into the total class and participate in group or team situations. They avoid individual competition.

When Indian children err, their elders explain privately the correct procedure or proper behavior. However, in school, teachers tend to scold and even verbally assault the child before his or her peers.

We must become more sensitive to the needs of Native students. We can:

- Discuss students' learning style with them.
- Be aware of students' background knowledge and experience.
- Be aware of how questions are asked.
- Remember that many students do not like to be "spotlighted" in front of a group.
- Provide time for practice before performance is expected.
- Be aware of proximity preferences (how close is comfortable?).
- Provide classroom activities that encourage both independence and cooperation.
- Provide immediate and consistent feedback.
- Give specific, meaningful praise.

Teachers, let your students (and their parents) know that you are also willing to learn.

In her article "Is There an 'Indian' in Your Classroom?" Lee Little Soldier makes the point that teachers might find it hard to determine whether there even are Indian students in their classrooms. Indians often have European names, and because of the high proportion of mixed-heritage individuals, there are wide variations in physical appearance. Some are easily recognized as people of color; others have light skin, light eyes, and brown or blond hair and may be identified as white. Those who are products of black-Indian unions may simply be assumed to be African American. In parts of the United States with small Indian populations, many people may be surprised to discover that American Indians still exist at all. American Indian communities are typically portrayed as a thing of the past, not of the present or the future. This depiction prevails even in places where there is a large and visible Indian population.

The schools remain at fault. In Nome, Alaska, a community where Alaska Natives outnumber whites, but where the school board, faculty, and administration are all white, we look at Nome-Beltz High School as an example of this fault. At Nome-Beltz High School teachers and students maintained a veil of silence about Alaska Native history and culture except for the disparaging remarks about Alaska Natives as barbaric and ignorant that were part of the hidden curriculum. Teacher expectations of Alaska Natives were low, and in fact almost half of the Native students dropped out of high school before graduation. Several committed suicide. Those who did graduate were discouraged from attending college and encouraged instead to pursue vocational training.

We must reconstruct the curriculum in our schools to reflect not only teaching about traditional life but also about transitional life and the modern period. The inclusion of contemporary life is essential if our Indian students are to see that they have a future, not only a past. Such curricular interventions stand in stark contrast to the deculturalization that has been the legacy of American Indian education, reminding us that education does not have to mean alienation. We must realize that the Indian community is not a relic of the past but a growing community with a future.

Effective and appropriate programming and instruction must incorporate the beliefs, values, and traditions of American Indians, Native Hawaiians, and Inuit people. Our goal should not be to make these students "Anglo-American" but to make them bicultural by giving them the skills, pride, and self-confidence to enable them to move between cultures. Thus, the teacher's responsibility is to help build bridges rather than destroy cultures. Building bridges results, in part, from providing students with cultural understanding and respect.

Indian education has meant different things to different people. Once it meant the ways American Indians, Native Hawaiians, and the Inuit passed on their cumulative knowledge to coming generations. For years it meant forced assimilation to European ways. Today it is teaching that recognizes the educational needs of Indian youth as unique.

The purpose of education is the actualization of unique personal and cultural characteristics and potential. Educational experiences should be consistent with Indian values. It is essential that the nation's schools help Indian students acquire the knowledge, values, and skills needed to participate in the forging of a democratic and just society that fosters the common good.

Chapter Six

African American Students: A Castelike Minority

The ultimate measure of a person is not where they stand in moments of comfort and convenience, but where they stand at times of challenge and controversy.

—Martin Luther King Jr.

Africans have had a unique experience in the Americas. They came with the earliest European explorers and settlers and were gradually enslaved in the North American colonies in the 1600s. When the 18th century began, slavery was flourishing in North America. The African experience in the United States has strikingly revealed the gross discrepancies between American ideals and reality. Throughout their history, African Americans have called on America to make its dream a reality. Their cries have usually fallen on deaf ears. African American history and culture must be studied to enable students to understand and appreciate fully the great conflicts and dilemmas in American society and to develop a commitment to help make America's ideals a reality.

Africans have been in America for many centuries. Inconclusive evidence suggests that they established a colony in Mexico long before Columbus's voyage in 1492 (Takaki, 1993). Africans were with the first Europeans who explored America. Africans had been living in Europe for many years when European exploration to America began. The Moors, a North African people, invaded Europe in 711 and eventually conquered and ruled Spain. Other Africans were brought to Europe as slaves beginning in the 1400s. These African slaves worked in private homes as cooks, maids, and butlers, in banks and shipyards, and in mercantile establishments.

Diego el Negro was with Columbus on his last voyage to America in 1502. When Balboa arrived at the Pacific Ocean in 1513, a black man, Nulfo de Olano, was part of the crew. Africans also explored present-day Kansas with Coronado. In addition to exploring America, Africans were among its first non-Indian settlers. Africans helped to establish St. Augustine, Florida, in 1565 and others joined the French to settle the Mississippi Valley in the 17th century.

SLAVE TRADE

The Arabs invaded Africa and enslaved Africans long before Europeans arrived on the continent. Europeans became involved in the 1400s. However, black slavery never became widespread in Europe, but it grew by leaps and bounds when Europeans began settling in America in the 1600s.

The European discovery of America created a whole new demand for labor. The numbers of Europeans who came as workers did not meet the growing demand. The plantations of the South, which grew crops such as sugar, cotton, and tobacco, had heavy demands for labor.

By the 1600s slave trade became a very profitable movement. European nations competed aggressively to monopolize it, with England dominating the slave trade by 1700. For nearly 400 years slave traders shoved, pushed, and threw Africans aboard slave ships in the largest forced movement of people in history. According to some historians, the slave trade cost Africa nearly 40 million people (Takaki, 1993). Millions never made it to the Americas. They died at the hands of slave traders or as a result of conditions in the filthy cargo holds of slave trips. The nearly 20 million who survived the trip to the Americas came in chains. Although deprived of even the most basic human rights, these people helped shape the course of history in the Western Hemisphere.

The captive's life was terrifying, brutal, and shocking. Slave catchers, who were usually Africans, raided the interior of the West African coast looking for individuals who were healthy and could survive the passage and the backbreaking work on the plantations in America. Few colonists gave much thought to the question of whether one person should own another. Whites looked upon Africans as less than human. The colonists did this in order to justify the mass enslavement of Africans.

THE SLAVE RAIDS

Just before dawn broke, wooden drums sounded the alarm. Enemies had surrounded the village. Warriors grabbed their weapons, but it was too late. Intruders armed with heavy wooden clubs, knives, and guns overran the compound. Some villagers fled, others fought back and were killed, and most fell stunned by well-aimed blows to the head. When the battle ended, the invaders joined the captured villagers together neck to neck with heavy logs and ropes.

The villagers had fallen victim to slave traders. The traders marched their captives over mountains, through forests, and along rivers. Those who tried to rebel were killed. Those who fell ill were left to die along the way. Whip-carrying guards kept the slaves in constant fear until they were loaded onto ships for the next leg of their journey to America.

Conditions on the slave ships were degrading and dehumanizing. The captured Africans were packed into ships like sardines. Those who survived the long, nightmarish trip across the Atlantic recalled brutal whippings, forced feedings, and the smell of death and filth in disease-ridden holds. They were chained together with iron ankle fetters. The space for each slave was so small that they were forced to lie down. Because of the crowded and filthy conditions on the ships, diseases were rampant and took many lives. Hookworm, dysentery, malaria, smallpox, and yellow fever swept through the ships. Amid the suffering, many Africans went mad. Some killed each other fighting and clawing for breathing space. Others simply prayed for death to come to them. During the 40- to 60-day trip, more than half of the Africans died.

SLAVERY IN NORTH AMERICA

The first Africans to arrive in the English North American colonies came in 1619 on a Dutch ship. These first 20 Africans were not slaves but, like most of the whites who came to the colonies during this period, indentured servants. Once they completed a period of service they were free. The English colonists soon realized that they were not obtaining enough workers with this system and that slavery had many more advantages. With slavery, the worker received few benefits and remained in bondage for life. The slave's children would also be slaves.

American slavery was a unique institution in human history. It was designed to dehumanize Africans and convince them that they were inferior and deserved the treatment they received. The ideals of white supremacy were reinforced. Despite the attempts of slave owners to dehumanize them, Africans and their descendents forged a new culture from their experiences and succeeded in developing a sense of community and a social life apart from the world of whites. Family members taught their children to survive the harsh, white environment as well as to never totally submit to the whims of the master.

After the American Revolution, societies organized to agitate for the abolition of slavery. These societies were militant and aggressive and harshly denounced slavery and slave owners and demanded an immediate end to slavery. Life under slavery worsened in the 1800s, and enslaved African Americans fought back. To forget the pains of slavery, African Americans often sang and danced. They depended on their spiritual beliefs and gathered together in "invisible" churches to hold their own services.

We must remember that not all African Americans were slaves. Many in the North hired themselves out and earned their freedom. Nonslave northern blacks played an extremely important role in African American life. Free African Americans experienced discrimination and racism everywhere. Laws denied them the right to vote, to have a trial by jury, and to testify against whites. African American children could not always attend white school. Separation of the races existed. In many ways African Americans in the North were neither free nor slave.

THE THIRST FOR EDUCATION

Many free African Americans realized how important education was to success. They paid money out of their own pockets to educate themselves and their children. Schools were opened in the 1830s, and many were immediately burned down by the townspeople. In spite of the dangers, teachers continued to set up schools and African children continued to attend. Education was viewed as a way to a better life. This led to the founding of African American colleges. Out of these schools came doctors, dentists, teachers, ministers, writers, and poets. They were in the forefront of the battle to abolish slavery.

CIVIL WAR AND RECONSTRUCTION

African Americans viewed the Civil War as a God-sent conflict that would emancipate them from bondage. Most white Americans, including President Lincoln and Congress, viewed the war as a conflict to preserve the Union.

After four bitter years of war the blacks were finally free from slavery and recognized as citizens. But the conflict was nowhere near over. Some whites were determined to "put blacks in their place," and violence against them was widespread. The goals of this violence were to intimidate blacks to keep them from voting and to reestablish the caste system that had existed before the Civil War. The Ku Klux Klan was operating during this time, and many blacks were killed or maimed. Jim Crow laws were passed requiring segregation in schools, parks, restaurants, theaters, and other public accommodations.

Reconstruction has been called America's unfinished revolution. African Americans took advantage of freedoms denied them under slavery. They formed their own churches, worked through political action to achieve full citizenship for males, and eagerly took advantage of the education available to men, women, and children. But, generally, African Americans remained poor and dependent on white landowners. Many laws were passed during Reconstruction that held out great hope for African Americans. Yet, for nearly a century after the end of Reconstruction, the federal government failed to enforce them.

After the Civil War, African Americans migrated to northern cities in large numbers because of the severe economic, political, and social conditions in the South. Southern states had stripped African Americans of most of their legal rights. When the African Americans arrived in midwestern and eastern cities, they had a rude awakening. Life was extremely difficult. They were the victims of white violence and experienced gross discrimination in housing and employment. Conflict and tension developed. Whites were determined to keep blacks from their jobs and out of their communities.

Organizations emerged to help African Americans adjust to city life and to fight racism and discrimination. The goal was to make African Americans feel proud of being black. The Harlem Renaissance during the 1920s and 1930s produced the works of African American artists, writers, and musicians. Gifted poets such as Claude McKay and Countee Cullen penned angry poems that reflected black aspirations and frustrations. Writers such as Langston Hughes, Jean Toomer, and Zora Neale Hurston wrote outstanding novels. African American musicians further developed blues and jazz.

World War II created additional jobs in the larger cities, and masses of southern blacks migrated during and after the war years. The problems encountered by earlier migrations were still alive. Segregation was increasing.

CIVIL RIGHTS MOVEMENT

In the 1960s, African Americans began a fight for their rights on a scale that was unprecedented in the nation's history. However, the civil rights movement of the 1960s was presaged in the slave rebellions and uprisings of the 19th century. Black Americans have always protested in ways consistent with the times in which they lived. The *Brown* decision of 1954 and the Civil Rights Act of 1957 set the pace. *Brown* established that separate schools for blacks were inherently unequal. But inequality persists today, and school districts still are planning for a more even distribution of black students and students of other races.

The early civil rights movement included four African American students, who sat down at a segregated lunch counter at a Woolworth's store in Greensboro, North Carolina, on February 1, 1960, and refused to leave when they were not served. They had launched the sit-in movement. This movement spread throughout the South, and African American college students were desegregating lunch counters and other public accommodation facilities in many cities in the South.

MALCOLM X

Early in life Malcolm Little learned that if you want something, you have to make noise. As Malcolm X, he emerged as a leader who preached African American solidarity and said that advancement would come through self-help. Initially in his thinking, whites were "blue-eyed devils" who were to be avoided at all costs. He became the most forceful spokesman of the Black Muslims. He saw in Elijah Muhammad's teaching a way to help blacks gain control of their destinies. Malcolm X urged young people to think of themselves as part of an African majority, not an African minority. As his thinking evolved, he declared, "There can be no black-white unity unless there is first black unity." He thus left the door open to cooperation with whites, but he stressed self-determination and self-defense by African Americans. One quality that he consistently showed in his life was his ability to change: to listen, to accept that he was wrong, to learn, and to grow. Ultimately this led to his own self-transformation. Malcolm X's life came to an end on February 21, 1965, when three gunmen shot him 15 times at close range.

STUDENT NONVIOLENT COORDINATING COMMITTEE (SNCC)

Student activists formed the Student Nonviolent Coordinating Committee (SNCC) in 1960 to coordinate their protest activities, support their leaders, and publicize their activities. Starting in 1961, the SNCC shifted its efforts from the sit-in movement to organizing voter registration campaigns in heavily black, rural counties of Mississippi, Alabama, and Georgia. Although composed of fewer than 200 college students, the SNCC's influence was widely felt because of its members' courage in challenging segregation in the Deep South. Out of the SNCC came some of today's black leaders, such as former Washington, D.C., mayor Marion Barry, U.S. Congressman John Lewis from Georgia, and former NAACP chairman Julian Bond.

In 1966 a faction of the SNCC committed to black separatism and headed by Stokely Carmichael took over the organization from John Lewis, who favored integration. The SNCC then began to eject its white members. Carmichael soon issued a call for "Black Power," a term used to describe a series of new tactics and goals, including an insistence on racial dignity and black self-reliance and the use of violence as a legitimate means of self-defense.

BLACK POWER

The concept of Black Power emerged during a time when the civil rights movement was losing momentum. Black Power had different meanings for most whites than for most African Americans. To most African Americans it meant political power, pride in blackness, black control of schools and communities, and black self-help organizations. To most whites, the concept meant retaliatory violence and "black racism."

Many African American leaders urged Carmichael to stop using the phrase. They felt it would frighten whites whose support they needed to get civil rights measures through Congress. Carmichael refused, and the split between the SNCC and more conservative organizations such as the NAACP widened.

Carmichael argued that African Americans did not want to be assimilated or merged into white society. They wanted to stand apart as their own people. Out of these feelings grew the slogan "Black is beautiful." Frustrated by poverty and police brutality, many African Americans embraced Carmichael's outspoken racial pride.

BLACK PANTHERS

In October 1966, in Oakland, California, Bobby Seale and Huey Newton founded a new militant political party, the Black Panthers. The Panthers demanded the right of African Americans to control their own communities. They asked the federal government to rebuild black neighborhoods in repayment for the years African Americans had spent in slavery. They wanted African Americans freed from jail and retried by black juries. Not everyone knew about the Panthers' political platform, but nearly all recognized their dress: black trousers, black leather jackets, blue shirts, and black berets.

MARTIN LUTHER KING JR.

During these years of turmoil and violence came a quiet voice in the wilderness, Dr. Martin Luther King Jr. King organized the Southern Christian Leadership Conference (SCLC), which gave him a base to pursue civil rights activities, first in the South and later nationwide. His philosophy of nonviolent resistance led to his arrest on numerous occasions. His campaigns had mixed success, but the protest he led in Birmingham, Alabama, in 1963 brought him worldwide attention. King emerged as the country's most influential civil rights leader ever. His "I Have a Dream" speech is quoted the world over: "I have a dream that one day this nation will rise up and live out the meaning of its creed, 'We will hold these truths to be self-evident, that all men are created equal.'" King's leadership of the civil rights movement was challenged in the mid-1960s as others grew more militant. His interests widened from civil rights to include criticism of the Vietnam War and a deeper concern over poverty.

By 1967, King had come to believe that the nation's main enemy was economic injustice. Poverty bred violence, he said. On April 3, 1968, King addressed a Memphis crowd. "I've been to the mountaintop," said King, "and I've seen the glory." He went on to describe his vision of a world free of poverty.

The next afternoon King stood on the balcony of his motel room, joking with members of his staff. Suddenly a shot rang out from a high-powered rifle. King fell, a bullet through his jaw. An hour later, the leader who dared dream of interracial peace lay dead.

Black frustrations, which reached new highs in the mid- and late 1960s, were manifested in a series of race riots in America's cities. Unlike the earlier riots in which whites attacked blacks, these riots were different because they involved little contact between whites and blacks. Rather, urban blacks directed their attacks towards the symbols of white society within their communities. They burned buildings owned by absentee landlords and looted stores run by merchants who they believed cheated them. Riots occurred in cities from New York City to Los Angeles. People lost their lives. Most of the victims were African Americans killed by white law enforcement officials.

The civil rights movement called America to look at itself in a giant mirror. Do black people who were born on this soil, who are American citizens, really feel this is a land of opportunity, the land of the free? America had to say no.

The 21st century reflects the past. The median income for African Americans is still less than that for whites. More African Americans than whites live below the poverty level. Black workers are disproportionately concentrated among low-skilled workers. Fewer low-skilled jobs are available because jobs now require technical skills and knowledge. African Americans from all cultures, social classes, and walks of life experience institutionalized racism and discrimination.

In some ways, the dream held out by Martin Luther King Jr. in 1963 has come true. Today, African Americans can be found in every walk of life, as teachers, doctors, nurses, lawyers, business executives, scientists, astronauts, entertainers, sports figures, and so on. Yet, in some ways the dream remains sadly unfulfilled. Cities teem with tension. Too few African Americans sit in the top offices of major corporations. Too many teenagers drop out of school and are unemployable. The nation has yet to see an African American president or vice president. To be sure, much remains to be done before all African Americans achieve Martin Luther King's dream. Still, all America can take pride in the achievements of African Americans today.

THE SECOND LARGEST ETHNIC GROUP

African Americans have received more attention than other culturally diverse groups, perhaps because they are currently the second largest ethnic group in the United States and have been the most active politically.

It is interesting to note that African Americans are the only culturally diverse group where the majority of the people came to the United States in chains. Other groups came by choice, to search for the American dream or to escape horrendous conditions in their homelands. Thus, African Americans are considered one of the "involuntary" culturally diverse groups in the United States. While different from other groups in this regard, African Americans nonetheless share dismal educational and employment outcomes with some Asian Americans, many Hispanic Americans, and American Indians, as well as whites.

Life on the margins is an all too familiar reality for black students.

More than other racially and culturally diverse students, black youth face social problems that inhibit their achievement, motivation, and educational outcomes. Racism is alive and well in many schools, and negative stereotypes of black students persist among teachers and school personnel. Beverly Tatum in her book *Why Are All the Black Kids Sitting Together in the Cafeteria?* (1997) speaks about stereotypes. She says that unfortunately for black teenagers cultural stereotypes do not usually include academic achievement. Academic success is usually associated with being white. Doing well in school becomes identified as trying to be white. Being smart becomes the opposite of being cool. When black students fail to achieve at high levels, a vicious circle ensues. In the minds of many educators, these black students fit into stereotypic roles assigned to blacks, when they fail in school they are destined to lives of economic disadvantage, unemployment, and underemployment.

Have we inadvertently reinforced the negative self-images of those students who are black? Why is academic success seen as a "white thing"? Have we, as white educators, assumed certain things about the future of culturally diverse students? Have we unconsciously communicated lower expectations to them? We must find some answers to what is happening in our schools. We are responsible for our curriculum, our teaching styles, and the experiences we can provide in our classrooms. We are responsible for the way we treat students, for how much we expect from them.

Society can avoid the costly problems associated with social and educational problems by investing in strategies about how to develop the potential of black students. Schools must recognize and nurture their talents (be they academic, leadership, creative, artistic). Schools must adopt prescriptive and proactive measures to increase students' well-being. Teachers need to hold high expectations for, and have positive attitudes about, their students. The curriculum must be realistic. Teachers must be prepared to meet academic and nonacademic needs.

For example, I find that black students often do not want to be reminded of their ancestors' arrival here in America. Without a context, without time to understand, read, and write, it seems too big, too powerfully melancholy for many students to understand. Rather than being presented with a cursory description of slavery, they seem to want to avoid any discussion of it altogether. Many textbooks leave out slave insurrections, successful lives of runaway slaves, whole countries run by Africans. Because the study of slavery is often simplistic, the little bits of truth thrown out to our students often provoke intense anger. Our students need to have a discussion of the lasting effects of slavery and how this has influenced the way people think, act, and perceive themselves and others today.

Essentially, the degree to which schools work to reduce or eliminate impediments (such as the slavery issue) to achievement is a barometer of a school's wellness. Contrary to popular opinion and practice, test scores are not necessarily the most important indicator of school wellness.

DESCRIPTION OF BLACK STUDENTS

Black students are overrepresented in special education, often in the lowest-ability groups and tracks, and among high school and college dropouts, the underemployed and unemployed, and therefore the economically disadvantaged. Low-track and low-ability classes usually have a poor quality of curriculum and instruction, and a negative classroom climate, as well as poor teacher interaction and low student expectations. Lower-track classes foster lower self-esteem, lower educational aspirations, lower levels of cognition (thinking critically, processing information, making inferences, synthesizing material), and, ultimately, few opportunities for economic mobility. It appears that the higher the level of education, the greater the degree of underrepresentation, and the lower the graduation rate.

Self-perception, attitudes toward school and curriculum, motivation, test anxiety (black students have some of the lowest standardized test scores nationally), study skills, and learning styles all affect academic achievement for black students.

Several social factors place black students at risk for educational disadvantage on a consistent basis: poverty, residing in a single-parent family, mother's level of education, racial status, and command of English. Many African American students come to school speaking black English (Ebonics). They use the verb *to be* extensively and omit other verbs. Experts believe some patterns of Ebonics are based on West African languages. The use of black English gained national attention in 1996 and 1997 when the Oakland, California, school district adopted and later dropped a plan to recognize it as a language. Today some schools employ it as an aid in the teaching of standard English. Proponents like Penelope O'Malley and David Corson say that African American students learn better when it is used in this manner. Opponents like Sondra Thiederman say that it could discourage students from learning standard English.

Some educators try to motivate black students by introducing courses of study based on an approach called Afrocentrism. These programs aim to encourage awareness of African culture and history and pride in the richness of African heritage. The curriculum emphasizes the present and past accomplishments of black people. Supporters correctly believe Afrocentrism improves self-esteem and promotes academic success (Tatum, 1997).

Certain environmental risk factors, along with other social injustices, further exacerbate the educational problems of black students. Although definitions of what it means to be "at risk" vary, there is consensus that many students lack the home and community resources to benefit from schooling. For some black students, survival takes a strong precedence over educational achievement.

The risk factors for black students include the following:

- *Race and ethnicity*: Black students are less likely to complete high school or be placed in upper tracks and ability groups, and are more likely to have lower standardized test scores, be retained, or placed in special education than are white students. Skin color is a powerful determinant of oppression in the United States and its schools.
- *Poverty*: Potential is limited by poverty. Singly or in unison, poverty and the other risk factors wreak havoc on any student's achievement and motivation. Black students face staggering obstacles for achieving decency, dignity, and success in America. These children suffer disproportionately from downward trends in the economy and from the lack of commitment toward alleviating problems in health, education, housing, and employment. Children in impoverished conditions have fewer resources and less access to formal learning opportunities; more and greater health problems and psychological difficulties; and more handicapping conditions (learning disabilities, speech impairments, emotional disturbances, and other health problems) that affect educational outcomes.
- *Single-parent families*: Role conflict and strain, differential priorities,

and struggles to meet basic needs often take precedence over academic needs for these families.

- *Educational level of the mother*: Major educational issues for mothers include less personal contact with school personnel and less knowledge about schooling, both of which contribute to less parent involvement. Consequently, children of parents who have low educational levels tend to have low levels of achievement and high dropout rates.

- *Limited English proficiency*: Language barriers contribute to social isolation from peers and teachers due to lack of communication, understanding, and sensitivity. Black English is the primary language of many students. Professionals frequently consider black English as inferior to standard English. When teachers hold this perspective, students who speak black English may be at risk for academic problems. Students who speak black English are likely to be seated farthest away from the teacher, called on less frequently, be given less time to respond, receive more negative criticism, get less praise for correct answers, and have responses interrupted more frequently. Teacher evaluation of reading comprehension also tends to be lower.

- *Social injustices*: Racism, prejudice, and stereotypes significantly affect the educational outcomes of black students. Racial attitudes and preferences are learned early in life. As early as age 3 or 4, children become aware of their racial and ethnic backgrounds. Avoidance, discrimination, and even physical attack can occur. Racism, discrimination, and oppression are the root of many of today's social problems. Racism is very complicated and constantly evolving. We do not need any more studies or sermons or White House conferences on race. We need good intentions and common sense.

What are some recommendations to alleviate these risk factors?

- *Reducing prejudices is essential.*
- *Black students must feel empowered and have a sense of belonging within and outside school.*
- *Students must learn to be aware of and cope with their angry feelings, which may result in violence, crime, substance abuse, depres-*

sion, and self-destructive behaviors, including suicide. Stress, anxiety, frustration, and anger often interrupt the learning process.

- *Encourage students to find a time-out area that is a safe environment where they can vent their frustrations.*
- *Students must learn how to deal with poor peer relations.* Loneliness and isolation make students vulnerable to depression, juvenile delinquency, gang involvement, physical illness, and suicide.
- *Peer tutoring can be effective in maximizing positive classroom interactions, friendships, and pro-social behaviors, as well as self-esteem building.* The best way to prepare students for a satisfying life is to give them a wide repertoire of techniques for lifelong learning.

When the values of black and mainstream cultures mesh, black students are more likely to reach their academic potential than are students of other cultures. However, when the values are inconsistent or conflicting, underachievement may prevail.

School norms consistently include conformity, passivity, cooperation, quietness, individualized instruction, independence, competition, and teacher-directed instruction. Although teaching styles may reflect the dominant cultural establishment, they do not necessarily reflect what is best and most productive for black students, too many of whom are unwilling and unable to conform to the aforementioned norms.

The model student sits quietly in his seat, asks few questions, works passively and independently, completes assignments in the prescribed manner, and does not challenge the teacher. Some black students have difficulty staying in their seats and being immobile. Their culture styles do not fit school norms and expectations. Thus, part of the school failure of black students can be attributed to their inability to master social codes of behavior, codes that they are expected to adopt but are seldom taught in school.

Communication styles between school and the black students also become an issue. Blacks are more persuasive and theatrical, show great emotion, have high levels of energy, and ask more questions, particularly when inconsistencies and injustices are noticed. Similarly, the communication styles of black students are often misinterpreted as confrontational, especially when verbal communication is accompanied by nonverbal communication (body language, facial expression, intonations) that adds strength or momentum to the words.

BLACK RACIAL IDENTITY

Many black children in our public school system see blackness as having an insignificant role in their daily lives. In the first stage, they often see their racial orientation as something to be ashamed of. Some students even loathe other blacks, feel alienated from them, and do not see the community as a support system.

In stage 2 (encounter) students may experience an "identity metamorphosis." They become aware of their blackness and may even feel guilty at having minimized the significance of race.

Stage 3 (immersion-emersion) deals with becoming the "right kind of black person." White is perceived as evil and oppressive, and black as superior. African Americans immerse themselves in a world of blackness. In the emersion phase, blacks learn to abandon romantic notions of blackness and move toward a deeper, more serious understanding of black issues.

The fourth stage (internalization) is marked by the integration of a new identity. There is a sense of belonging, and communication occurs with other cultures.

The fifth and final stage (internalization/commitment) is characterized as action-oriented. Time and energy are devoted to black affairs and improving the lives of both individuals and the community members as African Americans.

A teacher who is aware of these stages will begin to understand and deal with the baggage brought into the classroom. We must remember that when African Americans were slaves, the struggle to learn to read and write despite legal prohibitions was the focus of education. Later Booker T. Washington and W. E. B. Du Bois debated whether the appropriate education for African Americans would be a vocational track, because those were the jobs blacks were most likely to get, or a university degree, which might lead to aspirations that were less likely to be fulfilled. Today, African Americans still experience limited access to economic opportunities that sparked the original discussion (Takaki, 1993). Prospects for health, employment, and education are circumscribed by their race.

AFRICAN AMERICAN CULTURAL VALUES

As a cultural group, black students are socially oriented as reflected in strong kinship networks and large extended families. There is a strong need to belong and for affiliation. There is a need to bond with others who share similar concerns and interests. In many ways, group support represents a mechanism for cultural preservation and social identity. Today, black Americans want to do more than adopt outward signs of ties to Africa. They are studying and embracing African values, standards, or principles that have guided African people for hundreds of years. One way this is done is through the celebration of Kwanzaa, a yearly festival held from December 26 through January 1. Kwanzaa came about in 1966 when a black professor, Maulana Karenga, conceived of it as a way to restore the African American cultural legacy. He observed that other immigrant groups brought their holidays and feasts to America but that African Americans enjoyed no such days.

The word *Kwanzaa* means "first fruits of harvest" in Swahili and borrows elements from harvest festivals enjoyed all over Africa. Kwanzaa is a time for food, music, and dance, for readings and family stories. Seven principles are stressed: unity, self-determination, responsibility, cooperation, purpose, creativity, and faith. These principles, especially unity, purpose, and faith, have allowed African Americans to withstand centuries of slavery and injustice.

We can further break these principles down to cultural values that include:

- Extended family/strong kinship bonds (versus white nuclear family)
- Spirituality (versus white religion)
- Cooperation; socially oriented, mutual interdependence; collectiveness (versus white competition, independence, task-orientedness, individuality)
- Multilingual/Ebonics (versus white monolingual)
- Situation orientation (versus white time orientation)

- High-context communication, verbal and nonverbal (versus white low-context communication, verbal)
- Obedience to elders and adult authority (versus white obedience to authority)
  African culture also includes:
- Expressiveness in language, emotion, and gestures
- Informality and flexibility to adjust to various conditions/situations
- Humor and imagery in language
- Ability to navigate between two cultures
- Belief that education as a means to a better life/achieving upward mobility and success
- Importance of music (for communication, self-expression, spirituality)
- Communicating with passion, expression, spontaneity, and animation

However, these values, especially the social identity connected to them, can make black students vulnerable. Black students confronted with racism often respond with anger and rebelliousness. They may deliberately perform poorly in school, rebel against authority figures (teachers and administrators) who are perceived as agents of oppression, and rebel against any behavior associated with mainstream society. To protect their self-esteem, African American students may develop ineffective coping styles that alienate them from school and hinder academic achievement. Many black children hide their academic abilities by becoming class clowns, dropping out, and suppressing effort.

Their poor academic and social competencies result in educational, social, and psychological adjustment problems. This identity is most likely to develop when the values, attitudes, and behaviors espoused in the home and school are incongruent. This incompatibility can cause considerable stress for black students, particularly if the schools attempt to assimilate black students by ignoring, trivializing, or eliminating their cultural differences. Black youth need to gain mainstream skills while remaining connected to their home and community environments.

African American students are field independent learners. The students have a short attention span, are easily distracted, do better on verbal tasks, prefer cooperative learning, are highly creative in telling stories, and appreciate information that has human content. Schools tend to respond best to field dependent learners who have a long attention span, do not get easily distracted, do better on analytical tests, prefer competitive learning, are not very creative in telling stories, and appreciate information that is impersonal.

Many teachers are shown to be field dependent learners; therefore most teaching styles are tailored to field dependent students (white) as they stress the quiet, formally structured atmosphere of their classrooms. If African American students are in these types of classrooms they will be less likely to pay attention, show low motivation, have little classroom participation, be seen as hyperactive, and be placed in special education when they should not be.

Teachers should consider the following strategies:

- Attempt to identify and match learning styles of the students.
- Assign group as well as individual projects.
- Deliver informal as well as formal instruction.
- Introduce material that is relevant to the learners.
- Vary their teaching styles accordingly to match student needs.

Learning styles to consider with African American students:

- Highly developed movement and kinesthetic abilities
- Value placed on imagination and humor
- Ability to express feelings and emotions, both verbally and nonverbally
- Richness of imagery in informal language
- Learn by doing
- Learn quickly through hands-on experience, manipulative materials, and multiple stimuli
- People oriented (focus on people rather than objects)
- Resourcefulness, unique problem-solving abilities
- Tend to view things in their entirety, not in separate pieces
- Preference for the oral mode of presentation in learning
- Use of inferences, approximate time/space/number
- Alert, curious, good retention
- Ability to navigate between two cultures

FAMILY STRUCTURE

Family structure/parents play important roles in student learning. Many times, these family structures may be the basis for a student's success or failure. African American families are often headed by single parents who have little time to spend with the children as they complete their schoolwork. They may be undereducated and do not value or understand the importance of education. And finally, they are often financially limited. They have no extra money to spend on supplemental educational materials such as books or computers.

Despite barriers, parents continue to play integral roles in student achievement. Respect, understanding, and effective communication begin at home and are key ingredients in active and proactive family involvement. Parents bring valuable insights and unique perspectives from which to enhance home-school relationships and student achievement.

Schools are ill designed to accommodate today's African American students. Almost every aspect of U.S. society has entered into the technological age but the U.S. school system remains in the industrial age. Most of the programs, curricula, and buildings are essentially the same as they were 100 years ago. The only thing that has changed is the learner.

As we study black students we find that they prefer to respond with thoughts, not automatic responses. They prefer inferential reasoning to deductive reasoning, focus on people rather than things, have a keen sense of justice, and are quick to analyze perceived injustices. Black students lean toward altruism, prefer novel approaches, and freedom (particularly relative to music, clothing, and speaking), and they favor nonverbal communication modalities. As educators we must allow our black students to be curious, creative, perceptive, evaluative, judgmental, and to explore social problems of interest. To truly understand and appreciate these strengths, we must get to know them as individuals as well as use students' strengths and proactive educational purposes.

Black students are social, spatial, visual, and active learners. The people in the schools are more important than the concept of school. Black students are better able to recognize faces and emotions and are extremely sensitive to social nuances.

Teacher preparation programs must emphasize diversity and demonstrate that it is integral to their faculty, staff, and curriculum. Teachers should be required to study the worldviews, histories, and cultures of their students (including myths, values, music, child-rearing practices, communication styles, interpersonal styles, and language). Teachers need to learn how to be reflective practitioners and develop the observational skills that are essential for evaluation and assessment.

Teachers should engage in self-awareness activities and examine their biases. They must examine their attitudes concerning black students, be exposed to accurate information, and be able to demonstrate effective interactions among colleagues, students, and families. Too many black students fail in school because the culture of the school ignores or degrades their families, communities, and backgrounds. Most of all, teachers must create a healthy learning climate not only for black students but for all students.

Teaching is an art. It requires great sensitivity to the needs of all students. It is the role of the educator to change conditions until opportunities for action and reflection are created that promote student learning. This includes preventative strategies (early, ongoing assessment, and examining peer pressures to resist academic achievement), not always intervention strategies.

African Americans are in trouble today. The gains made in the 1960s, 1970s, and 1980s appear to be eroded. The dream of black equality is giving way to the intense pressure simply to survive. People remain poor, children are growing up in poverty, and the black infant mortality rate in the United States is worse than the national rate of Bulgaria. Children are growing up underprivileged, undereducated, and underemployed. Hundreds of thousands are homeless, searching for shelter and food. The 400-year history of protest and struggle has tried to move society to treat people equally, but we remain a nation still gripped by racial and social prejudice.

The history of African Americans in the United States is overshadowed by their involuntary presence as slaves. A common misconception is that the slaves accepted their condition passively until freed by Abraham Lincoln. In fact, free blacks worked increasingly to abolish slavery while enslaved blacks exercised what resistance they could. This is reflected in the black community today as blacks resist discrimination and racial prejudice.

America must develop policies that will help blacks, and blacks will have to be at the table when these policies are negotiated. The best plan is to begin with education. African American economic survival is directly linked to quality education. More resources are needed to attract better teachers and to provide more specialized and personalized help for schoolchildren. The schools need better human resources too, teachers and administrators capable of teaching black children, who believe they can learn, and who insist that they learn.

There is no shortcut to improving our schools. The black community itself must take the lead in insisting on quality education. It is self-destructive to get hung up on wanting jive courses—courses that have no meaning or relevance, lower standards, and no tests. Children must be able to function in a fast-changing society. They have enough cards stacked against them without further handicapping them.

I'm talking about responsibility, accepting responsibility for their fate. Make demands, keep the pressure up, request resources and programs that are helpful and needed. At the same time, move forward and do what you can on your own. We must work together to cast out racism and injustice and to raise up fairness and equality. We need to root out the effects of discrimination. The children deserve the best that we can offer.

Chapter Seven

Hispanic/Latino American Students: An Ethnolinguistic Group

Success is achievable. It is right there for you to grab. But you have to want it and want it bad.

—Juan Ramando

Although conversations about race, racism, and racial identity tend to focus on black-white relations, to do so ignores the experiences of other targeted ethnic groups. When we look at the experiences of Latinos, American Indians, Arabs, and Asian/Asian Pacific Americans in the United States, we can easily see that racial and cultural oppression has been a part of their past and present and that it plays a role in the identity process for individuals in these groups as well.

Hispanic/Latino Americans are Americans of Spanish-speaking descent. Many are the descendants of Mexican people who lived in the Southwest when it became part of the United States. Almost all other Hispanic/Latino Americans or their ancestors migrated to the United States from Latin America.

The three largest groups in the United States are Mexican Americans, Puerto Ricans, and Cuban Americans. Hispanics are the nation's fastest-growing ethnic group. A substantial number of immigrants from Central and South America have entered the United States since 1970. They come from El Salvador, Guatemala, Colombia, Nicaragua, and Ecuador. Their medium age on arrival is 25.8 (U.S. Census Bureau, 2001).

Most live in California, Texas, Florida, and New York. The urban areas involved are Los Angeles, New York City, Miami, San Francisco, and Chicago, as well as many cities in the Southwest. About one third of all

Puerto Ricans live in New York City. Miami has the largest Cuban American population of any U.S. city. Large numbers of Nicaraguan immigrants have also settled in Miami and other Florida cities.

It is misleading to consider Hispanics/Latinos as one ethnic group. Even though they share a past influenced significantly by Spain and the Spanish language, there are tremendous historical, racial, and cultural differences among and within them. Hispanic/Latino Americans represent a mixture of several ethnic backgrounds, including European, American Indian, and African. Most Mexican Americans are mestizos (Indian), whereas some Cuban and Puerto Ricans are black. Some are native to the United States, others are recent arrivals.

Today, more than 35 million people of Hispanic/Latino descent live in the United States. They make up the largest cultural group in the country, with African Americans ranking second. Mexican Americans make up 59% of all Hispanic/Latino Americans. Puerto Ricans make up 10%, and Cuban Americans account for 3.5%. People from Central America, South America, and Spain together make up approximately 9%. Many Hispanic/Latino individuals did not specify a place of origin on their forms, which makes these percentages unreliable. Hispanic/Latinos are the fastest growing group as a result of a high birthrate and continuing immigration. Between 1990 and 2000, this country witnessed a 53% increase in their number. Projections indicate that this trend will continue (U.S. Census Bureau, 2001).

Most Hispanic/Latino Americans speak English but continue to use Spanish as well. Spanish has become the next most commonly spoken language after English in the country today. In addition to their language, Hispanic/Latino Americans have preserved many other traditions of their homelands. The foods, music, clothing styles, and architecture of these countries have greatly influenced U.S. culture.

Like other culturally diverse groups, Hispanic/Latino Americans are confronted by high poverty and unemployment rates, as well as poor educational outcomes. Dropout rates are alarming. Unofficial reports indicate that one in two Hispanic/Latino students leave the public school system without a degree. They are hampered by not having skills that are important for competing in the job market. For example, many new Hispanic/Latino immigrants cannot speak or understand English. Discrimination and the lack of such skills have contributed to a high rate of unemployment and, consequently, a high rate of poverty among Hispanic/Latino communities.

Let us take a closer look at our three major Hispanic/Latino groups. Each group is a distinct population with a particular historical relationship to the United States.

MEXICAN AMERICANS IN
THE UNITED STATES

> It would be a disservice to portray the future in idealistic terms. Hope is important, but the falsification of reality can immobilize a community.
>
> —Rodolfo Acuna

Mexican Americans are part of the largest ethnic group of color in the United States. They are also the largest part of the Hispanic/Latino culture. Mexican Americans attribute their rapid growth to a higher birthrate than other racial groups and a significant and continuing immigration from Mexico.

Historical Perspective

More than 25 million Indians were living in the Western Hemisphere when the Spanish conquistadors arrived in 1517. The Mayas and the Aztecs developed some of the most complex societies in the region. Gradually the Spanish soldiers conquered the Indian groups and settled in the area known as Mexico and the Southwestern United States. Because few women came to the colonies from Spain, most of the Spanish men had Indian concubines or wives. The offspring of these ethnically mixed unions were known as mestizos. The unique characteristics of the Spanish settlers significantly influenced the physical and cultural development of the new "race" that was formed in the Americas. The biological and cultural heritage of Mexican Americans includes African strains. Moors came with the Spanish, as well as African slaves.

At the beginning of the 19th century, Mexico was in a perpetual state of political turmoil. Greatly concerned with the declining population in

Texas (at that time a part of Mexico), the Spanish encouraged Anglo Americans to settle there by making impresario land grants. Because Texas was geographically close to the United States, it attracted a large number of Anglo immigrants. They were interested in rich resources and open territory. Anglo Americans totally ignored the terms of the land grant agreements (becoming loyal Mexican citizens, adopting the Catholic religion, learning Spanish, and giving up their slaves). The new settlers were not interested in Mexican culture and really wanted to establish and control Anglo institutions in the Mexican province.

When the Mexican government took serious steps to halt Anglo immigration to the Southwest, the United States began an aggressive campaign to annex all of Mexico's northern territories. War broke out and Mexico was defeated. Anglo Americans gained control of all the Southwest territories and reduced the native Mexicans to the status of second-class citizens. Rioting, lynchings, burnings, vigilante action, and other forms of violence were directed at the country's "newest aliens" during this period of turmoil. At the same time state legislation in Texas and California outlawing the use of Spanish in the schools was enacted. Though the Mexican population declined during the conquest (due to forced relocation), it increased again during the early 20th century when U.S. farmers actively encouraged Mexican immigration as an inexpensive source of agricultural labor. Mexican immigrants found jobs in truck farming, cotton and sugar beet fields, mines, industry, and the railroads. Subsequently, political and economic conditions in Mexico have fueled a steady stream of immigrants to the United States.

When the Great Depression hit in 1929, jobs became scarce. White immigrants fled to the Southwest and took the few available jobs. Mexican citizens were "encouraged" or forced to return to Mexico. The civil rights of the U.S. citizens of Mexican descent were seriously violated. Violence and race riots broke out again. This led to the Chicano movement. Prior to the civil rights movement of the 1960s, *Chicano* was a term used to refer to lower-class Mexican immigrants from rural areas and small towns. The term was viewed negatively by middle-class and elite Mexicans, as well as whites.

However, at some point, Chicanos stopped thinking of themselves as Chicanos in a negative sense and became culturally aware of their language, heritage, and values. They became politically aware of and reviewed their history in the United States. Many Hispanic Americans tell me that they go through stages of racial identity. Stage 1 is forced identification, where individuals are identified as Hispanic or Mexican Americans by others, stimulating a search for their cultural roots. Stage 2 is acceptance of their group. Stage 3 is affiliation; in this stage Hispanic students and families develop a deeper sense of belonging and a desire to contribute to a sense of personal and familial well-being.

The term Chicano was also used to link Mexican American political activists and intellectuals to their Mexican Indian heritage. The Chicano movement had economic, educational, religious, and cultural goals. The push for bilingual education in the schools was one of its major goals.

The Chicano movement was also political. Many believed political clout was the best way to attain their goals. They would be able to overcome oppression in the United States only when they had political power and control over the schools and courts that influenced their lives.

Students need to be made aware of four young men who epitomized the movement in the public vision. Cesar Chavez unionized the farm workers and led various strikes. Reies Lopez Tijerina demanded that Anglos in New Mexico return the lands they had taken from the Mexican Americans in the 1800s or compensate them. Rodolfo "Corkey" Gonzales organized the Crusade for Justice in 1965. The crusade initiated successful projects related to improved education, better housing, and the elimination of police brutality in Mexican American communities. Jose Angel Gutierrez organized the political party La Raza Unida in the 1970s.

Mexican Americans Today

Most Mexican Americans continue to live in the Southwest in urban areas. Mexican-origin Latinos are the youngest of all Latino subgroups with a median age of 24.1 as compared to 33.5 for non-Hispanic/Latinos. Education and family income remain below the U.S. average (only 45% of Mexican Americans aged 25 and older have completed high school, and 26% of all Mexican-origin families live in poverty) (Suarez-Orozco & Suarez-Orozco, 2001, p. 50).

Mexican Americans, like African Americans and American Indians, made important educational and economic gains during the 1960s. However, many of these gains faded in the 1970s and 1980s owing to conservative national politics and changes in the economy. As the nation became more technologically advanced, groups with few skills could no longer find jobs.

By 1990, a new movement began. The various Hispanic/Latino groups (Mexican Americans, Puerto Ricans, and Cubans) joined together to form political, cultural, and business organizations to push for their collective rights and to improve the economic and educational status of the Hispanic/Latino Americans. Mexican Americans were reaping the benefits in local and state elections.

The Mexican American population is becoming urbanized. Large populations are concentrated in Los Angeles, Houston, Dallas, Denver, and Chicago. Among this urban population has developed a new middle-class group of Mexican Americans who are professionals and businesspeople.

Mexican Americans face several important challenges in the years ahead including the need to improve the educational status of its youth, close the income gap between Mexican Americans and the total U.S. population, and work with other Hispanic/Latino groups to influence political elections and national policy. Let us hope that the Mexican American community will face these challenges creatively.

PUERTO RICANS IN THE UNITED STATES

Colonialism has played an important role in the Puerto Rican experience. We are connected to you through colonial ties, making us unique.

—Sonia Nieto

Puerto Ricans are the second largest Hispanic/Latino group in the United States. The Puerto Rican population on the U.S. mainland is growing faster than the population in Puerto Rico.

Content about Puerto Ricans should be included in our curriculum because Puerto Ricans are an integral part of our society. Knowledge of their experiences on the mainland can help students master social science concepts such as *migration*, *cultural diversity*, *racism*, and *colonialism*. Students can also compare and contrast Puerto Rican experiences with those of other cultural groups.

Puerto Ricans are culturally uprooted and their migration is unique. They are U.S. citizens. Other groups coming to America must be naturalized. Puerto Ricans can enter the United States without restriction since they became citizens in 1917. Between 1940 and 1960 more than 500,000 arrived on the mainland looking for jobs and a better life. By 1970 over 70% of all Puerto Ricans in the United States settled in East Harlem in New York City.

Historical Perspective

Puerto Rico, called San Juan Baptista by Christopher Columbus, is a beautiful, small tropical island in the Caribbean Sea. It is smaller than the state of Connecticut. Spain ruled the island country from the 16th century until the Spanish American War in 1898 when the United States took control. Puerto Rico is neither a state nor an independent nation but a U.S. territory.

Like the conquered Mexicans, Puerto Ricans did not choose to become U.S. citizens. Puerto Rico became an unincorporated territory of the United States in 1898, ceded by Spain at the conclusion of the Spanish American War. Puerto Rico, which had struggled to become independent of Spain, did not welcome subjugation by the United States. An active policy of Americanization of the island population was implemented, including attempts to replace Spanish with English as the language of instruction on the island. The attempts to displace Spanish were vigorously resisted by Puerto Rican teachers and students alike.

In 1917, the U.S. Congress passed the Jones Act, which imposed citizenship and the obligation to serve in the U.S. military but denied the right to vote in national elections. In 1951, Puerto Ricans voted to accept commonwealth status, which allowed them greater control of their school system. The Spanish language was subsequently restored in all schools on the island.

Puerto Ricans began migrating to the mainland in large numbers after World War II. Economic conditions on the island have driven many Puerto Ricans to New York City and other northeastern U.S. cities. Puerto Rico has a high level of unemployment. City slums, housing congestion, and below-poverty-level incomes were also a factor. Fluctuating employment conditions have contributed to their migration, which has been called "the revolving door migration." This is a pattern of circular motion in which Puerto Ricans go back and forth between the island and the mainland depending on economic conditions in the two places.

The lack of legal barriers is a major factor in Puerto Rican migration to and from the U.S. mainland. As U.S. citizens Puerto Ricans can move freely. They are not limited by quotas as are Mexicans and other Hispanics/Latinos. Easy and inexpensive transportation to the mainland also facilitates Puerto Rican migration.

The Americanization of Puerto Ricans has also played a major role in their migration. Since Puerto Rico became a territory, U.S. culture and institutions have profoundly influenced Puerto Rican culture and lifestyles. English was initially forced on the students, and textbooks venerated George Washington and Abraham Lincoln rather than Puerto Rican leaders.

Puerto Ricans Today

The family, which is very important in traditional Puerto Rican culture, is changing. Values such as respect for authority and youth work ethic are changing. Puerto Ricans are clinging to respect for the elderly and the extended family. The Puerto Rican community is very poor and its members' educational status is comparatively low. The poverty rate is close to 60%, and approximately 50% of Puerto Rican adults over age 25 have not completed high school (U.S. Census Bureau, 1999). Puerto Ricans are a multicultural population descended from European colonies, enslaved Africans, and the indigenous Taino Indians, and a significant number of them are dark skinned and so may experience more racism and discrimination than light-skinned Latino populations.

The future of the Puerto Rican community must be shaped by educational, political, and social action. More young people are working to strengthen the community. Organizations are promoting educational achievement and leadership development among the youth. The Puerto Rican Youth for Social Action is one example of this shaping process.

The future of Puerto Ricans in the United States will be heavily influenced by the political, economic, and social developments on the island. These two communities are integrally bound. Status on the island influences the ideologies, debates, and visions of mainland Puerto Ricans.

CUBAN AMERICANS IN THE UNITED STATES

> If in things concerning my country I should be given a choice, I would choose to want the cornerstone of our Republic to be the devotion of Cubans to the dignity of human kind.
>
> —Jose Marti

As a group, Cuban Americans are older and more affluent than other Latinos, reflecting a different immigration history. Although Cuban communities have existed in Florida and New York since the 1870s, the majority of Cubans emigrated to Tampa, Key West, Miami, and New York City in the years after Fidel Castro assumed power in the 1959 revolution. As a group, Cuban Americans have low visibility because their relocation has occurred almost exclusively in a few large urban areas.

The first wave of immigration was upper-class, light-skinned Cubans who left in the first days of the Castro revolution in 1956. They were able to bring their personal fortunes with them and established businesses in the United States. The second major group, largely middle-class professionals and skilled workers, left after Castro had been in power for a few months. Though many were unable to bring possessions with them, they received support from the U.S. government and charitable organizations. The last major group of Cuban immigrants was known as the Marielitos. They arrived in 1980, having lived most of their lives under a socialist government. Marielitos are typically much poorer, less educated, and darker skinned than earlier refugees. Many also had criminal records.

Those who left the island in search of a political haven are not a representative sample of the Cuban population at large. A disproportionate number of refugees come from middle-class and upper-strata prerevolutionary society. They were threatened by government-mandated changes that eroded their economic position. Many are elderly because barriers to their exit from the island were considerably fewer than those faced by younger Cubans.

On average, Cubans have higher educational levels than Mexican Americans and Puerto Ricans. Approximately 17% of Cubans over age 25 are college graduates, as compared to less than 10% for Chicanos and Puerto Ricans (U.S. Census Bureau, 1999). Because the early Cuban immigrants viewed themselves as people in exile who might return to

Cuba when Castro is no longer in power, they have worked to keep Spanish an integral part of their lives in the United States.

Life in Cuba

On January 1, 1959, the city of Havana, Cuba, rocked with the effects of a drastic change. The regime of dictator Fulgenico Batista had been deposed by a revolution led by a bearded young rebel named Fidel Castro. His triumphal entry into the capital city was seen by nearly everyone as the coming of a new messiah. His popularity was more than that of a political figure; he had all the makings of a charismatic leader.

As the course of the revolution drifted politically left, a marked polarization of Cuban society began to occur. A person either supported the revolution or was thought of as a *gusano* (worm). The latter was a parasite to progress and the revolution was better off without him or her. The revolution affected all Cubans, regardless of their place in society. Fundamental changes reached to economic, political, social, and religious sectors of Cuban life.

The educational system was affected greatly. The number of schools in rural areas was increased in a campaign to end illiteracy. School was required for at least six years (ages 6 through 14). The government also provided a strong adult education program. Cuba has developed one of the most extensive networks of schools in Latin America, from preschool to graduate and professional programs. Nearly all adults can read and write. New high schools were built in rural areas. Instruction in the humanities and the natural and physical sciences was fraught with political socialization, which placed a premium on loyalty to the revolution.

The Cuban economy today deemphasizes consumer goods in favor of products for export. As a result of this emphasis, as well as of production lags, rationing is fairly common.

Since the collapse of the Soviet empire, most of the trading agreements Cuba had with former communist nations have collapsed. New goods must be purchased with hard currency, and the Cuban peso is not a hard currency.

Leaving Cuba entails many sacrifices. Relatives are left behind, a significant point when one realizes the close-knit nature of the Cuban extended family, which makes it difficult for members to break from the family unit. Forfeiture of all possessions is another factor to consider. Everything a person has worked for goes to the government. Also, there is the prospect of starting over in a strange environment without command of the English language. Despite all these difficulties more than a million Cubans have felt compelled to leave their homeland.

In the early 1960s, the United States accepted as a political refugee any Cuban who could reach its shores. Between 1959 and 1962 about 200,000 anti-Castro Cubans immigrated to the United States. After commercial air flights were suspended in 1962, many Cubans risked their lives as they came by small boats or rafts. In 1980 the flood of refugees was housed in temporary quarters ranging from holding shelters to the Orange Bowl in Miami. Despite tighter laws limiting the arrival of Cuban refugees, many continue to enter the United States any way they can.

Most immigrants to the United States have come with the unwavering intention of making this country their permanent home. Many Cubans arrived here with the thought of returning to their homeland as soon as the political climate changed. Most of them never expected Castro to remain in power for very long. Although the refugees were grateful to the United States for asylum, their ultimate plans were not in this country. Thus, they did not feel the immediate need to assimilate into the mainstream culture.

The adaptation of Cubans to American life has often been difficult. One problem encountered by Cuban parents was trying to raise their children to adhere to Cuban values, norms, and customs. These customs and values permitted less freedom than their American peers enjoyed. The children had to make major adjustments, as did the school systems that were to receive them. Along with a new language and curriculum, some students had to learn a new value system. Cuban youth lacked self-discipline and also the concept of private property (Suarez-Orozoco & Suarez-Orozoco, 2001). Authority was equated with people one does not trust and taking someone else's property was synonymous with "need" not "bad." With time and the patience of teachers, these students have adjusted to the new value system and have progressed well in their studies.

Cuban Americans Today

Cuban Americans, while making economic, social, and cultural contributions to the United States, also seek to maintain their cultural identity. In doing so they want their children bilingual. Cuban parents feel that bilingual education is a necessary bridge for those with limited or no English-language ability to succeed in American classrooms.

Today, Cuban Americans are the third-largest Spanish-speaking group in the United States (Mexican Americans and Puerto Ricans rank first and second). The Cuban experience indicates that Cuban Americans have been a viable and beneficial addition to U.S. society. The pattern can be expected to continue.

OTHER HISPANICS/LATINOS IN THE UNITED STATES

One thing is certain, racism is everywhere in America. Whenever a person of one race factors in skin or ethnicity or religion to make a decision about another human being, the racist card is being played.

—Maria de la Cruz

"Other Hispanic/Latinos," as the U.S. government classifies those Latinos who do not trace their family background to Mexico, Puerto Rico, or Cuba, are an extremely heterogeneous group. They include South Americans as well as Central Americans, well-educated professionals as well as rural farmers, those who immigrated for increased economic opportunities as well as those escaping civil war. Among this category of other Hispanics/Latinos, the largest groups are from the Dominican Republic, Colombia, Ecuador, El Salvador, Guatemala, Peru, and Nicaragua.

They arrive with a wide range of educational backgrounds. In El Salvador there is widespread poverty, and not enough schools. Children are supposed to be required to attend school from ages 7 to 12 but many do not attend at all. Only one half of those who attend school graduate. In Nicaragua a literacy campaign was started and then dropped due to lack of funding. In the Dominican Republic 60 percent of the people live in rural areas where there are few schools (*The Great World Atlas*, 2004). In the United States, these students suffer from the same racism and discrimination attacks as do all other Hispanic/Latino students.

Hispanic/Latino Cultural Values

Overall, the cultural value of *familism*—the importance of the extended family as a reference group and as providers of social support—has been identified as a characteristic shared by most Hispanic/Latinos independent of their national background, birthplace, language, or any other socioeconomic/demographic characteristic. For example, achieving in school and at work were considered important by Latino teens because success would allow them to take care of family members. Conversely, white American teens considered education and work as a means of gaining independence from their families (Takaki, 1993). The most critical task facing the children of all immigrants is reconciling the culture of home with the dominant American culture.

Spanish is often spoken in the home and is a very critical piece of the Hispanic/Latino culture. Who are you if you don't speak Spanish? Language is inextricably bound to identity. Jose, a young Puerto Rican man, said, "I think the only thing Puerto Ricans preserve in this country is the language. If we lose that we are lost. I believe that being Puerto Rican and speaking Spanish go hand-in-hand."

Large inner-city schools have failed to address the educational needs of Hispanic/Latino students. The dropout rate continues to be unbearably high. The matriculation rate in higher education is decidedly low, and the high school completion level is abominable.

The Latino students you have in your classrooms may have lived here for a generation, immigrated recently leaving many relatives behind, or arrived as war refugees with no option to return to their home country. These origins affect the extent to which they have learned English and the family's desire to maintain Spanish at home.

Cultural values play a huge part in the lives of Hispanic/Latino students and their families. Traditional Hispanic/Latino American cultural values include:

- A strong extended family system that is more pronounced than among other ethnic groups (versus white individualism)
- Relaxed/permissive child-rearing practices; independence and early development of skills are not pushed in young children (versus white authoritative child-rearing practices)

- Interdependence, cooperation, personal and interpersonal relationships are highly valued and come first; emphasis on social relations (versus white independence, competition, emphasis on task)
- Concrete thinking and learning experiences (versus white passive learning)
- Social learning in pairs and small groups (versus white independent, individual learning)
- Relaxed, present-time orientation (versus white future-time orientation)
- Commitment to the Spanish language, bilingualism (versus white monolingualism)
- Direct physical contact accepted, affectionate hugging and kissing on the cheek are acceptable for both the same sex and opposite sex
- Very strong religious beliefs
- Saving face, use of indirect communication
- More traditionally defined family structure (father as head of the house) and more defined sexual roles
- More overt respect for the elderly
- Past orientation, listens to experience
- Uses nonverbal communication, gestures, and expressions

Hand-in-hand with culture are learning styles. Hispanic/Latino learning styles involve:

- An inclusive approach
- Cooperative learning/peer tutoring
- Sensitivity to communication needs; are students "tuned in" to the class?
- Performance-based learning, ability tasking
- Hands-on learning
- Involvement of extended family
- Use of the Spanish language
- Less independent and more modest about accomplishments and abilities
- Youth-initiated and maintain meaningful interaction and communication with adults
- Use of intuitive reasoning (making inferences)
- Value of history, oral tradition, and visual/kinesthetic learning

In general, Hispanic/Latino American students value nonmaterial possessions, family bonds, active real-world learning experiences, social and cooperative learning, and student-centered classrooms.

I have found several strategies that work for Hispanic/Latino American students regardless of age. The following really do work:

- Use the overhead projector and videos to help students visualize. Include pictures, diagrams, and interest-related materials.
- Let the students sit where they feel comfortable as long as their behavior is constructive.
- Engage the students using the "whole class" method; do not single students out.
- Give constant praise.
- Explain directions in many ways, give a demonstration, and have the patience to repeat directions.
- Never assume that, because the students do not ask questions, they understand. Go to the student, ask, and make sure.
- Use hands-on materials, building things together.
- Offer extended time for assignments and tests.
- Make statements and ask questions in more than one way.

Educating and empowering Hispanic/Latino American students for school success necessitates developing their appreciation for their own culture, adapting teaching styles to learning styles, increasing students' sense of belonging in school settings, and focusing on strengths while reappraising weaknesses. Efforts must also continue to target language acquisition. Bilingual programs, Spanish-immersion programs, English as a Second Language (ESL), or Limited English Proficiency (LEP) are most helpful. Language is a major barrier for culturally diverse students, not just Hispanic/Latino students in U.S. schools. Teachers' beliefs about foreign languages can play a role in their ability to see the verbal strengths of these students.

For many years, the educational achievement of most Hispanic/Latino American students has lagged behind that of non-Hispanic students, despite early programs designed to help boost achievement. Under bilingual programs started in 1968 students were taught in Spanish such basic subjects as math and science, and studied English as a second language. When the students were ready, the classes were then taught in English. By 1990, many schools had replaced that traditional approach with two-way bilingual education, which combined native Spanish speakers with English-speaking students in all classes. The students progressed through the grade levels with some subjects taught in Spanish and others in English. The participants helped each other learn. This program remains controversial because some educators feel all academics should be completed in English.

Discrimination continues to plague many Hispanic/Latino American students. Educators like Suarez-Orozco and Suarez-Orozco (2001) and Takaki (1993) have shown that these students have often been assigned to classes for low achievers, forced to repeat grades, or classified as special needs because they do not speak English well enough or because of cultural differences.

Hispanic leaders support the hiring of more Hispanic/Latino teachers for Spanish-speaking students. Such teachers tend to be more sensitive to the linguistic and cultural backgrounds of Hispanic/Latino students. Leaders also call for improvements in English-language courses and counseling services for these students. Many schools have developed dropout prevention programs, career guidance programs, and multicultural educational programs aimed at providing better educational opportunities for Hispanic/Latino American students.

To help Hispanic/Latino students achieve academic excellence, we must utilize bilingual education. Leading educational researchers have found that bilingual education has a positive impact on student achievement levels. It is a tool for encouraging critical thinking, abstract problem solving, and cognitive development. We must also use progressive teaching methods by combining high academic standards with a focus on the individual child's needs and learning styles.

Hispanic/Latino American students also benefit from multicultural learning. We should provide intensive exposure to culture and community. Multicultural learning is also an important part of the child's cognitive and social development.

Finally, we must encourage and support family involvement. Research shows a direct correlation between student achievement and parental involvement in school. Hispanic/Latino parents want to commit themselves to intensive involvement in both curricular and extracurricular programs. We must seek excellence and equity for our Hispanic/Latino American students, acknowledging in the process that these students are an integral part of our future and are worth educating.

Chapter Eight

Asian American Students: The Model Minority

What has been spoiled through man's fault can be made good again through man's work.

—I Ching

Ronald Takaki in his book *A Different Mirror: A History of Multicultural America* (1993) wrote, "In America, Asian immigrants and their offspring have been actors in history. Their dreams and hopes unfurled here, before the wind, all of them. . . . [F]rom the first Chinese miners sailing through the Golden Gate to the last Vietnamese boat people flying into Los Angeles International Airport . . . [Asian immigrants] have been making history in America" (p. 5).

Asian Americans, one of the most diverse and interesting ethnic groups in the United States, are rarely studied in the public schools. When discussed in the textbooks and other media, they are often used to illustrate how an ethnic group of color can succeed in the United States. Yet curiously absent is a discussion of why Asian Americans outperform white students in schools. Because of their tremendous educational, occupational, and economic success, Asian Americans are often called the "model minority." It is true that some Asian American groups are better educated, have a higher occupational status, and earn more money than other Americans, including white Americans. However, the model minority concept is problematic for several reasons.

A focus on the economic success of Asian Americans obscures the tremendous economic diversity within Asian American communities. The model minority concept also obscures the stories of successful members of other groups, such as upwardly mobile African Americans and Hispanics. Finally, when overemphasized, the model minority argument can divert attention from the racism that Asian Americans still experience in the United States. As with all groups, Asian Americans have not escaped the ravages of poverty. Many hold menial, low-skilled, service and blue-collar jobs. Others attain managerial and technical positions.

Asians have immigrated to the United States from various countries: the Philippines, China, Japan, Korea, Vietnam, Laos, Cambodia, and so forth. During the 1980s, Asian Americans grew faster than any other racial group in the United States. This group included Korean Americans, Asian Indians, Pakistanis, and Southeast Asians (Hmong, Vietnamese) who fled to the United States in the aftermath of the Vietnam War. There was a 99% increase in the number of Asian American students compared to an increase of 53% for Hispanic students (U.S. Census Bureau, 1993).

The Koreans are one of the largest and fastest-growing ethnic groups in the United States. Many are college-educated professionals. Many Asian Indian and Pakistani immigrants are English speaking and highly educated. The Southeast Asians came for different reasons than the early Chinese and Japanese. Singular political, economic, or personal concerns motivated many of the refugees to leave their homelands. Most had been directly touched by the trauma of the Vietnam War (1954–1975) or its aftermath.

Historical Perspective

White racial ideologies during the late 1800s define Pacific immigrants as aliens ineligible for citizenship, unfair economic competitors, and socially unassimilated groups. For the first 100 years of Asian American immigration (1840s–1940s) the images of each community were racialized and predominantly negative. The Chinese were called "Mongolians" and depicted in the media as heathens, gamblers, and opium addicts. The Japanese, Chinese, and Koreans were viewed as the "yellow peril.".Filipinos were derogatorily referred to as "little brown monkeys." Asian Indians were called "rag heads."

In the late 1960s, as a part of the transformation of the civil rights era, the racial identity and ethnic consciousness of Asian immigrants were brought to the front burner. The polarization of civil rights protests required Asians in America to consider their identity, their self-definition, and their place in racialized America. They discovered that racial quotas and legal inequalities applied to them just as they did to other culturally diverse groups. "Colored" was clearly defined as anyone nonwhite.

Consequently, the terms *Asian American* and *Asian Pacific American* emerged as a unifying political construct, encouraging individuals to work across ethnic lines for increased economic, political, and social rights. Asian American groups have lobbied for bilingual education, curriculum reform, Asian American studies, improved working conditions for garment and restaurant workers, and support for community-based development. They have also opposed media misrepresentations and sought more opportunities for Asian Americans in theater, film, and television. Racial politics have continued to foster this unifying panethnic identity, though the large influx of new immigrants has changed the character of the Asian American community from the stable third- and fourth-generation community of the 1960s to one now composed largely of newcomers.

As we have said, Asian Americans have been called the model minority. Young Asians are routinely depicted as star students (especially in math and science), supported by industrious, entrepreneurial, upwardly mobile parents. For individual students, the stereotype of success may have negative consequences for the quality of instruction they receive. For example, I watched a five-year-old Asian American girl in a charter school kindergarten class dutifully engaged in the task the teacher had assigned, placing a number of objects next to the various numerals printed on a card. The child worked quietly without any help from the teacher and when the time was up she put her work away. The only problem was that at the end of the session, no numeral had the correct number of objects next to it. The teacher said that Mia, like other Asian American students she had taught, was one of the best students in her classroom. In this case, the stereotype of good Asian students meant Mia had not received the help she needed.

Asian Americans: A Diverse Group

What do we mean when we say "Asian"? Asian Americans are one of the most highly diversified ethnic groups in the United States. They vary greatly in both cultural and physical characteristics. The attitudes, values, and ethnic institutions often differ within their communities.

The U.S. government includes in its definition of Asian people from East Asia (Chinese, Japanese, Korean, and Filipino), from Southeast Asia (Vietnamese, Laotian, Burmese, Cambodian), from the Pacific Islands (Samoan, Guamanian, Fijian), and from South Asia (Indian, Pakistani, Nepali). The Asian Pacific population in the United States has increased from less than 1 million in 1960 to more than 8 million in 2000. It includes 43 ethnic groups with religious beliefs that vary greatly and include Buddhism, Islam, Christianity, Hinduism, Shintoism, ancestor worship, and animism. Those from communist countries where religion was outlawed may be without any religious tradition.

The largest Asian Pacific American groups are the Chinese (23% of the Asian population), followed by the Japanese (12%), Asian Indian (11%), Korean (11%), and Vietnamese and Hmong combined (9%), the fastest-growing Asian community in the United States (Uba, 2000).

Because of tremendous diversity among Asian Americans and their unique experiences in the United States, studying them can help students increase their ethnic literacy and develop a respect for cultural differences.

The Asian American groups also have important similarities. All came to the United States seeking the American dream, satisfied labor needs, and became victims of an anti-Asian movement to prevent their further immigration to the United States. Chinese Americans, Japanese Americans, and Filipino Americans have also experienced tremendous economic, educational, and social mobility and success in U.S. society.

The stories told by these groups can help students understand how the American dream can be pursued and attained. However, when these groups are studied, the problems that Asian Americans still face in the American society, such as cultural conflict, identity, and attaining a balance between their ethnic culture and the mainstream culture should not be glossed over. The poverty that exists in the urban communities and the new wave of racism that has been directed against Asian Americans, as well as against other groups of color, must be analyzed.

CHINESE AMERICANS

Talk does not cook rice. Learning is like rowing upstream. Not to advance is to drop back.

—Chinese proverb

When the news reached Guandong Province in southeast China that there was a "Golden Mountain" across the Pacific, a number of young men violated both Chinese law and tradition and headed for the promised land. The decision to leave China for a foreign land was a serious one because it was illegal to emigrate and violators could be severely punished. Also, Confucian doctrine, which was an integral part of Chinese life during this period, taught that a young man should value his family above all else and should not leave it. However, both the promises of the land and the mountain of gold, and the living conditions in Toishan district in Guandong, from which most of the first Chinese immigrants hailed, helped push the young immigrants across the Pacific.

Political upheaval, famine, local warfare, excessive taxes, a severely depressed economy, and the rugged terrain in Toishan that made farming difficult motivated young Chinese men to seek better opportunities in an unknown land where one could easily strike gold and return to China a rich man.

The Chinese were the first Asians to emigrate to the United States in large numbers, arriving in California in 1850 as part of the rush for gold. The journey across the Pacific was rugged and hazardous. These first arrivals were single men who paid their own way to the California gold fields, hoping to get rich and then return home to China.

On their arrival in California they experienced a rude awakening. White Americans considered them strange and exotic because of their traditional Chinese clothing, language, queue hairstyle (which whites called pigtails), and skin color. Almost from the beginning, the Chinese were objects of curiosity and victims of racism.

As the gold rush waned, many Chinese did not have enough money to go home. Hired at wages one third below what whites would have been paid, Chinese immigrants were able to find work in a wide range of occupations that most whites found unpalatable, such as work on railroads (they built the Pacific portion of the transcontinental railroad), domestic work, and intensive farming.

It did not take long for whites to become alarmed at the numbers of Chinese entering the United States, and a vicious movement developed to keep them out. Anti-Chinese activities took the form of racist newspaper stories, violent attacks against defenseless men, women, and children, and highly discriminatory laws, such as the Foreign Miners Tax, which forced the Chinese to pay a highly disproportionate share of the taxes collected under the law.

Immigration was severely restricted in 1882 and completely forbidden by the 1924 Immigration Act. Like African Americans and Indians, the Chinese were viewed as a threat to white racial purity. Laws prohibiting marriage between a white person and a "Negro, Mulatto, or Mongolian" were passed. These laws and discrimination in housing and employment limited the growth of the Chinese population.

A second wave of Chinese immigration occurred after World War II. In an effort to promote an alliance with China against Japan, the U.S. government allowed a few thousand Chinese to enter the country. Chinese scientists and professionals and their families escaping from Communism were part of the second wave.

A third wave occurred after the passage of the 1965 Immigration Act. Quotas were eliminated and entire families immigrated at once. Tens of thousands of Chinese have come to America every year, and the reestablishment of diplomatic relations between the People's Republic of China and the United States has provided new immigration opportunities for Chinese students.

JAPANESE AMERICANS

A teacher for one day is like a parent for a lifetime.

—Japanese proverb

By contrast, more than three quarters of the people of Japanese ancestry in the United States are American born, descendants of those who came to the U.S. mainland or Hawaii before 1924. Because of overpopulation, depressed farming conditions, and political turmoil in Japan in the early 1860s, its citizens began emigrating to Hawaii and the U.S. mainland in search of better economic opportunities. The arrival of 148 Japanese contract laborers in Hawaii in 1868 to work on the plantations violated Japanese law. By 1886, Japan, because of internal problems, legalized emigration and the exodus to Hawaii and the U.S. mainland began in earnest.

These early immigrants were attracted by higher U.S. wages. Because the Japanese government encouraged women to emigrate as well, often as "picture brides" in arranged marriages, Japanese families quickly established themselves. While Japanese workers were welcomed on the plantations of Hawaii, there was considerable anti-Japanese feeling on the West Coast. In 1906, the San Francisco Board of Education established a separate school for Chinese, Japanese, and Korean children, and the California Alien Land Law prohibited Japanese immigrants and other foreign-born residents from purchasing agricultural land because they were ineligible for citizenship.

The Japanese arrivals on the West Coast worked in a variety of fields, including agriculture, the railroads, domestic work, gardening, small businesses, and industry. Because of job discrimination, they were mainly self-employed. Their greatest impact was in agriculture, gardening, and small industry. Of all these areas, their accomplishments in agriculture, and especially truck farming, were the most impressive. Most of the land they were able to farm was considered unarable and largely useless by most white farmers. With a great deal of ingenuity and the use of intensive farming techniques, the Japanese dominated certain areas of California truck farming. They produced a large amount of the state's peppers, strawberries, celery, peas, cucumbers, tomatoes, cabbage, carrots, lettuce, and onions.

Japanese immigrants were often praised for their industry and eagerness when they first arrived in California. However, their tremendous success alarmed the white farmers, who viewed them as tough competitors and chose to drive the "yellow peril" out of California. "The Japs Must Go" became the rallying cry of the anti-Japanese movement led by the white farmer's unions and supported by the new media of the times.

Pressure built up. Then, on December 7, 1941, Japan bombed Pearl Harbor. Hysteria emerged on the West Coast as anti-Japanese groups spread rumors about espionage activities among the Japanese. The uproar on the West Coast and the fear that spread throughout other parts of the nation resulted in government action in March, 1942. Executive Order 9102 established the War Relocation Authority, which authorized the secretary of war to forcibly remove Japanese Americans to federal concentration camps. Without a trial or hearing, 120,000 Japanese Americans were removed from their West Coast homes and confined in camps as far away as Idaho, Colorado, and Utah. The internment showed how a dehumanizing experience could demoralize a group that had traditionally had high group solidarity and trust and cause mistrust and suspicion within it. There was a question of loyalty as Japanese leaders accused each other of participating in the oppression.

One response to this internment was for Japanese families to encourage their children to become as "American" as possible in an effort to prevent further discrimination. For this reason, as well as their longevity in the United States, Japanese Americans as a group are the most acculturated of the Asian Pacific American communities.

Japanese Americans today are one of the smallest of the Asian American groups. However, they have been called a leading force in the so-called model minority because of their success in education, social class mobility, and low levels of crime, mental illness, and other social deviances.

FILIPINO AMERICANS

The most important tool for success is the belief that you can succeed.

—Filipino American student

Filipino Americans also experienced a pattern of male immigration to Hawaii and then the mainland United States in the early 1900s. Like other groups they came seeking work and better opportunities. An early community of Filipinos in Louisiana was documented by Marina Espina in his 1988 book, *Filipinos in Louisiana*. Espina's research cites October 18, 1587, as the date when Filipino sailors aboard a Spanish galleon jumped ship on the Louisiana coast. They formed a settlement in the bayous of Louisiana and developed a shrimping industry.

Significant numbers of Filipinos did not settle in the United States until the first decades of the 1900s, after the Philippines became an American possession as a result of the Spanish-American War. Many were government-sponsored students who returned to the Philippines to apply the knowledge they acquired in America. Others were laborers who were recruited to work in the Hawaiian sugar cane fields. Because the men were not allowed to establish families, there are few descendants from this wave of immigration. This pattern ended in 1930 when Congress set a Filipino quota of 50 per year. Tens of thousands have immigrated since 1965 when the 1965 Emigration Act abolished national origin quotas, and more Asian immigrants were allowed into the country. Some Filipino immigrants were quite affluent in the Philippines, while others were extremely poor. In general, because of the U.S. military presence in the Philippines during most of the 20th century, Filipino immigrants are much more familiar with U.S. culture than most Asian immigrants.

Because of chronic unemployment and widespread poverty at home, like the Chinese and Japanese, thousands of Filipinos were lured to the United States in search of the American dream. But they largely worked as cheap and exploited field hands. Even though Chinese and Japanese immigration had come to an abrupt halt with the passage of the Immigration Act of 1924, Filipinos were allowed into the United States because of the U.S. annexation of the Philippines in 1898. Once the Philippines gained independence in 1946, immigration was severely limited.

Filipino immigrants in the United States had some unique group characteristics that made their lives on the West Coast and Hawaii harsh. As the third wave of Asian immigrants, they were victims of accumulated anti-Asian racism. They were also on average much younger (16 to 30) than other Asian immigrants. Also, most Filipinos were sojourners who hoped to return to the Philippines after gathering the riches of America. The Filipinos emigrated from a country that was a U.S. colony where the American myth of "all men are created equal" was taught in the schools. Thus, unlike other Asian groups, they came to the United States expecting to be treated as equals. Their acceptance of this myth made their adjustment in the United States more difficult (Takaki, 1993).

Like other Asian immigrants they did the work the whites disdained and refused to do. They were contracted to do stoop labor, like picking asparagus and lettuce, and to work as domestic servants. Some worked in the fishing industry and in canneries.

Unlike the Japanese and Chinese, the Filipinos were unable to develop tightly knit ethnic communities because their jobs kept them moving. They turned to recreation and entertainment that reflected the sociological makeup of young, unmarried men searching for meaning in life in a hostile and racist atmosphere. Cockfighting and gambling were favorite pastimes of the lonely, alienated men, who also often frequented prostitutes.

Filipino-owned dancehalls, in which white girls danced and sold or gave sexual favors to the immigrants, were popular and a source of widespread tension between Filipinos and white men.

Today, the majority of the immigrants from the Philippines are professionals, technical workers, and specialists. Current success was attained and is maintained by hard work, tenacity, and the will to overcome.

KOREAN AMERICANS

> Those who have it all never stop seeking. Those who stop seeking never have it all.
>
> —Korean elder

Korean immigration to the United States occurred in three distinct waves, beginning with fewer than 10,000 laborers who arrived between 1903 and 1905. While there were some Korean "picture brides," most male immigrants were unable to start families because of the same antimiscegenation laws that affected the Chinese and Japanese. Another small group of Korean immigrants came to the United States after World War II and the Korean War. This group included Korean adoptees and war brides. Korean immigration dramatically increased between 1970 and 1990 with more than 30,000 Korean families arriving on U.S. soil.

These Koreans came from a wide range of socioeconomic and educational levels. Most Korean families currently living in the United States are part of families consisting of immigrant parents and children born or raised in the United States, families in which differing rates of acculturation may contribute to generational conflicts.

SOUTHEAST ASIAN AMERICANS

Southeast Asian refugees are quite different from other Asian immigrant groups in their reasons for coming to the United States and their experiences in their homelands. After the end of the Vietnam War in 1975, a large number of mostly educated Vietnamese arrived. After 1978, a second group of immigrants, many of them uneducated rural farmers traumatized by the war and its aftermath, came to the United States largely to escape persecution by the Communists, the ravaged countryside of their homeland, and refugee camps. Many continue to arrive today from the refugee camps in Cambodia and Thailand. This group includes Hmong, Vietnamese, Chinese Vietnamese, Cambodian, Lao, and Mien. Chapter 9 is devoted to these new arrivals from Southeast Asia.

ASIAN INDIANS

Asian Indians have also experienced a dramatic population growth in the United States. Over 1 million are currently residing in various areas of the country. The first immigrants were farmers from India who settled on the West Coast in the 1850s. Like other Asians, they encountered a lot of discrimination and did not gain a foothold at that time. The contemporary wave (1986 to present) of Asian Indian immigration includes many highly educated English-speaking adults and their children. In addition this wave of immigrants also includes rural families who are less fluent in English and are having more difficulty adjusting to the American culture.

Asian Pacific Americans, Latinos, and American Indians are disparate groups, but they all share with the people of African descent the need for meaningful education. This education must lead to finding one's ethnic identity. This will help deal with negative stereotypes, resist negative self-perceptions, and affirm oneself.

Many of our Asian refugees and immigrants are scared. Fear is a powerful emotion, one that immobilizes, traps words in our throats, and stills our tongues. In order for meaningful dialogue to occur, fear of what they experienced in their war-torn countries must eventually give way to risk and trust. A leap of faith must be made. It is not easy. Breaking the silence requires courage.

As educators, we must encourage all groups to identify their strengths and to use them. We can also learn from the history we were not taught, view the documentaries we never saw in school, and speak with culturally diverse community members.

All of us can "do the right thing" once we discover what our own right thing is. We must share the vision. Sharing leads to a support network. There is strength in numbers. Strength leads to courage. Courage allows us to speak. Meaningful dialogue leads to effective action. Change becomes possible.

ASIAN AMERICAN RACIAL IDENTITY

Ethnic awareness becomes the first stage of identity for Asian Americans. This occurs during elementary school as students interact with family and community members. Positive racial identities develop with family support and exposure to the family's culture and heritage.

White identification is the second stage. Asian students begin to develop a heightened awareness that they are different from their white classmates. Racial prejudice contributes to negative feelings. Feelings of inferiority cause students to attempt to adopt or internalize white values. Further, they begin to alienate themselves from other Asian Americans.

The third stage is awakening to social political consciousness. In this stage students develop a new perspective of themselves, seeing themselves as a minority in society.

In the next stage, redirection to Asian American consciousness, students immerse themselves in their Asian culture and racial heritage. They often become angry, resentful, and outraged about white racism.

The final stage, and the stage we hope all culturally diverse groups will reach, is incorporation. Students' identity is strong, balanced, and secure.

ASIAN AMERICAN CULTURAL VALUES

Traditional Asian American cultural values include:

- Confucian ethic: Strong work ethic centered on effort and persistence (versus white Protestant work ethic centered on ability and personal characteristics)
- Academic orientation: Status by effort (versus white status by ability)
- Family honor and tradition (versus white individualism)
- Past and tradition: (versus white future, change)
- Nonaggressive, cooperativeness (versus white aggressiveness)

- Multilingualism (versus white monolingualism)
- Mutual interdependence, collectiveness, group welfare, public conscience (versus white independence, self-reliance, individuality, privacy)
- Harmony with nature (versus white mastery over nature)
- Conformity, correctness, obedience to adult authority and elders (versus white obedience to authority rather than elders)

Additional American culture includes:

- "We" over "I," support the group
- Use of self-control, self-denial, and self-discipline
- Cooperation, nonconfrontation, and reconciliation are valued
- Formality and rules of conduct
- Direct physical contact (particularly between men and women) should be avoided, public displays of affection are not acceptable
- Honor/status is given to position, gender, age, education, and financial status
- Spiritual, humanistic, often believe in fate
- Contemplative, circular thinking (to start at a given point and work your way back to that point after you have considered all options), never making decisions in haste
- Traditional hierarchical family roles; children are extensions of parents
- Parents provide authority, expect unquestioning obedience
- Emotionally controlled, modest, stoic
- Indirect and nonverbal communication used, often implied meanings
- May avoid eye contact as a mark of respect to authority figures
- High value placed on education, reverence/status given to teachers

ASIAN AMERICAN LEARNING STYLES

- High achievement motivation
- Use of intuition in learning and problem solving
- High degree of self-discipline, self-motivation, self-control
- High level of concentration and persistence in academics

- Disagreeing with, arguing with, or challenging the teacher is not an option; this has to do with respect
- Attitude toward discipline as guidance
- Modest, minimal body contact preferred
- Ability to listen and follow directions
- Excellent problem-solving ability (female Asians have higher math scores than any other female ethnic group)
- Indirect and nonverbal communication used, attitudes unfavorable to participation in discussion groups
- Keen awareness of environment
- Strong valuing of conformity may inhibit creative thinking

Asian students prefer a global learning style with a holistic view. They prefer experiential learning and learning through communication. Children often are already in kindergarten at age three if they live in Japan or China. They are not there to play but to develop language skills. There is a strong component of what we may refer to as "rote learning." We often view this as mechanical memorization. Chinese educators view it as memorizing with understanding.

Asian students perceive themselves as being competent in learning. They take responsibility on themselves for success in their subjects. They work hard and go over and over problems until they understand them. Asian American students lack anxiety, which has been proven to be a major hindrance to learning.

In general, Asian American values include mature self-control, a Confucian ethic (the belief that people can be improved by effort and instruction), a strong work or achievement ethic, strong family bonds, a respect for obedience and authority, and a strong commitment to education and achievement.

Although many Asian groups are excelling in U.S. schools, some educators argue for a reevaluation of education for Asian Americans to address the development of talents in leadership, the arts, and creativity. Other educators recommend an emphasis on cooperative learning, self-paced instruction, and values awareness. It is also essential that Asian Americans address issues of assimilation and acculturation, dual identities as American and Asian, in positive and proactive ways.

Motivation alone does not guarantee that Asian American students will achieve to their potential. As educators we must include such factors as learning styles, study skills, work ethic, attitudes toward school, and the quality of the learning environment. Rely on the students to help mold their learning. Remind the students that knowledge is the key to their future and determination, the key to their goals.

Chapter Nine

Hmong/Southeast Asian Students: Spirits of Tomorrow

Though I am different from you, we were born involved in one another.

—Tau Ch'ien

For as long as it has been recorded, the history of the people of Southeast Asia has been a marathon series of bloody scrimmages, punctuated by occasional periods of peace, though hardly any of plenty. Over and over again, Southeast Asians have responded to persecution and to pressures to assimilate by fighting or migrating, a pattern that has been repeated so many times, in so many places and eras, that it begins to seem almost a genetic trait.

The refugees coming from Southeast Asia (Vietnam, Cambodia, Laos, and Thailand) after the Vietnam War ended were accustomed to living in the mountains, plains, river valleys, and lowlands of Vietnam, Cambodia, Laos, and Thailand. They had never seen snow. Almost all Southeast Asians were settled in places in the United States that had flat topography and freezing winters. To encourage assimilation and avoid burdening any one community, the Immigration and Naturalization Service adopted a policy of dispersal rather than clustering. Newly arrived Southeast Asian refugees were assigned to 53 cities in 25 states. Group solidarity, the cornerstone of Asian culture and social organization for more than 2,000 years, was completely ignored. The majority were sent to cities like Minneapolis, St. Paul, Chicago, Milwaukee, Detroit, Hartford, and Providence. Some nuclear families, unaccompanied by their extended relations, were placed in isolated rural areas. Disconnected from traditional supports, these families exhibited unusually high levels of anxiety, depression, and paranoia. The customs they were expected to follow seemed so peculiar, the rules and regulations so numerous, the language so hard to learn, and the emphasis on literacy and decoding of unfamiliar symbols so strong, that many refugees were overwhelmed.

Many Southeast Asians later migrated to California because refugee services, health care, language classes, job training, and public housing were concentrated there. The refugees under the age of 35 became employed as grocers, carpenters, mechanics, merchants, teachers, nurses, and interpreters. Others became lawyers, doctors, dentists, engineers, and computer programmers. Those over the age of 35 are immovably wedged at or near entry-level jobs. They can't get jobs that require fluent English, and they can't learn English on their current jobs. Many have no jobs at all.

Many Southeast Asian refugees were criticized for accepting public assistance. This is unsettling because they feel they deserve the money. Many speak of "the promise," an oral or written contract made by Central Intelligence Agency personnel stating that if they fought for the Americans, the Americans would aid and take care of them if the Communists won the war. After risking their lives to rescue downed American pilots, seeing their villages flattened by American bombs, and being forced to flee their countries because they supported the "American war," many refugees expected a heroes' welcome in the United States. They felt betrayed when the American airlifts rescued only the officers from Long Tieng, leaving nearly everyone else behind. Others felt betrayed when those in the Thai camps who wanted to come to the United States were not automatically admitted. For those refugees who were allowed to enter the United States, betrayal came in the form of ineligibility for veterans' benefits, condemnation for "eating welfare," and the threat that welfare would cease. In reality, most Southeast Asian refugees would prefer almost any other option than welfare, if other options existed.

Southeast Asian refugees came to America to save not only their lives but also their ethnicity. There is no other group of immigrants whose culture has been so little eroded by assimilation. Hmong, Vietnamese, and Cambodian refugees still marry among respective clans, marry very young, and have large families. Clan and lineage structures remain intact, as in the ethnic group solidarity and mutual assistance. Their essential temperament—independent, insular, antiauthoritarian, suspicious, stubborn, proud, energetic, loquacious, humorous, hospitable, and generous—has so far been ineradicable. They put faith in their children. Families say that we must use our heads, our intelligence and our knowledge to the fullest to bring about success. If one child is well educated and successful, then the rest of the family will be successful, too.

Southeast Asian children rarely cause disciplinary problems and are regularly on academic honor rolls. Students spend more than twice as much time on homework and have had better academic success than non-Asian students. The Vietnamese show superior performance probably because adult Vietnamese refugees had completed an average of 12.4 years of education compared to other Southeast Asian groups who had completed an average of 1.6 years of education. Hmong students do very well in math but score lower than other Southeast Asian groups in reading comprehension. There is still an issue with relatively high dropout rates for Hmong, especially girls, since, even if they are promising students, they often conform to the cultural expectations to marry young and start bearing children. Female dropout rates have improved in the last few years (Walker-Moffat, 1995).

Overall, Southeast Asian students are hardworking, quick-learning students. Most parents are eager to attend school conferences, in spite of language barriers. On several occasions students have acted as interpreters for their parents.

Southeast Asians have become a part of the vast diversity of people who have come to America, searching for security and a better life. They arrived as Southeast Asian refugees, gradually became Asian Americans, while still trying to remain Vietnamese, Cambodian, or Hmong. At first glance, Southeast Asians display great variety and important divisions. A closer look reveals underlying similarities and significant unity. Religion, history, politics, location, climate, and many common cultural traits have united the people who live there.

Life was, and still is, hard. Southeast Asians have gone through many miserable experiences, trying to live a normal life and trying to fit into a new environment. At the same time, many had to discard some of the mores learned from their culture in order to adjust to the new surroundings.

Let us look briefly at the countries that send us Southeast Asian immigrants and refugees today.

VIETNAM

Vietnam is a country in Southeast Asia with its eastern coast on the South China Sea; it is bordered by China to the north and Laos and Cambodia to the west. Most Vietnamese are farmers who live in small villages raising rice as their main crop. Vietnam has 54 ethnic groups, who organize their lives around cultivation of crops. However, since the Vietnam War many villagers have migrated to the cities in search of jobs and a higher standard of living.

Nearly all Vietnamese (94%) 15 years of age and older can read and write. Children begin elementary school at age 6 and are required to attend seven years of classes. After this, all students are given a choice of attending either secondary school, where they study history, science, math, music, and either Russian or English, or vocational skills schools where they learn job skills. Secondary students can go on to choose from more than 100 colleges (universities, agricultural colleges, technical colleges, or private business colleges).

Since 1990, the economy has grown to include agriculture (rice and cashews), manufacturing (textiles), mining (copper and gold), fishing, and service industries (barbers, clerks, computer technicians, taxi drivers, and waiters in restaurants).

The Vietnam War tore the country apart when it began in 1957. It is still called the American War by the Vietnamese. Communist-supported rebels in the south began a revolt against the government, which was backed by the United States. American military and civilian advisers rushed to aid South Vietnam. Through the years, South Vietnam received extensive assistance from the United States, including cash, military equipment, and more than 500,000 troops. Despite this support, South Vietnam collapsed.

The Vietnam War caused enormous destruction. The United States dropped tons of chemicals on central Vietnam to clear the jungles and forests. Rice fields and villages were destroyed. The result was the deaths of millions of Vietnamese, many of them civilians.

With the collapse of the southern regime, many Vietnamese fled the country. They settled in the United States, Canada, and Australia. Many of the refugees left Vietnam in boats, risking drowning. They were the "boat people." They went to Thailand and other Southeast Asian countries where they lived in refugee camps until they could be relocated. Over 500,000 have entered the United States since the Communist takeover in 1975.

CAMBODIA

Cambodia is chiefly a farming nation with relatively flat land, plentiful water, and a tropical climate ideal for growing rice. The country has few factories and imports most of the manufactured supplies it needs.

Cambodia is a monarchy with a king as head of state. The king has ceremonial powers while a prime minister heads the government. Most of Cambodia's people are Khmer, one of the oldest ethnic groups in Southeast Asia. They speak Khmer, a language with its own alphabet. Vietnamese make up the second largest ethnic group.

One quarter of the men and over one half of the women cannot read or write. Many parts of the country do not have schools. However, there is a long tradition of education for boys in Buddhist monasteries. The French, who built many schools, including some for girls, expanded education. The educational tradition was destroyed during the war years by the Communists, who believed that education was unnecessary and that the citizens should merely listen to and obey the orders of their government. The schools were closed and the teachers were executed. Since 2001, some attempts have been made to rebuild the schools, but shortages of teachers, books, and funds continue to plague the educational system.

During the 1950s and 1960s Cambodia tried to remain neutral in the struggle between Communist and non-Communist nations. But the United States and South Vietnam charged that North Vietnam had troops and supplies in Cambodia for use in the war. In 1969, U.S. planes began to bomb Communist targets in Cambodia and continued to 1973. Ground fighting continued until Cambodia fell to Communist control in 1975.

Most Cambodian citizens were forced to move to supervised work camps in rural areas. Over 1 million Cambodians died as a result of execution, starvation, disease, or hard labor under the Khmer Rouge (Communists); others fled to Thailand. The Khmer Rouge movement did not end until 1999.

THAILAND

Thailand is a tropical country in Southeast Asia where most of the people are farmers living in small rural villages. However, Thailand has one of the fastest-growing economies in the world, and its urban centers have expanded rapidly. Thailand is also the only nation in Southeast Asia that has never been ruled by a Western power. A constitutional monarchy, a form of government in which the constitution limits the power of the king or queen, remains in existence.

More than 85% of Thailand's people 15 and older can read and write. Children are required to attend school from ages 7 to 14. Elementary students study math, science, history, geography, religion, music, dance, and the Thai language. Only a small percentage of Thai students continue on to a private secondary school where tuition is charged. There are 15 universities, several institutions of technology, dozens of teachers' colleges, and numerous vocational colleges. Boys must also spend one month in special training, learning to serve in the military.

The economy is based on free enterprise, in which businesses operate largely free of government control. Agriculture, manufacturing, fishing, mining, and tourism contribute greatly to Thailand's national income. There is also an extensive highway and railroad system in place. Bus lines reach every part of the country, and Bangkok International Airport provides daily flights worldwide. Several other cities have international as well as domestic service.

Thailand was invaded by Japan in 1941, but by 1944 the Japanese military had been forced out. Civilian-led governments ruled from 1944 to 1947 and military dictatorships were in control from 1948 to 1973. A university student revolt in 1973 led to open democratic policies by 1980. This openness allowed about a million refugees, who had fled to Thailand from Cambodia, Laos, and Vietnam after the Vietnam War ended, to find shelter until they found other homes in the 1990s.

LAOS

A great deal has been written about the Hmong from Laos, but little about Laos in general. What follows is a brief synopsis of Laos today.

Laos is a landlocked country in Southeast Asia bordered by China to the north, Vietnam to the east, Cambodia to the south, and Thailand to the west. Much of Laos is mountainous territory, especially in the north and east. The Mekong River forms the western border.

More than 60 ethnic groups live in Laos, residing mainly in rural areas where the villages are extremely poor. About 60 percent of the Laotian people 15 years of age or older can read and write. Most children attend elementary school for 5 years from ages 6 to 11. Some attend an additional 6 years of secondary school. Laos has one university.

Buddhism has influenced education. Until the French started a major school system in the early 19th century, the Buddhist monks taught Laotian boys to read and write and to memorize stories of Buddha in Pali, the language of the sacred texts. Girls did not attend school. Once the Lao People's Revolutionary Party assumed control of the country in 1975, it set a goal of providing a basic education for every child and teaching all adults to read. By 1986, there were more than 7,000 schools in which more than half the school age population was enrolled. The current government appears sincere in its commitment to increase educational opportunity. Teacher training schools are preparing teachers that the country desperately needs.

Laos has little industrial development and the country is the poorest in Southeast Asia. Laos has no railroads and few roads, most unpaved. The government controls the newspapers, radio, and television.

◆ ⭐ ◆

Southeast Asian immigrants continue to arrive at our shores. They arrive scared and lost but with hopes and dreams of a better life. They are coming prepared to find a place for themselves in the multicultural society that is America.

Chai, a second-year University of Minnesota student, who has been in the United States about two years, sums up the feelings of many Southeast Asian immigrants and refugees:

I believe I am living an American life with an American dream. Yet it is still hard for me to consider myself an American. Why? Is it because there is a part of me that is not American at all? Is it because I look different? But what is an American, especially an Asian American? I am Asian and I look Asian, but I'm not an Asian of Asia anymore. I am no longer part of the lowlands. I no longer hold strong cultural values. Could I ever go back? No, it is very unlikely. Since I am no longer totally Khmer, nor am I a real American, what am I?

Chai paused to stare out the window. He continued slowly.

I believe that being an American means being something different from what I used to be, having different values and living a different life. People who choose to make their home in the United States are American because they have chosen to live differently from their ancestors. They have become something different, something new. Of course they can never be completely like other Americans because there are so many different Americans. In short, Americans can never be completely alike even if they are all Americans because America is a country of diverse people." Chai wiped his eyes. He went on. "Whether I like it or not, I am a new Asian American, a Khmer American. That is my identity."

Have the Southeast Asians suffered so much and yet gained so little? Despite their suffering, the people I have spoken with gave me the sense that they are happy to have the privilege of living in a free country, knowing that their children and grandchildren will never have to experience the same kind of suffering, agony, and fear that they themselves have experienced.

Let us now welcome two of the largest Southeast Asian groups to the United States, Hmong and Vietnamese, and hear their stories.

HMONG MEANS FREE

When you come across a tree that you do not recognize, learn its name before you consider chopping it down.

—Hmong student

The Hmong are a mountain people from southern China and northern areas of Laos, Myanmar, Thailand, and Vietnam. Hmong communities are also found in other countries including Australia, Canada, France, and the United States. Worldwide there are about 8 million Hmong. Over 150,000 Hmong live in the United States, more than 70,000 of them in Minnesota. California ranks next with 50,000, and Wisconsin has over 30,000.

Hmong is a monosyllabic language that had no written script until Western missionaries devised one for it in the early 1950s. The full name of most Hmong men consists of three words (Nao Kao Lee, Vu Pao Tcha). In Laos the clan name is placed first; in America it is last. A Hmong male is also given two names, one in childhood and another when he goes through puberty and is considered an adult. Examples are Xia Shoua Fang, Buoa Neng Moua. A married woman keeps her father's clan name and does not adopt her husband's, even though she becomes a formal member of the husband's clan. Most women do not receive an adult name and use only the one given them during childhood.

Hmong Experience in Asia

Many of the Hmong living in the United States today came from Laos or Vietnam. Their ancestors originated in southwestern China. Political persecution, along with increasing population pressure, led many Hmong to migrate southward into mainland Southeast Asia where they settled in the mountainous regions of northern Burma, Thailand, Laos, and Vietnam.

The word Hmong means *free*. However, older generations of Western scholars and the lowland Lao have referred to the Hmong as Meo, which means *savage*, a term the Hmong find derisive and unacceptable. The Hmong have always farmed for a living. Most cultivate dry upland rice and corn as staples and the opium poppy as a cash crop. When French colonists arrived, they introduced coffee and cotton as cash crops. However, it is the opium trade more than any other product that has drawn Laos into the modern, capitalistic world economy.

Hmong culture originated in what is now central China about 4,000 years ago. For several thousand years, the central Chinese government, dominated by Han Chinese, basically left the Hmong alone as long as they paid tribute to the Chinese leaders. The last dynasty in China, the Qing (1644–1911) followed a different policy. Qing armies and officials oppressed the Hmong, who rose in rebellion. In the early 19th century, this political persecution, along with increasing population pressure, led many to migrate and settle in the various mountainous regions of Southeast Asia.

The Hmong lived under various kings until Western civilization/colonialism arrived in the late 15th century when the Portuguese set up trading posts. The Spanish (claiming the Philippines), British (settling in Malaysia), and Dutch (colonizing Indonesia) arrived over the next two centuries. The French were relative latecomers, arriving in the mid-19th century.

Regardless of which external power was acting as overlord, the Hmong have consistently played a significant role in the political life of Laos for several reasons. First, they lived in the strategic border region between North Vietnam and Laos, one of the most fiercely contested terrains during the successive phases of the Indochina conflict. Second, they have been extraordinarily hardy soldiers, capable of operating effectively both as guerrillas in the jungles and mountains and as regular troops in positional warfare. Third, they grew the opium that helped finance the French colonial adventure from the 1890s to the 1970s, including the Japanese occupation from 1941 to 1945 and the American involvement in Southeast Asia in the 1960s and 1970s.

Opium

Opium, an effective analgesic, has been used medicinally in small quantities for thousands of years. Asia did not have a large population of opium addicts until the British smuggled increasing quantities of the drug into China during the 18th and 19th centuries in an effort to reverse Great Britain's negative trade balance with China. Widespread opium addiction became one of the scourges that came to Asia with Western imperialism, and opium continues to be a major source of revenue. Opium production equaled wealth.

Raw opium is the resin from a particular species of poppy. The active ingredient in opium is morphine, a potent painkiller that also creates a sense of euphoria in those who use it. Repeated use leads to addiction. In the remote mountains of Southeast Asia, where no modern health facilities existed, opium was usually the only drug available to treat a variety of ailments, and its use was widely accepted.

The Hmong learned to cultivate the opium poppy and grew small amounts for their own use and for trade. Modern opium use remains a critical issue. Not only have French colonists, Japanese imperial troops, Nationalist Chinese soldiers, American counterinsurgency forces, and certain military and political leaders been involved in and benefited from the opium trade, so also have the more moralistic communists. The hard currency obtained from the sale of opium paid for modern weapons from the Soviet Union or the People's Republic of China. Likewise, the Pathet Lao who controlled the mountainous regions also used the profits from opium to finance their revolutionary movement. Thus, the hands of every nation and group that has vied for political power in Southeast Asia in the last century have been stained by opium. The Hmong and the people, who did the actual hard work of growing the opium, have merely been pawns in this dangerous illicit trade, and through it, in international politics.

Although the opium that the Hmong and others grew was traded in the world beyond their villages, they did not get entangled in world politics until the 1940s. Occupation by the Japanese finally pushed the emerging nationalist leaders in the Southeast Asian countries to proclaim their independence. This led to war against their colonial masters. Battles took place in Vietnam and Laos.

American foreign policy during the Cold War against Communism caused the United States to become involved in the affairs of the Laotian people. At the time the French pulled out of Southeast Asia, the official American presence in Laos was a lone Foreign Service officer who did not even have a secretary to type the reports he sent to the U.S. State Department. Yet within a few short years, the United States had become inextricably entangled in Laotian politics.

How did this happen? Why did this happen? To answer these questions it is necessary to examine developments in Southeast Asia between 1954 and 1975. Unfortunately, these developments were so complex, with many players actively competing with each other in the political arena and much conflict among the individuals who formulated U.S. policy, that it is impossible to summarize in a cogent manner. We do know that the United States began sending economic aid in 1951. Military aid was channeled entirely through the French until their defeat in 1954. Under the

Geneva Accords, only France could station troops in Laos. To circumvent this, the United States used retired military officers or officers on temporary reserve status to administer the military aid program. Wearing civilian clothes, they soon began training troops. Both the State Department and the Pentagon believed the best way to prevent the spread of Communism was to build up the military program. Accordingly, the United States agreed to pay all the salaries of the troops in that army (Ackland, 1983).

Frustrated by the conditions under which they had to operate, some Americans in Southeast Asia turned for help to the CIA, whose agents could operate covertly. By 1961 the CIA began systematically recruiting Hmong into the mercenary army. U.S. Army Special Forces trained these men after they began fighting. When the Hmong were asked to help, they did so because they believed that the United States would help them in return. They were undereducated and without skills and had no military training before they went to battle. They fought first and trained later.

The Hmong were the only effective indigenous fighting force in Laos, but they paid a high price for their valor. Estimates say that 25% of the Hmong who enlisted in the military were killed. Over 50,000 Hmong civilians were also killed during the war. Another report said 17,000 Hmong troops and 75,000 civilians perished during the conflict. Despite official denials, countless numbers of people were killed and entire villages wiped out during this unpublicized war (Hamilton-Merritt, 1993). With the men fighting in the military, traditional slash-and-burn agriculture no longer existed. The Hmong now had to depend on the CIA for supplies and survival.

Meanwhile, a civil war between Communist North Vietnam and anti-Communist South Vietnam broke out and soon became a testing ground for the larger Cold War between the Communist bloc of nations and the Western allies.

The United States first sent military advisers, then air support, then bombing raids, and ultimately a half million ground troops to Vietnam. To impede the southward flow of men and armaments, American planes bombed not only targets in North Vietnam but also the Ho Chi Minh Trail, which was in Laos. In this manner Laos was drawn inexorably into the Vietnam War. Whenever there was a pause in the American bombing of North Vietnam, the bombing of Laos intensified. The Americans called these air operations in Laos reconnaissance flights, even though over 2 million tons of bombs were dropped on Laos in the 1960s. There was an average of one bombing sortie every eight minutes for nine years. This was more than the total tonnage dropped by American planes in both Europe and the Pacific during World War II (Stevenson, 1972).

The Hmong who survived also suffered greatly. While the men fought in the jungles and on open plains, their wives and parents moved from place to place trying to farm while keeping one step ahead of the Communists. Often they could not stay long enough in one place to harvest the crops they had planted. Many fled into the jungles and ate leaves, wild fruit, tree bark, and whatever else they could find in order to survive. The Hmong reacted to these upheavals as they had to calamities throughout their history, by grasping their traditional culture even more tightly.

The United States was determined to end its involvement in Southeast Asia and was looking for a way to extricate itself "with honor" from a conflict that had cost more than a million lives (all participants combined). After three years of secret talks, on January 23, 1973, President Nixon's national security adviser, Henry Kissinger, and North Vietnamese negotiator Le Duc Tho finally reached an agreement. The United States withdrew, the Communist Pathet Lao took over, and the Hmong had to flee. Those caught were persecuted and imprisoned.

During the last 4 days of the war, between 1,000 and 3,000 Hmong, mostly high-ranking army officers and their families, were airlifted by American planes to Thailand. During the previous month, airlifts and sealifts had evacuated more than 45,000 South Vietnamese. The Hmong fought hard to board the aircraft. Several times the planes were so overloaded they could not take off. Dozens of people standing near the door had to be pushed out onto the airstrip. After the last American transport plane disappeared, more than 10,000 Hmong were left on the airfield fully expecting more aircraft to return. When it became apparent that there would be no more planes, a collective wail rose from the crowd and echoed against the mountains. A long line of Hmong, carrying their children and old people, started to move across the plateau, heading toward Thailand (Fadiman, 1997).

The Flight to Thailand

Most Hmong families never considered staying in Laos. They and the 150,000 other Hmong who fled to Thailand after the war were exercising their immemorial Hmong preference for flight, resistance, or death over persecution and assimilation. The Hmong rapidly learned that because most of them had supported the United States, they were viewed as enemies of the state.

The fiercely independent Hmong found their lives changing dramatically. They simply began walking. Some traveled in small extended family bands, while others traveled in convoys of up to 8,000 people. No one fled alone. Many carried children on their backs. The babies presented problems. They made noise. Silence was so essential that one Hmong woman, now living in Wisconsin, recalled that her son, who was a month old when the family left their home village, didn't know a single word when they arrived in Thailand two years later, because no one had talked during that entire time period except in occasional whispers. Nearly every Hmong family I met had a story to tell about a baby, a relative's child, a neighbor's child, who had been drugged with opium to keep it quiet. If given too much opium by mistake, the baby died. Able-bodied adults usually took turns carrying the elderly, the sick, and the wounded until they were no longer able to do so. People who died en route were left to rot. It was too dangerous to take time to bury them.

On the way to Thailand, families walked through abandoned villages and untended fields. They passed piles of jewelry, silver bars, and embroidered garments, which had had to be discarded to make travel easier. Most refugees eventually had to cross the Mekong River, which is up to a mile wide and forms the Lao-Thai border for more than 500 miles. Most refugees did not know how to swim. Some attempted to float across with bamboo stalks placed under their armpits, on banana-wood rafts, or in inner tubes purchased from Lao traders. Many babies and small children who had survived the journey thus far drowned while crossing the river strapped to their parents' backs. Their bodies were left in the Mekong River. Many refugees were shot by the border patrol as they tried to cross. An unknown fraction who attempted to flee died en route from Communist bullets and mines, as well as from disease, starvation, exposure, snakebite, tiger mauling, poisoning by toxic plants, and drowning.

Those who reached Thailand were placed in a string of makeshift camps near the Lao border. Officially they were illegal immigrants because the Thai government had not signed the 1951 Geneva Convention on the status of refugees. However, Thailand was willing to grant them temporary residency as long as other nations paid the bills and promised them permanent asylum.

Depending on how you looked at it, life in these camps was either a catastrophic deracination or a useful dress rehearsal for life in the American inner cities to which many refugees would ultimately relocate. Though they lacked electricity, running water, and sewage disposal, the camps were so densely populated that they were, in effect, urban. Like other poor urban communities, there were problems of inadequate health care, overcrowding, welfare dependency, unemployment, substance abuse, prostitution, suicide, abandonment, and loneliness.

A large portion of the refugees who found their way to the refugee camps in Thailand endured harsh living conditions for months, and in many instances years, before being resettled in a third country. Refugees settled in France, Canada, Australia, Argentina, French Guiana, and elsewhere, but because of their American military ties they preferred the United States by huge margins.

As with Vietnamese and Cambodian refugees, the best-educated Hmong and Lao came to America in the first wave of immigrants and the least educated in later waves. Because for several years the United States refused to accept extended family groups of more than eight people but did not limit the size of nuclear families, the Hmong and other groups, none of whom had birth certificates, grew accustomed to lying when immigration officials interviewed them. Second wives became daughters or sisters, nieces, and nephews became daughters and sons. As the refugees from Laos, Vietnam, and Cambodia kept arriving in Thailand, the older the refugees were, the less willing they were to leave. Their cultural tradition was still there. Many were forced to leave Thailand and return to their own countries, where they were persecuted or killed.

Thousands of Hmong and other Southeast Asians spent years in Thai refugee camps. Unlike the 130,000 Vietnamese who were evacuated in late April 1975 by the Americans and allowed into the United States under the authority of the U.S. attorney general, the other refugee groups were not given the privilege until 1977. Even then several thousand more Vietnamese also entered. By the early 1980s over 50,000 Hmong had resettled in the United States. The numbers were close to 1 million when the 2000 U.S. Census was taken.

Adapting to Life in the United States

Questions are asked about Hmong acculturation (literacy levels, health, mental health) and their economic status. What was noted was the almost universal failure of adult Hmong to learn English and find employment.

We must remember that long before the Hmong came to the United states they had already encountered great disruptions in their lives. As men left home to become soldiers, the extended kinship network lost some of its importance, young people were able to meet a broader range of potential marriage partners, and women left alone became more independent to survive.

Since their arrival in the United States, the Hmong clans have faced even greater changes in their material culture, means of livelihood, social organization, religious practices, and patterns of political leadership. In America, they cannot practice slash-and-burn agriculture or depend on Air America to drop them food. Clan elders no longer control how land is used or when clan members should move to another locality. Many now depend on federal refugee assistance or welfare. The only feature of the traditional Hmong economy that survived was the sharing of food and basic necessities among members of an extended family.

In terms of social organization, most Hmong in the United States can no longer live as extended families. American landlords, government housing authorities, and fire and health department codes forbid too many individuals from living in an apartment or house. Thus, Hmong extended families have had to split up physically. Social service agencies view the nuclear family, not the extended family, as being the most important when it comes to distribution of various kinds of assistance.

One of the most subversive effects of the surrounding Euro-American culture on the Hmong social organization is the greater equality accorded women in the United States. Despite the crucial contributions made by women to economic subsistence and childbearing and rearing, they had a very low status. Women had to obey their menfolk in every aspect of life. Bride kidnapping was acceptable, as were wife beatings and polygamy.

Tensions are growing because men feel they are losing their basis of command. Because they have few transferable job skills, can't find jobs that pay them enough to support their families, and consequently are forced to depend on welfare, many men suffer from depression. In households where the wives have found employment, however marginal, the husbands often experience a loss of prestige, self-esteem, and authority (Goldstein, 1995). Even disciplining children can be an issue when the family believes "a good beating" will teach them what is right. The ability of the police to intervene in family affairs is something that troubles many adult Hmong. Parents can be thrown in jail for beating their children. A husband cannot beat his wife.

Given the greater freedom and greater protection that women in the United States enjoy, it is not surprising that Hmong women, like most Southeast Asian women, are adjusting more eagerly than men to life in America. "No Hmong woman has ever told me she wanted to live in Laos again" (Donnelly, 1999, p. 148).

Christianity, particularly its Protestant form, has also played a role in undermining traditional gender relations in some Hmong families. The various denominations involved do not approve of polygamy, which continues to exist within Hmong communities in the United States. Christianity has also affected other marriage practices. The payment by a groom's family of a bride price to the bride's parents, arranged marriage, bride kidnapping, and the tradition of girls marrying within a year or two of reaching puberty are all frowned upon and deemed uncivilized by the churches.

While Euro-American culture and Christianity have helped to change gender relations, certain American institutions, particularly the public schools, are eroding traditional intergenerational relations. Children acculturate (learn values, behavior that is considered appropriate, and what is considered the real world) much faster than adults.

Children are a focal point of the integration of cultures. They move in and out of home and school environments that are in sharp contrast with each other. Immigrant schoolchildren quickly learn that what their parents expect is not necessarily the same as what their teachers and classmates approve of. The children also sense that the two cultures are not only different but are considered unequal: the Euro-American one is almost invariably treated as superior, the immigrant one as inferior. Until recently, many teachers in American classrooms considered it their duty to help eradicate all traces of foreign cultures.

Unlike many Hmong adults, who received no education at all and are therefore illiterate and lack basic classroom skills, the children are able to benefit more from their schooling in America. In a study of Hmong first-, second-, and third-graders in Minneapolis, Renee Lemieux found that there is a positive correlation between a child's English proficiency and his or her perceived degree of self-esteem and level of adjustment to school (Lemieux, 1994). Thus, from a Euro-American middle-class perspective, the faster the children of refugees master English and internalize American values and norms, the better they will feel about themselves and the more easily they will fit into the larger society.

What is seldom recognized, however, is that Hmong families are paying a heavy price for their children's acculturation. Some children have become a source of distress to their parents and a cause of family disunity. The dilemma that parents face is that while they want their children to become educated (good academic performance is viewed as an achievement in and of itself and as the only means of ensuring future economic security), they realize that school is the very place where children are learning behavior that contradicts the parents' own teachings.

One final difference is the contrast between Hmong culture and American culture in the honor accorded the aged. Old people are very much respected among the Hmong. In American society, old people are often pushed aside to make room for those who are younger and more vigorous.

Every Hmong Has an Exodus Story

Chou Nou Xiong, Interview, April 8, 2005, Garden Grove, California

I was born in a small village called Muong Cha in Laos in 1962. At the time, my father was a soldier actively fighting alongside the American Central Intelligence Agency against the Communists. Although war was in progress, life seemed peaceful. We farmed with only a few simple tools. Each village had only two or three axes and hoes, which people used in turn.

We did not think of ever leaving Laos, but one day our lives were changed forever. We found ourselves without a home or a country and a need to seek refuge in another country. Laos became a Communist country in 1975 and my family fled in fear of persecution. Because my father had served as a commanding officer for 11 years with the CIA in what is now known to the American public as the "Secret War," my family had no choice but to leave immediately. My father's life was in danger. We were forced to leave loved ones behind, including my grandmother who was ill and unable to leave her bed.

For three months my family walked through the dense tropical jungles and rice fields, along rugged trails through many mountains, and battled the powerful Mekong River. We traveled in silence at night and slept in the daytime. A lot of people died along the way. Some people stepped on mines along the trail and were either killed or badly injured. We tried to buy food but it was very expensive. When we ran out of food we ate bamboo shoots and jungle plants. People who were too weak to walk were left behind to die.

The weather was very bad. It rained heavily. When we reached the Thai border after three months of travel, the Thai officials would not let us cross. They did not want us to take refuge in their country. A young man who could speak Thai finally convinced the officials to let us enter for a price.

We reached a makeshift refugee camp near the Thai border and lived there for about a year. Life was not easy. When our food ran out we went hungry. We survived on what little the Thai government gave us. I was not used to being hungry in Laos. But hunger was so common in the camp that I got used to it. Each day was like the day before, hard work, just trying to survive, with no future ahead for us.

One day we were told to pack our things and get on a bus that would take us to Bangkok. There we stayed another three months because our papers had not arrived so we could not leave for the United States. We lived in a camp downtown near a square where four streets intersect. There were a lot of soldiers so we were afraid to go out and see the city. We lived like caged animals. Our papers finally came. We went to the airport at three o'clock in the morning. Since it was still dark, we never saw what Bangkok looked like.

On our way to the airport, 32 of us were squeezed into a tiny bus. Our luggage consisted of a few clothes, a blue blanket, and a wooden mortar and pestle to pound rice. Two Americans greeted us at the airport and took us to a big plane. We flew in the air but did not know where we were going, only that it was someplace in America.

The air flight was fraught with anxiety and shame. Some people got air-sick but they did not know how to use the airbags. They didn't know how to use the bathroom but were afraid to soil themselves. They thought they had to pay for their food but had no money. They even tried to eat the Wash 'n Dries.

Our destination was Portland, Oregon, where we lived for two years before moving to St. Paul, Minnesota, and then Garden Grove, California.

Our first week in Portland was miserably disorienting. We spent a week with relatives, sleeping on the floor, until a local refugee agency placed us in a small rented house. There were 11 of us.

We didn't know anything so our relatives who had lived in America for three months told us what to do. They told us about electricity and said not to touch the plugs in the wall because you could get hurt. They told us the refrigerator is a cold box where you put meat. They showed us how to turn on the television. We had never seen a toilet before and we thought maybe the water in it was to drink or cook with. When our relatives told us what it was we didn't know whether to stand on it or sit on it. At the store we did not know that the cans and boxes had food in them. We could tell what meat was, but the chickens, cows, and pigs were all cut up in little pieces and had plastic on them. We were told the stove was for cooking food but were afraid to use it because it might explode. We were also told that in America the food you don't eat you just throw away. In Laos we always fed it to the animals. It seemed strange to waste it like that. Life was difficult. When we moved to St. Paul it became a little better. Now that we are in Garden Grove it is very good.

One thing we did very quickly was to learn how to use the telephones and drive cars because these skills allowed us to communicate with other Hmong. Once we could comprehend the language a little we could look for jobs but we had no professions or trades and we suffered from culture shock. The American language is very difficult. Many words have the same meaning. Many words sound the same but are spelled differently and mean different things. I still cannot read or write as well as you.

I am now working as a carpenter (I swept floors in St. Paul) and am getting by. My children are in school and doing well. For them education is the key to their future. For me, I am trying to accept the American way of life.

Hmong Today

Minnesota hosts the largest Hmong population in the country—the largest outside Thailand, according to the Council on Asian Pacific Minnesotans. Approximately 65,000 to 70,000 Hmong live in the Twin Cities area. The Hmong have become an integral part of the community since arriving in the 1970s. However, their history and culture are relatively unknown.

Many Hmong believed that the United States would help them establish an independent homeland after the war. In exchange for the promise of this homeland the Hmong had joined the United States in fighting against the North Vietnamese. After U.S. troops pulled out of Vietnam, the dream of a Hmong homeland disappeared. The Hmong were suddenly vulnerable to persecution because of their involvement in the war.

Throughout most of their history the Hmong have been an agricultural people. This close connection with nature has shaped their worldview. Each animal has a spirit and plays an important role in their shamanistic beliefs. A growing number of Hmong are converting to Christianity. New religious practices are just one sign of the growing diversity within the Hmong community. Along with traditional clan and regional differences, adapting to life in a new country has added another layer to cultural diversity within the Hmong population.

St. Paul, Minnesota, welcomed approximately 5,000 Hmong newcomers in the summer of 2004. These refugees from Wat Tham Krabok refugee camp in Thailand arrived suffering from malnutrition, a lack of basic health care, lack of education, and low job skills; many had mental health issues. Many arrivals were 18 or younger, many were young teen mothers. Chronic malnutrition in Wat Tham Krabok may have led to developmental cognitive delays in many children. Despite all hardships the Hmong arrived with a strong work ethic in place. Adult educational programs and job training will be vital in helping these refugees make the transition from the camp's poverty to self-sufficiency.

St. Paul Public School District has developed a comprehensive, thoughtful education plan for the new arrivals. The district set up five transitional learning centers where children can come first for individual skills assessment. In these centers the children will learn about classroom norms and expectations before they are gradually mainstreamed into the schools of their family's choice. The strong Hmong education programs that already exist in St. Paul give the schools a foundation upon which to build. The programs will be paid for with the per pupil state aid given to all districts.

Hmong Americans are thriving in our communities. St. Paul schools have graduated over 4,000 Hmong students. There are approximately 400 Hmong students enrolled at the University of Minnesota. The new generations of Hmong Americans are clearly poised to become an integral part of America, while maintaining a solid connection to the past.

There is a new wave of Hmong immigrants following the original trailblazers of the 1970s. Times are changing. In 1976, Paul Kong remembers, his parents were so scared that they would wait for days for their church sponsors to take them shopping even though a grocery store was two blocks from their home. Kong-Thao remembers how kids in school asked if she were Chinese or Japanese and she had no idea what they were talking about. Paul Kong is now an insurance salesman and president of the Hmong 18 Council, a nonprofit mediation service. Kong-Thao is a St. Paul School Board member.

As new groups of Hmong émigrés arrive, they find Hmong grocery stores, Hmong school teachers, Hmong legislators, Hmong mental health advocates, Hmong clothing shops, Hmong language signs in government buildings, and Hmong groups offering everything from English classes to soccer tournaments. But the resettlers from the Wat Tham Krabok settlement camp will also find entrenched Hmong gangs with histories of teen prostitution and rape. They will also find school districts laying off teachers and closing schools, a housing crunch, and money-drained social service agencies reeling from budget cuts.

There will be a warm welcome as families reunite, but there will also be a backlash from people who have e-mailed public officials and punctuated town hall meetings with "We don't need any more of those people coming to my country" sentiments.

The existing Hmong community will take a strong hand in providing for newly arrived relatives. They will help with English instruction and job placement. Just because they don't speak the language doesn't mean that they're not going to be able to work. They are going to be working next to relatives who will help them with the language and simple jobs. The strength and creativity within the Hmong community is awesome.

We all have a role to play in making these newcomers feel welcome and in easing their transition from dependence to self-sufficiency.

VIETNAMESE: SPIRITS IN AMERICA

To be well rounded, one must know both sides of the circle. (Children who have never known success must be taught how to succeed.)

—Thien Tau

Most of the Vietnamese people in America came as refugees in the wake of the Vietnam War. Their journey to the United States was often dangerous and difficult. After they arrived, many faced problems settling in a country where language and culture were so different from their own. Like many immigrants, the Vietnamese were determined to make better lives in a new land.

History of Vietnam

Vietnam has been a land often dominated by other countries and cultures. China ruled over Vietnam for a thousand years (111 BC to 939 AD) and attempted to convert the people to Chinese ways. The Vietnamese resisted and retained most of their own customs. When the Chinese were finally forced out, Vietnam enjoyed several centuries of independence from outside rule.

In 1535, outside forces again intruded when the Portuguese became the first Europeans to enter the area. At the time, Southeast Asia was the object of commercial competition among European powers. The French prevailed and unified Vietnam in the early 1800s. During this French colonial period the Vietnamese suffered many hardships. Extremely high taxes were levied on the poor, and the French tried to impose European ways of life on the people. But the Vietnamese had always been fiercely independent and the longer the French remained, the more the opposition to them grew.

During World War II, the European colonial forces were driven out of Southeast Asia by the invasion of the Japanese. It was while the Japanese occupied Vietnam that a veteran Communist leader called Ho Chi Minh organized an independence movement whose purpose was to fight the Japanese and to oppose any more French rule.

When World War II ended, the French were determined to resume rule over Vietnam, and they reestablished themselves in the south. Ho Chi Minh forces controlled the north. The Vietnamese refused to accept French control, and in 1954, after eight years of fighting, both sides agreed to meet at a treaty conference in Geneva.

Concerned about the spread of Communism in Asia, the U.S. government had supported the French forces in Vietnam and took a major role at the treaty conference in Geneva. The result was the division of Vietnam. A line was drawn at the 17th parallel, dividing the country into two zones, a northern region with a Communist government under Ho Chi Minh, and a southern region with a non-Communist government headed by Ngo Dinh Diem as premier. Elections and reunification were to take place by 1956. Both governments claimed exclusive right to rule Vietnam and both looked for allies. In the south, the Saigon government asked the United States for assistance. In the north, Ho Chi Minh received aid from the Soviet Union. Hostilities continued, and by 1960 a full-scale war was under way.

The war and the American involvement continued to grow. In 1964, Congress passed a resolution giving President Lyndon Johnson power to act in the national interest of the United States in Southeast Asia. Two hundred thousand troops were sent; by 1968, the number had risen to 500,000.

The war in Vietnam became a subject of bitter debate in the United States. Members of Congress argued about whether it was right to fight a war without actually declaring war. Students protested, sometimes violently, against a conflict that they saw as immoral. Some young men drafted to serve in the army fled to Canada. Others believed America had a responsibility to combat the spread of Communism in Southeast Asia.

The debate continued. A cease-fire agreement was signed in 1973 and President Richard Nixon announced the removal of American troops from Vietnam. In 1975 the southern government fell, Saigon was overrun by northern troops, and the entire country was governed by Communist rule.

The cost of the prolonged conflict was high for everyone involved. Over a million North and South Vietnamese military personnel were killed, and the number of civilian casualties is unknown. Approximately 57,000 Americans died in Vietnam.

Who Were the First Vietnamese Refugees?

The first Vietnamese refugees to enter the United States were those who came in the months just before the fall of Saigon. They included university and medical students, wives of U.S. servicemen who had been stationed in South Vietnam, and many officials of the South Vietnamese government. Once Saigon collapsed, members of the military forces and employees of American companies in Vietnam were given top priority.

Thousands of others escaped any way they could. Those who had small boats ferried passengers out to sea where they were picked up by American ships. Pilots in the Vietnamese air force loaded their planes with relatives and friends and flew them to U.S. bases in Thailand. Approximately 150,000 people went to the United States and 50,000 to other countries like France, Australia, and Canada.

The Vietnamese refugees who entered America in the first massive wave were more highly educated (three fourths had attended high school and one fifth had studied at a university) and were much wealthier than those who came later.

Officially, the immigration laws of the United States allowed for the entry of refugees in unlimited numbers. There were no quotas restricting the number of people entering the United States from Southeast Asian countries. The Vietnamese refugees, however, did have to be sponsored in order to resettle in America. Sponsoring agencies helped the Vietnamese locate housing, learn English, find jobs, and enroll their children in school.

Who Were the Second-Wave Refugees?

Unable to take flights out of Vietnam after 1975, most of the fleeing refugees had to use boats. Those with money found reliable boats to take them to ports in Malaysia or Hong Kong. Those with little or no money boarded leaky, dangerous vessels for any destination as long as it was away from Vietnam. Every kind of floatable vessel, from small fishing boats to large cargo ships, from homemade rafts to empty oil drums, was used to ferry refugees. The boats were jammed with three to four times the number of people they could safely carry.

The "boat people" endured many horrors in their efforts to leave Vietnam by sea. Food and water were scarce; prices were exorbitant; Thai pirates and Vietnamese coastal patrols would attack and take food, water, and possessions and then beat and kill the men and assault the women. Some were left adrift on sinking ships. Estimates of people lost at sea and presumed dead are as low as 40,000 and as high as 200,000.

What About Those Left Behind?

An estimated 15,000 children of American soldiers and Vietnamese women were left behind. Most of these children were orphaned. They

were looked down upon by the Vietnamese, who called them *bui doi*, or
"dust of life." Their mothers often had been forced by circumstances into
prostitution, and these young people were the result. The children grazed
for food and other needs among the scrap heaps because not even their
relatives wanted them around as reminders of the war. More than 300,000
children were orphaned. Over the years, many of these orphaned Vietnamese children have found their way to the United States, adopted by
white families.

Vietnamese Stories

One of the best ways to understand the difficulties of the trip out of Vietnam is to hear the stories of individuals who made the long journey to
freedom and now live in America.

> Van was born in Saigon and remembers 50 people crowding into a
> small boat. After six days of sailing on the South China Sea, it
> became apparent that they were lost. They ran out of food and water.
> After 15 days an Indonesian freighter rescued them. Twelve had died,
> including Van's mother and sister.
>
> Thien was 16 years old when his family left Vietnam. He remembers
> an overcrowded boat and a huge storm. The boat broke apart and he
> held on to a piece of wood to keep afloat. He watched most of his
> family drown. He treaded water for three days, hanging on to the
> piece of board until an American ship rescued him. He was brought
> to the United States on that ship. Thien has now graduated from col-
> lege and is glad to be in America.
>
> Ba is a wife and mother who got herself and eight others out of Viet-
> nam by walking. They looked for food and water en route, often
> going without. After eight months they reached a relocation center in
> Thailand. She remained in the camp for several years before Catholic
> Charities sponsored her trip to the United States.
>
> Heiu was only 6 years old when he left Vietnam. He still has night-
> mares about the horrible events of his escape. Several days out to sea
> Thai pirates attacked them. The boat's captain was shot and killed,
> all food and water was taken, and several young girls (including his
> sister) were kidnapped. Two days later a second pirate ship stopped

the boat and took people's clothes. A storm broke up the boat, causing the remaining people to abandon ship and swim to shore. Heiu's father and Heiu were washed up on a beach. The rest of the family was never found.

Those Vietnamese who made it to America were settled in ten states: Washington, Oregon, California, Texas, Minnesota, Illinois, New York, Massachusetts, Pennsylvania, and Virginia. They found jobs in low-paying areas like convenience stores, maintenance, and fishing. Many are locked into low-paying, dead-end jobs and socially segregated by limited English skills. Despite the odds, they kept their families, customs, and religion intact. They had left everything behind and risked their lives for an unknown that they hoped would be better. "We looked for freedom. That is why we are here," says Thu, a refugee who arrived with his family in 1978.

In the early days, adjusting to life in America was not easy. Thu recalls that he bought milk based on the shape of its container, since he could not read any of the writing on the carton. Then there was the night his wife tried to deice the car windshield for the first time, with boiling water, and shattered the glass. "We can laugh now, but we learned a lot."

The end of the Vietnam War was actually the beginning for many Vietnamese immigrants. Many Vietnamese people escaped the ravages of the Communist government and resided in refugee camps. They had no idea what their life would be like. Imagine being forced away from one's homeland where simplicity ruled.

In contrast, life in the United States was complicated. A whole new language to learn, a radically different culture to adapt to, and slow acceptance by the American people were some of the challenges that the Vietnamese newcomers had to face. But they persevered. They realized that education was important and that it was the key factor for success. Education was the only way to move up the ladder in the American social world.

The first generation of Vietnamese people living in the United States faced severe cultural differences. The second-generation Vietnamese children encountered communication problems with their parents, who spoke little English. Children often became the translator for their parents.

Parents worked hard in jobs such as assembly lines and meatpacking plants in order to raise their children. Parents were adamant that Vietnamese children had to preserve their culture. The children were expected to learn to speak and write in Vietnamese to learn who they were.

Many of these children are very intelligent. They are often the smartest in their classes and can do quick arithmetic. But as these Vietnamese children grew up, many realized that they were different from other people. Vietnamese students have had to struggle against fear and ignorance as they try to fit into the classroom environment and begin the task of learning English and the American way of life. At the same time, community leaders began to form group movements to bring back the culture from Vietnam to America and unite the Vietnamese living in the United States. However, some Vietnamese teenagers did not feel that they fit into any culture and formed their own groups, gangs. Perhaps the formation of Asian gangs was inevitable. Parents simply did not understand what their children were facing and feeling and did not know what to do.

Culture and Education

Both the Hmong and the Vietnamese culture place a high value on education. As persons of knowledge, teachers are considered some of the most important members of society. When they attend American schools, refugee children find conflicts between Vietnamese and Hmong methods of education and those used in the United States. In Southeast Asia children listen to and learn from the teacher, who is always correct. In America, students learn from the teacher but are also taught to think for themselves. Many refugee children find this difficult and confusing. The children always agree with everything the teacher says because to do otherwise would show disrespect.

There are other aspects of U.S. education that are unfamiliar to Southeast Asian students. Activities such as individual research, classroom debates, learning by doing, and group projects are new and strange to these students.

Many students have their first experience in education when they arrive in America. Their first attempt at writing or reading is in a language with which they have no familiarity. These students have never seen a calendar, read time off a clock, or made or kept an appointment. They have never held a pencil or saved a paper for later reference. One parent said that the distance between life in Laos and Minnesota is comparable to Minnesotans adjusting to life on the moon. All rules for living, and even survival, have changed.

The following are educational strategies that we can introduce into our classrooms that will help Southeast Asian students become more successful:

- Give students the opportunity to learn independently and to take risks.
- Adopt changes in curriculum to fit student needs.
- Be willing to change your instructional methods.
- Focus on study skills and time management skills. Do not emphasize the urgency of getting the task done.
- Introduce test-taking skills.
- Allow for demonstration of mastery of material.
  As educators, we must affirm:
- The students' sense of worth
- That success is possible
- Positive learning experiences
- Self-initiation, independence, and self-efficiency
- Racial identity
  We can enhance achievement by:
- Meeting with parents to address concerns
- Making accommodations for learning styles
- Giving positive reinforcement
- Creating student-centered classrooms
- Having high teacher expectations
- Utilizing mentors and role models
- Creating relevant and meaningful coursework (language, folktales, traditions that are passed on from generation to generation)
- Creating flexible and nurturing classrooms
- Exploring feelings, attitudes, and behaviors

As educators we must also remember that ability does not always determine performance. Children of all cultures may be put at risk because of external disadvantages. Many Southeast Asians have a society based on a centuries-old system of nations and clans. The clan system shapes their life. Ancestry is also traced through the male ancestors. Men lead the clans. Women lead indirectly. They give advice behind the scenes. To see women in high public profile brings a mixture of ridicule and praise.

Reverence for ancestors and the elderly is another important component of Southeast Asian culture. Each clan or extended family has its own way of offering respect to its ancestors. The husband determines the clan affiliation. A woman becomes part of her husband's family when she marries, often living with them until she and her husband can afford to establish a household of their own. A basic family unit can have three or four generations living together. Women may control the home but defer to men in most matters outside the home.

Decision making is influenced by the astrological or lunar calendar. Wrist strings around the neck, ankle, or waist prevent soul loss, which is also thought to cause illness. Some of these practices and beliefs have come into conflict with those of their new country. Yet the Southeast Asian refugees have managed to hold on to the essence of their identity. They have remained extremely cohesive and connected to their past. Perhaps their turbulent history has taught them how to remain constant amid changing circumstances.

Public housing practices have broken up many of the extended families. The American emphasis on youth has undermined the power of the clan elders. Difficulties with English have also diminished the sway of elders, who are often slow to adjust to the new environment.

Is there room for both new and old leaders, for economic and political leaders who understand the American ways as well as cultural leaders who know Hmong or Vietnamese customs? The young people are moving farther and farther away from tradition. Still many clan leaders cling to the hope that old ways will enjoy a resurgence and find a place in America. Others are prepared to accept and let go. No matter the path, Hmong and Vietnamese culture in America are rapidly changing under the pressure of youth, assimilation, and the need to survive.

Over time, gender and generation gaps have developed. Young people tend to put money and material wealth first; family is farther and farther down the list. One of the areas in which Southeast Asian refugees have been most successful is the business arena. Though they may begin as short-order cooks or janitors, through hard work and family support they will often move on to better jobs in manufacturing, accounting, social service, and technology. A significant number of the refugees find jobs in high-tech fields such as engineering and computer science, where fluency in English is not as important as other kinds of skills.

Vietnamese entrepreneurs are successfully operating tailoring shops, gift shops, and many other small retail shops. The Hmong do equally well in grocery stores, cleaning services, and sewing endeavors. Vietnamese restaurants are one of the most common business ventures developed by the refugees. Hmong restaurants are also gaining a stronghold. A demand for Vietnamese and Hmong food is growing.

Southeast Asian refugees have come to the United States at great personal risk. They have left their homeland, they have suffered great hardships on the journey to America, they have endured many difficulties in adjusting to the American culture. However, Southeast Asians feel that the sacrifices they have made to reside in the United States are worth it. Many echo the words of Mia: "I am happy to be an American. I am a Vietnamese person by birth but I made the choice to come here and I am glad. America is my home."

The history of the Southeast Asian refugees yields several lessons for anyone who works with them as employer or teacher. Among the most obvious of these are that the Hmong and Vietnamese do not like to take orders; that they do not like to lose; that they would rather flee, fight, or die than surrender; that they are not intimidated by being outnumbered; that they are rarely persuaded that the customs of other cultures, even those more powerful than their own, are superior; and that they are capable of getting very angry. They are angry that the most drastic change bred by the Vietnam War was the loss of the single asset the Hmong and Vietnamese prized most highly: their self-sufficiency.

The Parents Speak

My experiences in schools have allowed me to meet many Southeast Asian parents. I would like to share some comments they have made to me as I listened to their stories about life in their homeland and in the United States. Some chose to allow me to use their names, others preferred to remain anonymous.

> *Foua*: What I miss in Laos is that free spirit, doing what you want to do. You own your own fields, your own space, your own plants. I

miss that feeling of freeness. I miss having something that belongs
to me.

Jon Yee: I am just a worker who wants to survive. I am not ambitious.
I do not want to get rich. I am poor, but I am happy and do not envy
others. I like living quietly and simply with my children.

Xang Mao: I am homesick and I miss my country. The mountains,
trees, flowers, and animals here are all so different. There is nothing
here to remind me of my country and that makes me sad.

Ka: I have had to discard some of the morals I learned from my culture
in order to adjust to life in America. This is sad.

Nao Kao: I experienced what it was like to be discriminated against and
hated simply because I look different. This made me realize what
kind of people I would have to face every day here in America. I
can't protect my child from that.

Vu Pao: Life is hard for us adults in the United States. We live in a
place that is strange to us. We are not educated and it is not easy to
make a living here.

Lee: Racism is probably the hardest challenge and most difficult obstacle that I have encountered in the United States.

Thek: America is a country with golden opportunities. We were lucky
we managed to get out of the chaos and reestablish our lives in
America.

Pang: I am thankful that the American people let us stay in their country. They are very nice. I am honored to have them as my neighbors.

Mai: It is good to be Americanized, but we should never forget our
heritage, our traditions, our way of life. We should always remember
where we come from.

Parent: We Hmong believe that if one child in a family is well educated
and successful, then the rest of the family will be considered successful also. I tell you, please strive hard and do the best you can. Back
in Laos, food and money were separate. Even if we had no money,
we could still produce our own food. But here in America, without
money, there is no food. Everything in America comes down to
money. I want you children to study hard so that all of us can live
well and be happy.

Parent: I have become part of the vast diversity of people who have come to America, like swarms of mosquitoes, searching for security and a better life for me and my children.

Parent: I was a refugee and have gradually become an Asian American although I am still Vietnamese. Life was, and still is, very hard. I have gone through many miserable experiences, trying to live a normal life and trying to fit into a new environment. At the same time, I have had to discard some of the morals that I learned from my culture in order to adjust to my new surroundings because I was—no, I still am Vietnamese.

Two Students Showed Me Their Spirit

Toua Moua shares his story:

Being a newcomer in a strange land and seeing very unusual-looking people was exciting. Some of the students were really nice to me, but others were not so friendly. They yelled and made faces at me. I did not know what they were saying but sensed that they felt great hostility and hatred toward me. I experienced for the first time what it was like to be discriminated against and hated simply because I looked different. This made me realize what kind of people I would have to face every day here in America. It made me realize I would be surrounded by hatred and hostility. I longed for Laos and its beautiful countryside where prejudice did not exist.

I began to develop a certain hatred for those stupid kids who had no idea what suffering we had gone through. It took a long time for the anger I felt inside me to begin to dissipate.

I also encountered a lot of people who encouraged me. In high school I had a really great teacher (Bruce Turnbaugh) who encouraged me to pursue my education as far as I could. He told me that being myself is unique because there is no one exactly like me on earth. He meant that I should be proud to be Hmong. From that day on, I have tried always to remember what he told me. The unfortunate experiences I have had in Laos and Thailand and the prejudices and animosity I have had to deal with in American society all set me apart from other people. I am proud to be Hmong.

Mia Xiong shares her story:

I believe I am living an American life with an American dream. Yet it is hard for me to consider myself an "American." Why? Is it because there is a part of me that is not American at all? Is it because I look different? Yes and no. But what is an American? What does it mean to be an American, especially an Asian American? I agree with what my Asian American peers tell me. Although I am Asian and look Asian, I am not an Asian of Asia anymore. I am no longer a Hmong of the mountains of Laos. I no longer hold strong Hmong cultural values. What I once treasured is no longer important to me. Since I am no longer totally Hmong, nor am I a real American, what am I?

I believe that being an American means being something different from what I used to be, having different values, and living a different life. People who choose to make the United States their home are Americans because they have chosen to live differently from their ancestors. They have become something different, something new. They can never become completely like other Americans because there are so many different Americans. In short, Americans can never be completely alike even if they are all Americans because America is a country of diverse people. It is harder to deny any new identity than to accept it. I know I have become an American even though I am different. Whether I like it or not, I am a new Asian American, a Hmong American. So why not make that my identity? Hello, my fellow Americans.

There are many aspects to the Southeast Asian migration experience. In a larger sense, it is not so different from that of other immigrant groups in America. Like other newcomers, these refugees have tried simultaneously to hang on to some facets of their culture and heritage while adapting to American society with the hope of achieving economic success, social acceptance, and a measure of political power. It will be some time before these goals are achieved. But the day will come and Southeast Asians will become an integral part of American society.

The Southeast Asian culture in the United States is in a period of transition and refinement. Clothing style, status, and cultural evolution are being redefined. Will Vietnamese and Hmong cultural groups be a dominant factor in the future, or will the next generation produce an Americanized people lacking culture and tradition? Only time will tell.

Chapter Ten

Arab Students: Surviving the Storms

Acquire knowledge. It enables its possessor to distinguish right from wrong, it lights the way to heaven, it is our friend in the desert, our society in solitude, our compassion when friendless. It guides us to happiness; it sustains us in misery; it is an ornament among friends; it is armor against enemies.

—Prophet Muhammad, Hadith

Early on a summer night, a white ice-cream truck rolled down a tree-lined street, luring children with its tinny rendition of "The Entertainer." A moment later, an undercover police officer wearing a red-white-and-blue bandana was kneeling over the prone body of an Arab American who had just been driving the truck. The officer was pointing a gun at the man's head.

How did this suburban scene jump so quickly from American to American Gothic? According to Arabs and Muslims, it has to do with another day, one that featured lightning-quick assaults on the American psyche: hijackings, jetliner crashes, and falling skyscrapers.

The terrorist attacks of September 11, 2001, unleashed a torrent of hatred and ugliness against Arabs and Muslims. Some say they have suffered small indignities, while others talk of blatant discrimination that violates their civil rights.

Abedulah Alkhateib, the Jordanian who was selling ice cream to supplement his salary as an engineer at Daimler Chrysler, was approached by an undercover detective dressed in a tank top and cut-off shorts. He also wore earrings and sunglasses. The detective was responding to calls from residents of the neighborhood who were suspicious of the dark-skinned man. They thought Abedulah was selling drugs because of a

215

backpack on the seat. The backpack was full of books. Abedulah was working on his doctorate at a local university.

The detective drew his gun and ordered Abedulah out of the truck and to his knees. He then kicked the Jordanian in the back so he was lying prone on the ground. "Are you Arabic?" asked the detective as he kicked Abedulah's legs and pointed his gun at his left temple. Abedulah was then handcuffed, and a police dog was used to search the truck for drugs. After an hour Abedulah was released. He was badly shaken and his ice cream was melted and spoiled. The police defended their actions.

Other Arabs and Muslims can relate to Abedulah's experience. They, too, are nursing bruised and angry feelings since 9/11. The complaints range from job discrimination to violence and name-calling. The alleged discrimination has come from all directions: employers, neighbors, police officials, and passers-by in the street. Arabs and Muslims have been insulted unknowingly by friends and openly by strangers. They feel constantly on the defensive to explain Islam. Arab immigrants feel like outcasts. They have to constantly prove their loyalty to their adopted homeland. The irony is that many came to America to escape just this sort of thing.

Discrimination has grown since 9/11. Lives have been changed. Some Muslim women are less likely to wear their headscarves, called hijabs, worried that it could prompt an angry outburst by strangers. Others Americanize their first names to fit in better. Ibrahim becomes Abe, and Muhammad is Mike. They are afraid to exercise their freedom of speech, worried that any criticism of the United States' actions in the Middle East or here at home may make them look like enemies of the state.

Local imams now preach in tones similar to those of the Reverend Martin Luther King Jr. in the early 1960s. They tell followers that they are being closely watched so their behavior must be beyond reproach.

To understand our Arab wave of immigrants we look at land, people, history, and culture. Arabs follow many ways of life, but they are united mainly by their history and their culture. Most Arabs live in the Middle East, which spreads across southwestern Asia and northern Africa. Arabs have also migrated to such countries as Brazil, England, Canada, France, and the United States.

Approximately 200 million Arabs live in the Arab world, which is defined politically and linguistically. Politically, the Arab world is usually said to include the following countries: Algeria, Bahrain, Egypt, Iraq, Jordan, Kuwait, Lebanon, Libya, Mauritania, Morocco, Oman, Qatar, Saudi Arabia, Sudan, Tunisia, the United Arab Emirates, and Yemen. The people and their governments regard themselves as Arab. In a linguistic sense, the term *Arab world* refers to those areas where most people speak Arabic as their native language.

Originally, the word *Arab* was probably associated with the camel-herding nomadic tribes of the Arabian Peninsula and nearby parts of the Middle East. Later, it was applied to settled people who spoke the Arabic language. Today almost all Arabs live in cities, towns, or villages.

Many aspects of their culture today unite Arabs, above all their language, literature, and music. Religious and historical factors also bond the people together. Most Arabs are Muslims, following a religion called Islam. Their rise to political and cultural importance during the Middle Ages was closely associated with the rise of Islam. The modern Arab identity emerged during the 1800s and 1900s, when most Arab lands were colonies of European powers.

Despite this common heritage, deep differences exist among Arab countries. For example, many Arab countries possess valuable petroleum deposits. The export of oil has made countries like Kuwait and Qatar extremely wealthy. Other countries, such as the Sudan and Yemen, remain poor. Some countries, including Jordan and Lebanon, have highly urban societies where many people work in industry or commerce. Others, such as Mauritania and Yemen, have rural societies that rely on farming or herding. Lebanon and Tunisia have been heavily influenced by Western culture, while Oman and Saudi Arabia remain strongly traditional. These and other differences have caused conflicts, and even wars, within the Arab world.

LIFE IN THE ARAB WORLD

When people think of Arabs, they often picture nomadic herders or Bedouins, living in tents and crossing the desert with their camels, sheep, goats, or cattle, in search of water and grazing land. Today, less than 1% of Arabs are nomads. Livestock herding now resembles ranching rather than nomadic life, and animals, even camels, are transported by truck.

About half of all Arabs live in cities or large towns, working in factories, businesses, government, and health care. Others live in villages and farm or work in local trades.

Arabs strongly value family ties and hospitality. Traditionally, Arabs have placed great importance on belonging to family or kinship groups, including the extended family, clan, and tribe. The extended family includes members of two or more generations, many of them sharing one home. A clan consists of several related families. A tribe might include hundreds of families.

Today, some kinship ties have loosened, especially in the cities. The impact of Western values and the need for some people to move far from home to earn a living have tended to weaken family relationships. However, grandparents, aunts, uncles, and other relatives, in addition to parents, raise many Arab children. It is still common for parents to arrange their children's marriages. Women still form the focus of family life. They supervise the raising of children, preparation of meals, and organization of family celebrations. Due to economic pressures and educational opportunities, a growing number of women are working outside the home.

Until the 1900s, religious authorities operated most schools in the Arab world. Today, all Arab nations have free, nonreligious primary and secondary schools. In most Arab countries, about 90% of all children receive at least an elementary education. Kuwait has 85% of its children attending secondary schools and even offers special education services for disabled individuals. More women attend school in Kuwait than any other Arab nation. In Jordan, all children are required to attend school through the 9th grade. The government controls all schools, and a United Nations agency operates several schools for Palestinian refugees. Most adults in Jordan can read and write. In Egypt, children between the ages of 6 and 14 are required to attend school. Attendance is enforced for ages 6 to 12. One half go on to high school. Overcrowding, lack of funds, and lack of teachers have hindered the Egyptian educational system. In Iran, little is known about the quality of education or the number of students attending school. The government requires children from 7 to 11 to attend school. Many teachers have left the system; others have been executed for counterrevolutionary activities. Girls and boys in Iran are educated separately at all levels. All education is free, but those students attending the university must agree to work for the government for the number of years equal to the time spent at the university. Arab institutions of higher education have existed for centuries. Al-Azhar University in Cairo was founded in 970. Today there are approximately 85 universities in the Arab world.

A BRIEF HISTORY OF THE ARAB WORLD

As we explore a brief history of the Arab World we find that the word Arab first appears in documents about 850 BC. The documents, written by the Assyrians (a people residing in what is now Iraq) suggest that the early Arabs were nomadic camel herders centered in what is now Jordan and Israel.

About 400 BC Arab families or tribes began to establish small states, often at centers for the overland caravan trade. Roman influence reached its height around 200 AD. The prophet Muhammad was born about 570 AD, and history saw the rise and spread of Islam. A sense of Arab identity emerged in connection with the spread of Islam. By the mid-1500s, nearly all Arab lands were under the control of the Ottoman Empire.

By the mid-1700s the rapid economic and military development of much of Europe gave the European states control of the Arab world. France controlled Algeria, Tunisia, and Morocco. England took over Egypt and the Sudan, and Italy took over Libya in 1912. By the 1920s nationalism grew into a major movement throughout the area. From 1920 to the 1970s, Arab countries struggled for independence. In 1945, seven countries founded the Arab League. Today 21 countries belong to the league, which works to promote closer political, economic, and social relations among its numbers.

The Arab-Israeli conflict can best be described and understood as a struggle between two nationalist movements, both of which claim Palestine as their national homeland. Tension between the Arabs and Jewish settlers has existed since Israel became a state in 1948. Thousands of people died in wars fought in 1956, 1967, 1973, 1982, and 1987.

ARABS TODAY

Arabs today continue to face major challenges. The problems of poverty, overpopulation, poor health care, and inadequate educational facilities are severe in some Arab states. In others, enormous oil wealth has provided high-quality medical care and education. Another challenge is to find ways to solve religious or ethnic conflicts, such as that between Arabs and Kurds in Iraq or among Sunni Muslims, Shiite Muslims, Christians, and Druses in Lebanon, as well as the Arab-Israeli dispute. Arabs must also deal with the powerful conflicts between Islamic tradition and the influence of the West.

With the exception of Arab Americans, the typical citizen of the United States has been exposed to little information that provides humanistic and realistic insight into the identity of the Arab peoples. Shaped by a lack of multicultural education and a prejudiced, uninstructed film industry and television media as well as newsprint, American perceptions about Arabs range from the overly romanticized to the harmfully negative. Terrorism, 9/11, and the war in Iraq have added to the negativity.

Many Americans narrowly stereotype Arabs as greedy billionaires, corrupt sheiks, terrorists, desert nomads, camel-riding chieftains, slave traders, oil blackmailers, sex maniacs, harem girls, enslaved maidens, belly dancers, and veiled women. Arabs are often described as barbaric, uncultured, uneducated, committed to a religion dedicated to war, quick to torture and behead, and responsible for the conflict with Israel. With little or no knowledge of the Arab peoples' rich heritage and accomplishments, the American public perceives Arabs as "anti-American," "anti-Christian," "cunning," and "war-like."

Despite, or perhaps because of, the continuation of negative Arab images, a countertrend to dispel misconceptions is rising today. This trend to combat defamation of both Arabs and Arab Americans has been influenced by a number of factors. Increasing numbers and visibility of Arab immigrants and the rapidly expanding relations between the United States and the Arab world have sparked a much-delayed interest in Arab Americans and their counterparts abroad. Educated immigrants as well as foreign students in colleges and universities have played an important part in the political and cultural revival of the Arab American communities and the revitalization of the doctrine and traditions of Islam.

Furthermore, the former Iran hostage situation, the invasion of Kuwait, the Israeli-Palestinian conflict, the Afghanistan conflict, civil wars between Christians and Muslims, oil boycotts, and the control of major natural resources of the area as well as 9/11, the current war in Iraq, and the war on terrorism have magnified the need for the American educational system to present accurate information about Middle Eastern cultures.

WHO ARE THE ARAB AMERICANS?

Arab Americans are a very heterogeneous group of people who are multicultural, multiracial, and multiethnic. Although "Arab" and "Muslim" are often linked together in the popular culture, many Arabs are Christians and many Muslims are not Arabs.

The first wave of Arab immigrants came between 1875 and 1930 from regions now known as Syria and Lebanon. Ninety percent were Christian and assimilated quickly and with relative ease into their new country. The first wave consisted largely of young unmarried men, not well educated. They came to America with little capital, limited skills, and speaking little or no English. The immigrants worked diligently as pack peddlers, and some achieved a large fortune quickly. They walked a fine line in trying to balance religious and cultural traditions with social pressures from the schools and the larger society. These men married into other cultures and gave up the Arab family structure.

A second wave of Arab immigrants began to arrive after World War II. They were seeking economic opportunity. Later they came because of the Arab-Israeli conflict and civil war. The second wave also practiced Islam, a religion that was not well known in the United States. Most of this group were college graduates or came in pursuit of higher education. Palestinians, Egyptians, Syrians, and Iraqis dominated this wave. They came to the United States with an Arab identity shaped by Cold War politics and the Arab-Israeli conflict. They were less likely to assimilate at the cost of losing their ethnic identity. A devout adherence to the practice of Islam has deepened their interest in Arab tradition and culture. Schools also began to teach Arabic.

The U.S. government does not classify Arabs as a minority group. They are not defined specifically by race but are united by culture and language. The anti-Arab sentiments and "terrorist" stereotyping in America today have increasingly impacted many of this group.

Arab Americans are citizens or residents of the United States who are immigrants or descendants of immigrants who came to the United States primarily from the countries that constitute the present Arab world. Arab Americans are extremely diverse with regard to their country of origin, the beginning of their family ancestry in America, and their religion. Estimates say approximately 3.5 million Arabs reside in the United States.

Religious diversity is characteristic of both the Arab world and the Arab American population. Although it is true that Islam is the religion of the majority of Arabs in the Arab countries, many Americans are often surprised to learn that of the 200 million Arabs living in Arab countries, including North Africa, nearly 14 million are Christians and 10,000 are Jewish. Arab Christians comprise the Catholic, Orthodox (Greek and Roman), and Protestant churches. It is significant to note that Arab Muslims are increasing in number among recent immigrant populations. It is also significant to note that Islam is (after Christianity) the second largest religious group in the United States at this time.

Arab Americans live throughout the United States, with the majority residing in California, New York, New Jersey, and Michigan. The top five metropolitan areas are Los Angeles, New York City, Detroit, Chicago, and Washington, D.C. Lebanese Americans constitute a larger number of the total population of Arab Americans residing in most states except New Jersey, where Egyptian Americans are the largest Arab group. Americans of Syrian descent make up the majority of Arab Americans in Rhode Island. The largest Palestinian population is in Illinois, and the Iraqi and Assynian/Chaldean communities are concentrated in Illinois, Michigan, and California (U.S. Census Bureau, 2000).

Descendants of earlier immigrants and more recent immigrants work in all sectors of society and are leaders in many professions and organizations. As a community, Arab Americans have a strong commitment to family, economic, and educational achievements and make contributions to all aspects of American life. Their Arab heritage reflects a culture that is thousands of years old and includes many diverse Arab countries.

To understand and appreciate Arab Americans, one must remember that Western civilization owes a large measure of its heritage to the Arab World of the past. One must also remember that people of Arab descent have made modern contributions in almost every field of endeavor. In truth, the impact of the Arab American has never been greater, and the reality of what is observed does not fit the stereotypes harbored by many Americans. Most Americans should recognize the names of Arab Americans such as John Sununu, U.S. senator from New Hampshire; George Mitchell, former U.S. Senate Majority Leader, Doug Flutie, former professional football player; Rony Seikaly, professional baseball player; Abe Gebron, Chicago Bears coach; Casey Kasem, Paula Abdul, and Paul Anka, music entertainers; Marlo Thomas and Jamie Farr, television entertainers; the late Danny Thomas, entertainer and founder of St. Jude's Hospital (recognized for research on and treatment of children afflicted with cancer and leukemia); Helen Thomas, senior White House correspondent and United Press International journalist; Najieb Halaby, former head of the Federal Aviation Administration and holder of the aviation record for the first transcontinental solo jet flight across the United States, also journalist and father of Lisa Halaby, Queen Noor of Jordan; Vance Bourjaily, prominent novelist and author of *The Man Who Knew Kennedy;* John Haggar, founder and CEO of Haggar Slacks; Emile Khouri, creator of the Disneyland architectural conception; Dr. Michael De Bakey, pioneer heart surgeon and inventor of the heart-lung bypass pump; Cindy Lightner, founder of Mothers Against Drunk Driving; Christine McAuliffe, first teacher in space and one of the seven crew members who died aboard the space shuttle *Challenger*; and Ralph Nader, consumer advocate.

For years, Americans ignored Arabs. In the fall of 1973, when Arab states cut back oil production while at the same time the Organization of Petroleum Exporting Countries (OPEC) raised prices sharply, Americans for the first time had great reason to think about the Arab world and the millions of American Arabs both American and foreign born. As the U.S. economy suffered and worldwide panic set in, many realized that a bridge between Americans, Arab Americans, and the Arab world was essential. Subsequent events of international significance, particularly the current U.S. military action against Iraq, brought this realization into greater focus. The American people are struggling to recognize and understand their newest, and one of their fastest-growing, ethnic groups.

THE MODERN ARAB WORLD: AN ERA OF POLITICAL, ECONOMIC, EDUCATIONAL, AND SOCIAL CHANGE

The 19th and 20th centuries brought new changes that impacted the Arab world's political and economic status, educational systems, and social life. Political and economic changes were influenced greatly by foreign interference. European colonial powers began to gain economic power in the Middle East and undermine the control and the power of the Ottoman Empire. The positive focus by the European powers on the Christian sects eventually led to an even more pronounced division between Muslims and Christians. The Arab world was faced with requests for the reform of Islamic law. Some of these reforms centered on equality for men and women. Numerous Arab sectors resisted the European domination, and struggles for independence ensued.

In 1948, lasting and devastating effects of the Jewish Holocaust influenced the British to play a key role in the creation of a Jewish state (Israel) in Palestine, causing the exile of thousands of Arab Palestinians from their homeland. The final conquest of Jerusalem by the Israelis in 1967 caused again the exile of thousands of Palestinians.

Since World War II, the modern Arab World has experienced many other changes. The desire for Arab nationalism, social justice, acquisition of education, and closer unity among Arab groups has been prevalent throughout the Arab countries. Economic growth has been rapid thanks to oil resources. Revolts, riots, and wars have taken their toll. Throughout the years, the goal has been Arab solidarity.

SOCIAL LIFE: FAMILY, HONOR, AND THE ROLE OF WOMEN

The roots of modern Arab family life are found in the ancient Arab traditions. Strong family ties and group loyalty were cherished. Family bound its members in work and leisure; food also tied families together.

Arab cuisine is known for flavor and its use of fresh ingredients. The staple in every Arab's diet is bread called *aish*, which is a darker form of the pita bread in the Greek culture. Fava beans are also important in the diet. At an Arab meal it is expected to have a soup, meat, vegetable stew, bread, salad, and rice or pasta. The desserts are mostly fruit.

Everyone works to preserve Arab status, honor, and welfare. Families provide economic and emotional support. The family's survival is placed above individual needs. During the 20th century, changes began with regard to the roles of women and the structure of the family. Change came slowly because of social customs that were deeply rooted in the core of the Arabic culture. Women were expected to yield their own interests and goals to the male family members. The education of Arab women lagged behind owing to political, historical, and economic reasons.

Currently, progress in women's education has accelerated and is given top priority. The rapid rate of women's enrollment in all levels of education is becoming more evident. Modernization has taken root, but for most Arabs, life is still organized around their religion, and their values are expressed in relation to the family.

IMPLICATIONS FOR AMERICAN EDUCATION

An old Arab proverb says, "To see yourself in a different light look through someone else's eyes." The presence of approximately 3 million Arab Americans that include increasing numbers of visiting Arab students and a burgeoning population of new immigrants from Arab countries all have noteworthy implications for the U.S. educational system. The problems faced include cultural and behavioral norms and the curricula of the U.S. schools. The displays of overt and covert prejudice and discrimination toward people of color and different ethnic backgrounds must end. Multicultural education should be the norm, and teachers must learn to become culturally responsive to the unique needs of students of Arab descent.

To accomplish outcomes teachers must have a broad and in-depth command of both the ancient and the modern histories that undergird today's Arab and Arab American culture. Thus the histories, cultures, religions, and contributions of Arab Americans, which are largely ignored in the pages of American textbooks, must be placed alongside those of other previously excluded groups in the school curricula. Respect for and acceptance of diversity and the inclusion of multicultural education within our educational institutions are the life-support systems to enable all students to define their role in history and to legitimize their own cultural values, beliefs, customs, and ideas, improving the educational, economical, and social survival of all students. While understanding Arab culture broadly, it is equally important that teachers also recognize the great diversity within Arab culture and see the child of Arab descent as an individual.

Children who have recently emigrated from the Arab world are coming from countries that are seeing deterioration in individual and political freedom. There are few preschools, and there are shortages of classrooms, lack of professionally qualified teachers, very few counselors, librarians, or technology. Dropout rates are high, and the matriculation rates less than 10 percent in many Arab states. The post 9/11 anti-Arab backlash and the fact that the United States won't grant visas has denied many young Arabs the opportunity to study in the United States. Access to digital media is among the lowest in the world. There are 18 computers per 1,000 students compared to the global average of 78 per 1,000 students. Only 1.6% of over 270 million Arabs have Internet access, also one of the lowest rates in the world (*USA Today Weekend*, 2005).

Are American teachers aware of the following:

- Some Arab students tap a pencil to help keep them on task.
- Many Arab students can't memorize spelling words unless they spell the words out loud.
- Many Arab students are kinesthetic learners; they move around and use their large muscles.
- Other Arab students are tactile learners and work best when they are able to feel using small motor muscles.
- Many Arab students only learn academically after they have formed personal relationships with the teacher.
- Still other Arab students are visual learners and work best when they are able to see, watch, read, and view.

Teachers should know, for instance, that Arab Americans and Arab "foreign" students often face social and psychological displacement when confronted with a new language, methods, and curriculum that are foreign to the culture they know. Many students feel it is their responsibility, their duty, to maintain their native culture, yet they need to feel comfortable with the culture of their new target language, English. In addition, behaviors reinforced within the Arab home are often not regarded in the same way outside the home, especially in school settings. The learning required by two different cultures (home and school) may lead to a lack of "fit," which may have detrimental effects on the development of adolescent self-esteem. For example, an important characteristic of Arab culture concerns the idea of "face." Teachers may find that the parents of Arab students are very sensitive to public criticism. Consequently, criticism should be shared in a way that will minimize loss of face and honor for both the student and the family.

Also, teachers must realize the problems of acculturation. Many Arab children are bilingual or trilingual; many speak Arabic, French, and English. Matters of religion, diet, hygiene, gender roles, social distance, and punctuality reflect cultural differences that are often misunderstood. Many may experience feelings of loneliness, hostility, indecision, frustration, sadness, and homesickness. They are caught between cultures, not sure which they belong to. Cultural stress or shock may linger.

Arab American students must confront harsh American perceptions of their way of life and the differences that tend to isolate them from the mainstream. For example, Arab Americans enjoy proximity to one another when talking. Members of the same gender are known to walk arm-in-arm or to hold hands, a behavior normal for Arabs but often unaccepted within mainstream America. Additionally, features of their language, such as loudness and intonation patterns, perfectly acceptable in their own mother tongue, unfortunately can have connotations of rudeness, anger, and/or hostility as they attempt to speak in a new language.

Teaching within a pluralistic society further requires educators to realize that traditional Arab customs and values, especially from students who have a Muslim heritage and sometimes other cultural religious heritages, pose unique difficulties in typical U.S. school settings. For instance, male students who have never been exposed to female authority figures may have difficulty following orders from women teachers and administrators. Also a lack of familiarity with deodorant has often led to the practice of washing hands and face with cologne, usually reinforcing the U.S. perspective of being unclean, when in reality cleanliness is greatly valued but culturally addressed from a different perspective. Punctuality, in contrast to the value placed on it by most middle-class Americans, may also present a problem. Some Arabs may place little significance on being late. Tardiness is not considered a sign of disrespect. With regard to food, Muslims, who are forbidden to eat pork, often find it served as an entrée in school cafeterias.

Again, their differences are often brought to the forefront without any attempt to understand the rationale that gives value to them. Many Arab students fast during the month of Ramadan and may appear tired or irritable during this period. Teachers should be understanding of the strength and endurance required by these young people to commit to the doctrines of their faith. Ramadan is a chance for Arabs to reaffirm their cultural traditions and values. Teachers need to be patient and supportive during this period when some students may withdraw from or be isolated by classmates who perceive difference as being strange, wrong, or unacceptable.

Arab Americans are bound by a common ancient heritage, language, and culture. In spite of the effects of enculturation and acculturation in American lifestyles, it is clear that family unity, honor, religious beliefs and practices, feelings of identity with their homelands, and many other traditional values and customs remain strong in Arab American culture.

Even though American schools need to change their instructional methods and curriculum, Arab students are surviving. Statistics show that 85% of Arab Americans have at least a high school diploma. More than 40% of Arab Americans have a bachelor's degree or higher compared to 24% of Americans at large. Seventeen percent of Arab Americans have postgraduate degrees, which is nearly twice the American average of 9% (U.S. Census Bureau, 2000). Many Arab Americans go on to use their degrees as they seek employment in managerial, professional, technical, sales, or administrative fields. Twelve percent are government employees.

Arab Americans are well educated, diverse, affluent, and highly entrepreneurial. Though Arab Americans are the least-studied ethnic group in the United States, they receive considerable publicity associated with political and economic events at home and in the Middle East. The media often put them on the defensive. Arab Americans simply want to enjoy America's riches while preserving the important parts of their native culture.

An Arab American high school student sums up the feelings of many Arab Americans: "I know now how to see below the surface of things in order to gain a deeper understanding of the world around me. I have learned to understand and gradually accept the American way of life."

Recognizing the great importance of preparing young Arab Americans for their roles as thoughtful and informed citizens of the 21st century challenges society to acknowledge that American involvement with the Middle Eastern nations and the world of Islam is certain to remain significant. Arab countries provide the United States with 80% of its oil, provide a place for employment for many Americans in the Persian Gulf area, and serve as a market for American goods and services. In turn, the United States opens its schools to provide quality education for Middle Eastern youth and continues to draw thousands of Arab immigrants to its shores annually. The Arab culture and population are becoming more visible.

Thus, an essential goal for educators ought to be to increase awareness and understanding of the Arab people through the study of their history, culture, religion, and contributions. An equally important educational goal should be to dispel the misconceptions and stereotypes about Arabs that continue to be promoted through the media. The Arab caricature in the United States continues to be dehumanizing, depriving the Arab American of much-deserved respect and ethnic pride. We, as educators, have a great opportunity as well as a moral and ethical responsibility to address aggressively these heinous forms of bigotry.

Living in a pluralistic society should not make it virtually impossible for ordinary people and highly sensitized educators alike to ignore the value of any of its citizens as contributing and distinctive members of American society. Education must become the vehicle for eliminating Arab stereotypes, as well as all stereotypes, and replacing them with understanding and acceptance. Educators are fortunate indeed to be in a position that allows them to reach out to all cultures in order to form bonds of friendship, savor shared memories, and create mutual respect for cultural traditions. In truth, the embracing of diversity is, and will remain, essential to America's social health and prosperity. Teachers should not fear diversity; rather, they should enjoy its gifts.

Chapter Eleven

Somali and 21st-Century African Students: Drums of the Future

When I dare to be powerful, to use my strength in the service of my vision, then it becomes less and less important whether I am afraid.

—Audre Lorde

From Senegal, Ghana, Ethiopia, Mali, Nigeria, Kenya, Eritrea, Somalia, and many other areas, Africans are making their way to America to start new lives, just as the first African adventurers and colonists did over 400 years ago. These new arrivals are coming in great numbers. However, there is a difference: they are not arriving in chains.

The new Africans are coming to a country that has seen dramatic changes during the past four centuries, and a nation that has been profoundly shaped by the long African experience in America. It is a country where people of African ancestry now hold positions of power, prestige, and influence as the nation continues to grapple with the aftermath of segregation and inequality. It is a country that has seen three of its more prominent black American citizens—diplomat Ralph Bunche, civil rights leader Dr. Martin Luther King Jr., and novelist Toni Morrison—awarded the Nobel Prize.

America is also a country that has been influenced in recent decades by the arrival of immigrants from the Caribbean, the descendants of Africans who were taken to those islands as slaves. The immigrants and their children have also made their mark on American life, including Shirley Chisholm, the first African American woman elected to Congress, and General Colin Powell, who has served as chairman of the Joint Chiefs of Staff and as U.S. secretary of state. Modern Africans, such as Kool D. J. Herc, were instrumental in the creation of hip-hop, which has continued African American music's ongoing conquest of the world.

AFRICA TODAY

The African continent is an immense plateau, broken by a few mountain ranges and bordered in some areas by a narrow coastal plain. Africa stretches 5,000 miles north to south and over 4,600 miles across at its widest part. It is a land of striking contrasts and great natural wonders, from dense tropical rain forests; to high mountain ranges; to the world's largest desert, the Sahara; to grasslands where elephants, giraffes, zebras, lions, and many other animals live.

Africa is divided into 53 independent countries and several other political units. The largest country, the Sudan, has an area of 967,500 square miles, and the smallest country, Seychelles, has a land area of only 176 square miles. The most heavily populated area, Nigeria, has more than 125 million people, and two fifths of all African countries have fewer than 5 million people each.

The African people belong to several population groups and have many cultural backgrounds. South of the Sahara, where most Africans live, blacks form the great majority of the population. They are divided into over 800 ethnic groups, each with its own language (over 1,000 languages are spoken), religion, and way of life. The large number of ethnic groups of uneven size has made it difficult for many African countries to develop into unified, modern nations. Ethnic differences have led to civil wars in several of the African nations.

About two thirds of all Africans live in rural areas where they make a living growing crops or raising livestock. In many parts of rural Africa, the people live as their ancestors did hundreds of years ago. However, since the 1960s and 1970s millions of rural Africans have flocked to the cities, where traditional lifestyles are being replaced by more modern ways.

Agriculture is the leading economic activity, but most farmers use outdated tools and methods to farm thin, poor soil. In case of crop failure or drops in world market prices, a country's economy suffers. The majority of African nations rely heavily on aid from countries outside the continent.

Nearly 200 million Africans practice local traditional religions. Each ethnic group has its own beliefs and practices. In general, however, local religions have many features in common. They teach what is right and wrong and define relationships between human beings and nature, and between young and old. Nearly 150 million Africans are Muslims, and about 130 million are Christians.

FAMILY

Strong feelings of loyalty and cooperation bind African families closely together. The family helps its members (parents, children, grandparents, aunts, uncles, and cousins) with business concerns, employment, legal matters, and other affairs. The family also cares for the sick and the elderly. Marriage is thought of as a way to acquire more relatives, and to have children. Bride wealth, in the form of money, livestock, or other valuables must be given to a woman's family before the man may marry her. Many African ethnic groups also practice polygamy.

EDUCATION

Education began hundreds of years ago when Muslim scholars established some of the first schools in Africa. These schools taught Islam, the Arabic language, and science. But for most Africans, education did not involve going to school. Parents taught their children what they needed to know to get along in the community and to make a living. Young Africans were trained in such skills as metalworking, wood carving, pottery making, and weaving. Christian missionaries taught some groups how to read and write as early as the 1500s. However, large advances in education did not begin until the 1900s when the European colonial powers decided that they needed more Africans to fill jobs in government and industry.

Today, many African governments strive to build schools and to extend education to as many people as possible. Over one half of all children in Ethiopia ages 7 to 11 attend school for 5 hours per day. Those who attend learn three languages, including English, as well as science, mathematics, reading, writing, and health. Still many children do not go to school at all. Education for them is learning to do what the adults do and finding adults with the time to show and train them. Because of the very high unemployment rates, many parents have adopted the "why bother with school?" attitude. The children will have no jobs anyway. Only 25 percent of the adults in Ethiopia read or write.

Ghana requires all children to attend school for six years (three in elementary and three in middle school). The students are taught reading, writing, math, and English, the official language of Ghana. Sixty-four percent of all adults read and write. In many areas of Ghana there are no school buildings so the students bring their own chairs and tables and set up outdoors. If it rains, they find shelter under trees.

In Nigeria children attend school from ages 6 to 12. The first three years they are taught in their native tongue. After third grade, math, science, reading, and history are taught in English. Bush schools still exist where students learn the ways of their ancestors. Men teach the boys to hunt, make tools, and care for animals. Women teach the girls about cooking, sewing, and making crafts.

In Kenya, 57% of the adults can read and write. Only half of the children in Kenya attend school. Schooling is not regulated by the government. Elementary school is offered from ages 7 to 11. One in every seven children goes on to high school. All levels of schooling are taught in Swahili and English. In some remote villages, children learn about farming and raising livestock. Elders come to the villages and teach tribal dance, crafts, and folklore. Most adults in Kenya over the age of 40 cannot read or write.

In South Africa, during the apartheid years, black and white children attended separate schools. Since 1993, all children have been taught in the same classrooms. The children are required to attend school from age 7 to age 16. South African children are taught all subjects in both their native language and English. In the urban areas and in most rural areas, 82% of the adults can read and write.

Most African governments are committed to education. However, crushing poverty is one of the most overwhelming problems these African nations face. Many adults throughout Africa cannot read or write. The literacy rate varies from country to country. In many rural areas there is a shortage of schools, educational materials, and qualified teachers. A significant number of children still do not attend school at all, and others leave after only a few years. Progress is being made, but the process is very slow.

HISTORY OF AFRICA

Africa has a rich history. One of the world's first great civilizations, ancient Egypt, arose along the banks of the Nile river over 5,000 years ago. Later, other powerful and culturally advanced kingdoms and empires developed in Africa. About the time of Christ, southward migrations began because of the constant need for more land to support a growing population. The rise of Islam was a very important development that helped shape African history. Kingdoms in Western Africa began to flourish about 1000 AD owing to trade routes and the increased use of gold, silver, and copper. The eastern, central, and southern kingdoms flourished because of trade routes to India, Indonesia, and China.

During the 1400s and 1500s Europeans began to establish trading posts in Africa. Gold and slaves became two of the continent's most valuable exports. By the 1800s, Europeans competed fiercely for control of Africa's resources. By 1900, Europe had carved almost all of Africa into colonial empires. Many Africans resisted colonial rule from the beginning, but the demands for independence did not become a powerful mass movement until the mid-1900s. Between 1950 and 1980, 47 African colonies gained independence. However, leaders in many of these new nations could not handle the social and economic problems that remained after independence. Military officers overthrew the governments of many nations. Military dictatorships emerged or a single political party became the ruling power. Civil wars broke out in the Congo, Nigeria, Chad, and other countries. Today, ethnic rivalries and territorial disputes continue to threaten the stability of Africa.

Africa today continues to face serious problems including poverty, illiteracy, disease, and shortages of food. One of the worst droughts in history struck Africa in the early 1980s. Thousands died of starvation, especially in Ethiopia.

In many African countries economic and social development is handicapped by dependence on one or two products as sources of national income. Inflation has caused Africa to pay more for the manufactured goods it imports. Ethnic rivalries continue to divide many countries.

WINDS OF CHANGE

Many people see signs of hope in Africa in spite of all its problems. More Africans than ever before are attending school and developing skills needed to improve their standard of living. The finding and mining of mineral deposits in Angola, Gabon, and Nigeria is helping these countries to attain greater economic strength.

African nations are also trying to work together to solve common problems. Various groups are trying to find peaceful solutions to disputes between nations and promote economic relationships. It is the hope that greater cooperation will lead to greater progress and stability throughout the continent.

Let us now look more closely at two groups of African immigrants who are arriving in the United States in large numbers in the 21st century, Somalis and Algerians.

SOMALIA

Somalia is the easternmost country on the mainland of Africa. Its coastline, which runs along the Gulf of Aden and the Indian Ocean, forms the outer edge of the horn of Africa. About 95% of Somalia's people share the same language (Somali), culture, and religion (the Sunni branch of Islam). More than two thirds of the population are nomads. During the dry season the nomads concentrate in villages near water sources. When the rains begin, the nomads disperse with their herds.

The basis of Somali society is the clan, a large, self-contained kinship group, consisting of a number of families claiming common descent from a male ancestor.

In the 1980s, Somalia had an influx of refugees numbering nearly 1 million driven by war and drought from Ethiopia. During the 1990s hundreds of thousands of Somalis died as a result of the violence, starvation, and disease that accompanied the drought and civil war. An estimated 1 million refugees fled the country. Many of the Somalia refugees came to the United States.

Education in Somalia

Because of the civil war and drought many children have never been in school. Fewer than 20% of all Somali children attend school, and most of the adult population cannot read or write, even though education at the primary level is compulsory in urban areas but not enforced in rural areas. At the age of 3 children go to Quranic school to learn how to read and write the Qur'an. At age 7 many can read and write Arabic. Secondary education is not compulsory so even fewer than 20% attend school. There is no special education program, and children born since the civil war are not receiving a reliable education.

Somalia Today

Somalia today is trying to regroup from the rebels who overthrew the United Somali Congress and dictator Mohamed Barro, who had been the ruling force in 1991. The fighting disrupted agricultural production, which was already suffering from the effects of a prolonged drought, and an estimated 1.5 million Somalis were threatened with starvation. By December 1992, about 270,000 Somalis had starved to death. In 1993, a multinational peace force, led by the United States, intervened to secure food supplies. This group of peacekeepers was forced to withdraw in 1995 in the face of violent clan assaults. Physical and social infrastructure (roads, bridges, water, law and order, education and health services) have virtually collapsed. Authorities are able to provide only the basic administrative framework (security and trade) while the needs of the people (health, education, and food) are largely unmet. In 1997, heavy rains caused flooding in the south, and floods killed about 1,300 people. More than 200,000 were forced from their homes. Again, many countries saw an influx of Somali immigrants, including the United States.

Somalis in the United States

Since 2002, by some estimates, more than 40,000 Somali immigrants have settled in the state of Minnesota alone (making Minnesota home to one of the largest Somali communities in the United States), leaving behind possessions, relatives, and a country ravaged by civil war, for a new life in a radically different culture in America. The largest communities are located in Los Angeles, San Diego, Atlanta, and Detroit. The one thing they could not leave behind was their Islamic faith. "We think, act, and live within the framework of Islam," said an elderly Somali man, newly arrived in Minneapolis.

As the Somali population grows, it is not uncommon for Islamic values to collide with the practices of American schools. Among the issues raised by the clash of cultures, the Islamic requirement to pray has proved a particular challenge for both Somali students and their teachers. Daily prayer is part of their way of life. Five prayers must be done at fixed times each day (approximately at noon, midafternoon, sunset, early evening, and at 6:00 a.m.). For a Muslim student, at least two of these prayer times fall during school hours. Another issue is food. Pork is strictly forbidden. Schools with Somali students must provide lunches to accommodate Islamic dietary requirements. Both issues can and should be accommodated in our American school system.

To better understand the Somali families and their children who are enrolled in our schools, we must explore and learn about their culture and beliefs as well as their educational background. Somali students can be divided into two groups: students who attended school in Somalia and students who are new to the educational system. The first group will have fewer problems in the American school system if their cultural needs are met. The second group will have more problems because they have never been in school before, have never spoken a language other than their native language, have never lived in large cities, and have never experienced a culture other than their own. These students need help to cope with their new education. They need more explanation about how and when to use a pen or pencil and how to use crayons, paper, scissors, and so forth.

Somali students can be successful in the American educational system without rejecting their culture. However, we must be aware of traditions that may create barriers that can affect the life of the Somali student. The meaning of dress, food, prayer, greeting, and other elements of tradition relates to educational performance. Understanding the Somali culture related to the behavior of Somali students will be helpful tools to American school staff who want to help Somali students reach their academic goals.

Somali Dress

In Islamic tradition, the form of dress is important for Somali women and men. The men wear Western pants or a flowing plaid ma'aiois (kilt), Western shirts, and shawls. They may wrap a colorful turban around their heads or wear a koofiejad (embroidered cap). Women usually wear one of the following: direh (long dress worn over petticoats), coantino (a four-yard cloth tied over the shoulder and draped around the waist), or hijab (a dress that covers the entire body except for hands and face). Both boys and girls start dressing this way at age seven.

With these traditions in mind, Somali families have the following expectations from the American schools:

- Schools should separate girls from boys when they have mixed or body-touching activities such as swimming.
- Girls should be allowed to dress in uniforms that reflect their culture if the school requires uniforms.
- Schools should give options to the students, especially girls, about any activity related to dress (gym sports dress).
- Schools should consult with parents should any conflict related to dress arise.

The families have high expectations from the American schools, especially with things related to culture and religion. Parents want to be consulted about their child's activities and education.

Somali Food

Like dress, food is important in Somali culture and religion. Because of the Islamic tradition, it is prohibited to eat any food related to pork or drink any alcoholic beverage. Pastries made from lard are also forbidden. Therefore parents expect the schools to listen to the following advice:

- Schools should send home their breakfast and lunch menus for the month.

- Schools should be aware of the cultural food traditions.
- Schools should give out a menu translated into Somali, which helps families understand American foods—for example, that a hot dog is not dog meat.

Somali Religion

As mentioned earlier, Muslim Somalis pray five times every day, wherever they are. Most Somali students and their parents have questions about where their children can pray and how American schools can meet their prayer needs. The following are the expectations of the Somali American families with regard to school and prayer:

- Students should be allowed to go to Friday prayer or have group Friday prayers in school.
- Schools should have resources or basic information about prayer in the Islamic faith.
- Schools should take seriously any advice about prayer coming from students and their families.
- Schools should provide a private area for prayer.
  Ramadan is the most important month for Muslims around the world.

Fasting is required and food can only be eaten between midnight and dawn. The student can attend school and observe fasting with no issues on the part of the student. At the end of Ramadan, holidays are celebrated and Somali students do not attend school. We must be aware of these days, excuse our Somali students, and wish them a happy holiday.

Somali Greetings

Every culture has its own way of greeting. Like other Muslims, Somali men and women do not shake hands unless they are spouses. Somalis use sweeping hand and arm gestures to dramatize speech. Many ideas are expressed through specific gestures (open hand means no, snapping fingers may mean "and so on"). It is impolite to use the index finger to call somebody to come to you, and the American "thumbs up" gesture is considered obscene.

As educators we have many things to learn about the cultures of our students. We must work diligently to narrow the cultural gaps among students, teachers, families, and community members.

ALGERIA

Algeria is a large country in northern Africa, second in size to the Sudan. Northern Algeria stretches along the Mediterranean Sea, and this area has a warm climate and rich farmland. To the south is the sun-scorched waste of the Sahara Desert covering four-fifths of Algeria. Beneath this desert surface lie huge deposits of natural gas and petroleum.

Most Algerians are of mixed Arab and Berber descent. However, the people form two distinct cultural groups, Arab and Berber. Each has its own customs and language. But nearly all Algerians are Muslims and are thus united by their religion. Algerians prefer to be part of the new African immigration rather than be called Arabs. This is thought by the Algerians to be due to the negative Arab feeling in the United States.

Algerian History

Algeria has a long and rich history. By 3000 BC nomadic Berbers were living in the region. In 1100 BC Phoenicians established trading posts along the Algerian coast. The Romans ruled from 200 BC until the Vandals and the Byzantines took control in 600 AD. Next came the Spanish Christians in 1500, followed by the Ottoman Empire, and shortly after, Islam became firmly entrenched.

France invaded and gained control of Algeria in 1830. The French ruled until World War II when Allied forces took control. Algeria was returned to France after the war. By 1954, Algerians were clamoring for independence. Fighting broke out, orchards and cropland were destroyed. This continued until peace talks began in 1961. Algeria was granted independence on July 3, 1962. Fighting resumed among groups within the country in the 1980s and 1990s. Muslim fundamentalist extremists protested against the government and terrorist attacks continued.

More and more immigrants are arriving from Algeria. They are coming from rural areas where society was organized around extended family, clan, and tribe.

Algerian Education

The current education system is in complete disarray. French colonial education had been imposed for centuries. French was the language pressed on Algerians. Teachers had been trained hastily or recruited abroad. Classrooms were located in the homes of former French residents. Rural areas had no schools. During the 1970s, the Algerian government set out to redesign the system to make it more suitable to the needs of the developing nation. All private education was abolished. Algerian law now requires all children from 6 to 25 years of age to attend school. More than 90% attend elementary school. However, only about a third go on to high school. One of the strongest features of this new reform was the creation of a variety of literacy programs for adults. Immigrants arriving in the United States today are still lacking a basic education, making success in American schools very difficult.

CONTEMPORARY AFRICAN IMMIGRANTS

The severe economic difficulties, increased poverty, and the political instability that have plagued many African countries in the last two decades have resulted in the large-scale migration of Africans to the United States. Unlike their counterparts in the 1960s and 1970s who were anxious to return home to Africa after acquiring an American education in order to contribute in the task of nation building, an overwhelming majority of recent immigrants are more interested in establishing permanent residency in the United States. The influx of African immigrants to the United States in the last two decades has been phenomenal. According to figures presented by the Immigration and Naturalization Service (INS), the numbers have quadrupled. These new immigrants can be found in major metropolitan areas in states like New York, Texas, Georgia, Illinois, Maryland, Colorado, and California; they are attracted to major cities like New York City, Atlanta, Chicago, and Los Angeles. Most recently they are found in increasing numbers in small and midsized cities in Ohio, Nebraska, Iowa, North and South Dakota, Idaho, and Maine.

To experience the sights, sounds, and flavors of Africa without leaving Minnesota, just step into a Somali minimal in Minneapolis or an African shopping center in St. Paul. There you will find the sweet, pungent smells of Somali dishes, the vivid colors of African clothing, and the rapid-fire, foreign-language conversations of Somalis, Ethiopians, and Liberians who moved to Minnesota in the past decade.

Africans also permeate all aspects of Colorado life. These African immigrants are doctors, lawyers, professors, engineers, students, cab drivers, clerks, security guards, and chefs. They reflect some basic American passions: politics, the Denver Broncos, day trading, eating burgers, and even skiing.

One of the motivations for the African migration to the United States was the hopes and disappointments of independence in their home countries. At independence, Africans were filled with tremendous hope and optimism. For many Africans, independence was seen as more than just a period of self-rule and freedom. In their campaign speeches and rhetoric, nationalist leaders led many to believe that independence would also lead to a significant improvement in their social and economic life, including improvements in education, health care, and greater employment opportunities. Unfortunately, more than four decades after independence, the economy of most African states is characterized by grinding poverty, epidemic corruption, and high rates of unemployment.

African immigrants are trying to live the American dream. Many are living with friends and relatives until they are able to find jobs and situate themselves. An advantage of this living arrangement is that they learn and receive advice on surviving in America. However, the most important factor influencing where they live is the prevailing racial climate, political tolerance toward immigrants, and employment opportunities (*USA Today Weekend*, 2005). That may explain why Atlanta, where blacks occupy important economic and political positions in the city administration, has become a mecca for African immigrants.

African immigrants are quick to take any employment opportunity they can get. They work as cab drivers, parking lot attendants, airport workers, waiters, waitresses, and cooks in restaurants. Many African immigrants have become entrepreneurs, opening small family-based business ventures , such as restaurants and grocery stores. They own health care agencies and specialty stores that cater to the needs of African newcomers. Some African-born physicians, lawyers, and accountants have opened offices in Atlanta, New York, Chicago, and Los Angeles targeting other African immigrants and the general immigration community.

Even African women, who have traditionally been in the background of the traditional African family structure, now find themselves at the forefront of economic opportunities. Many use their traditional skills like hair braiding, tailoring, and dressmaking as a basis for starting other small business ventures. African women, especially those from West Africa, have stopped waiting for their men to mail checks home from the United States and have joined them in America. These women are earning their own income. Other African women have come to the United States alone, leaving husbands and children behind.

Passing on ancestral traditions and customs to their children is becoming more and more important to most African immigrants. Religious beliefs play an important role in the lives of most African immigrants. Many are followers of Christianity, and equally as many are followers of Islam. Parents are concerned that children born or raised here will grow up to be part of the melting pot of the dominant American culture.

Most recently, African immigrants have started to publish newspapers and produce radio programs. They work as individuals or through groups with the dual purpose of serving the immigrant community and promoting African traditions and cultures. Some radio broadcasts provide news or information about events at home; others allow the recent African immigrant community to discuss issues affecting their lives.

The new African immigrants are no longer just interested in making money; they are also interested in building stronger relationships, stronger communities, and organizing themselves in order to become a more powerful political and economic force in their communities.

Despite their dedication, hard work, and determination to realize the American dream, African immigrants are often faced with the reality of what is called the "innocence about race relations" with which they had left Africa as they struggle to make a living in their new homeland. The new immigrants encounter some of the same stereotypes often associated with their African American counterparts. They are often perceived as lazy, criminals, drug dealers, and welfare cheaters. This perception often results in police harassment, intimidation, unlawful arrests, and even murder. The February 1999 killing by New York City police officers of Amadou Diallo, an African immigrant from Guinea, near his home in the Bronx has become a metaphor for the way African immigrants are perceived and treated by some law enforcement authorities.

Another problem faced by African immigrants is the lack of cooperation and acceptance by some of their African American counterparts. African immigrants are perceived by some African Americans as responsible for the fact that their ancestors were sold into slavery. There is also the accusation that African immigrants see themselves as better than their African American neighbors. Unfortunately, this perception has led to an uneasy relationship between some African immigrants and their African American brothers and sisters that continues to divide and paralyze blacks in America, thereby making them ineffective political and economic forces in national politics.

What the future holds for the continued flow of African migration to the United States is unclear. But from all indications it appears that African migration, immigration, and integration into American political, social, and economic spheres will continue.

AFRICAN IMMIGRANTS FIND CULTURAL CHASM IN THE UNITED STATES

Growing up in Nigeria, Lillian Obiara and her parents idolized aspects of black America: the vibrant culture, the dynamic music, and the movie and sports personalities they saw on television. When Lillian arrived in the United States recently, she was dismayed by the neighbors' lack of knowledge about Africa, the insulting comments about the way Africans live, and the hostility she encountered from some black Americans.

While some African Americans feel an emotional and spiritual attachment to Africa and give their children African names (Kwame, Kofi, Hakeem, Kamari), other African Americans are separated from African immigrants by a chasm widened by cultural differences and mutual misconceptions.

Many Africans believe that black Americans either romanticize the continent of Africa or snub its population as unsophisticated. African

Americans argue that many African immigrants do not make enough of an effort to integrate with black America and fail to appreciate how profoundly the legacy of slavery and the civil rights struggle has affected American-born blacks. Stereotypes are created by media images and misconceptions. A clash of culture, language, and class also plays a major role.

When immigrants from other parts of the world arrive in America, they can integrate into communities that share the same cultural perspective and typically speak the same language. Not so for Africans, who speak scores of different vernaculars and have distinct tribal affiliations, none of which American-born blacks can automatically identify with.

Like many other immigrants, Africans come to the United States in search of education and employment. Others are fleeing political instability or persecution in their home countries. Many are too caught up in the fight for everyday survival and for resources to support families back home to care about making an effort to get involved with black Americans.

Black Americans who visit Africa are trying to connect with home, the land, the spirit, the ancestors. By contrast, African immigrants are here for economic reasons, not to connect with African America. Being categorized by race stuns some Africans who come from predominantly black societies where ethnic affiliations and class override color.

Many are humbled by a downward assimilation. They come as university graduates and professionals but find they must take jobs as cleaners, janitors, or taxi drivers. "It is a shocking experience to find yourself down, down, down," said Yaw, an educated businessman from Nigeria.

OUT OF AFRICA

Young African immigrants must choose between being African and African American. Their parents pull in one direction and their peers pull in another. The bus that runs up and down Rainier Avenue in Los Angeles carries two types of East African youth. Their traditional clothes and Islamic politeness and diffidence distinguish the first type. They never speak loudly and always sit near the front of the bus for either safety or propriety's sake. Contrast the second, newer type of East African youth.

These young people always sit in the back of the bus, decked out in FUBU, Johnny Blaze, Ecko, and Mecca with sneakers as thick as Neil Armstrong's moon shoes. In the winter they wear puffy space jackets, their ears sealed in bulging iPod earbuds. In the summer they wear NBA vests and long baggy shorts or white undershirts with polka dot boxer shorts puffing out of their sagging "raw denim" pants. The girls have colorful nails done up at Hollywood Nails. The boys have tight braids and do-rags. No amount of scrutiny can separate them from African Americans. Only when they speak is the truth revealed.

Some say if the students come from Nigeria, Zaire, or Zimbabwe, they know they are African, not because their features are more recognizable, but because they are a year behind the trends. Their pants aren't sagging in the proper, lackadaisical manner, or worse, they are wearing a generic version of Tommy Hilfiger, a brand name already a thing of the past for African American youth.

African immigrants are in crisis mode. To become assimilated may be more detrimental than beneficial for their future in America. Black Americans represent the American underclass, and to adopt their ways is to adopt their fate. Blacks don't stand a chance of becoming white and benefiting from the institutions and connections available to white people. African immigrants, in order to survive in this country, must work hard to preserve their cultural distinctions rather than blend in with African Americans. To blend with African Americans is to engage in downward assimilation. In New York City, Miami, and Atlanta, the retention of foreign accents and culture has helped West Indian and Nigerian blacks get jobs.

Most African immigrants avoid thinking too deeply about what is really going on in America. The complex and unusual structure of their new society is broken down into basic parts: parts that work and improve their lot, and parts that don't work and don't improve their lot. Immigrants can't help but be scared because their world is a panicked world. They arrive in America fleeing desperate circumstances (war, famine, crazy dictators). They are usually forced to live in poor neighborhoods riddled with crime and bad cops, and if they have a job it's rarely stable or meaningful. African immigrants want to improve their lives as fast as possible, and they do not see many African Americans living the lives they want to live in America. Indeed, most black immigrants are as suspicious and critical of whites as black Americans, but they don't have the luxury of voicing their grievances.

East African youth are in transition; they may look black American, but their core is still African. Their children, however, will be African American in the deepest sense. Because America is the way it is, these African American children will experience the full brunt of America's brand of racism. The happy and prosperous life their grandparents dreamed about when they arrived here from "war-torn Africa" will become, for them, a nightmare of police harassment, job discrimination, and limited social and economic prospects. The African immigrants are trying to block the path to this bleak future by sustaining and imposing their Africanness. African American youth feel they're not being taught what they need to understand African immigrants' history, and their own.

On April 3, 1968, Martin Luther King Jr. said, "Something is happening in our world. The masses of people are rising up. And wherever they are assembled today, whether they are in Johannesburg, South Africa, Nairobi, Kenya, Accra, Ghana, New York City, Atlanta, Georgia, Jackson, Mississippi, or Memphis, Tennessee, the cry is always the same. 'We want to be free.'"

King's statement powerfully expresses the unity of people of African descent in worldwide liberation struggles in the late 1960s. It is therefore ironic as well as troubling that decades later, African American youth are finding it more difficult than ever to unify with their African immigrant peers.

> "We (African Americans) have our own struggle and they (African immigrants) have theirs," said Jamar, a senior at Roosevelt High School in Minneapolis, Minnesota. "It is still hard for us, just like it is hard for them. We still gotta work hard for ourselves, and better ourselves before we can help one another."
> "African Americans grew up in a whole other country," said Keyandre, also a senior at Roosevelt. "The things they (African Americans) do on a daily basis are completely different from what we (African immigrants) did when we were in Africa. We try to keep traditions. Our lifestyle is different. We eat different food, we view life differently. We are not the same."
> Shawontaya, another Roosevelt senior, was less sure about how to

define the difference between African Americans and African immigrants. "Some of them (African immigrants) come over here and practice their beliefs, others don't. Some try to dress like us (African Americans), others dress like they were still in Somalia or whatever."

Most of the students interviewed do not believe that African immigrants should have to assimilate to African American culture or white American culture just because they live here. These students also feel that African Americans should know more about where they come from.

"You should stay true to what you are. Just keep in mind where you came from," adds Jamar.

The students stated that although the obvious solution to this lack of understanding is education, they do not expect schools, community organizations, or other institutions to take the lead.

"The schools are not teaching too much of anything," said Tyana.

"They're teaching the same five or six people and mostly during February (Black History Month)," said Kamari.

The group agreed that the presence of more teachers who use hands-on instructional techniques and more culturally diverse teachers would go a long way toward bridging these cultural gaps.

"We shouldn't have to wait all the way to our senior year to have to take African American topics," said Shawontaya. "We need to understand each other. We are not being taught what we need."

Our African immigrant students arrive with a huge variety of learning styles and basic academic skills. These students, really all students, must be placed at the center of learning. More than ever, classroom climate for African immigrants must be characterized by empathy, understanding, acceptance, sensitivity, listening, authenticity, presence, immediacy, equity, and equality. Assure students of these characteristics and they will thrive.

African immigrant students must be empowered. Empowerment brings a sense of belonging and connectedness. Empowerment comes from having teachers who understand and respect cultural diversity and who promote multiculturalism.

As educators, we must nurture the African immigrant culture in order to promote healthy, safe, and respectful environments for these students and their families. What better way to capture the minds of these young people than to enroll them in schools that are tailored to their individual interests and needs.

Chapter Twelve

Strategies Aimed Toward Culturally Diverse Students

The important thing is this: to be able at any given moment to sacrifice what we are, for what we could become.

—Charles DuBois

In a first-grade classroom at PS 62 in Queens, a borough of New York City, Tatyana Ahmed, an American-born black student, sits on the floor sharing a book with a recent Indian immigrant, Jyot Singh. Tatyana glides her finger slowly along a page of *Who Eats Leaves?* as she helps Jyot spell out "koala."

The little girls bend their heads companionably over the book, but a mere glance indicates a gap much wider than their levels of English comprehension. Tatyana, sitting cross-legged in sneakers and jeans, looks every inch the contemporary American. Jyot, by contrast, wears a red patterned dress tucked carefully over lacy tights and patent-leather shoes. It is a challenge for their teacher to understand the differences between these children in ways in which they will learn.

The first step is a tighter focus on how to absorb burgeoning numbers of immigrant children into schools in the United States. We are confronting the largest wave of immigration in the history of our country.

Although federal funding is available to schools with immigrant students, it hasn't increased as immigration has grown. There have been state and local efforts. Some cities, such as Chicago and St. Paul, have experimented with gateway/transitional learning centers for newly arrived immigrant children. The centers are located in existing schools and serve as a first step for the newcomers. The students' English and learning skills are assessed at the transitional centers before they are placed in existing language programs at the district schools. The length of time spent in the transitional program before they can enter mainstream classrooms will depend on their academic ability and learning plan. However, most individual schools still lack support, especially in neighborhoods where demographics have changed dramatically in recent years.

Many classrooms have an influx of students who speak no English, know little of American culture and customs, and in some cases have never attended school before. Simply becoming accustomed to cold weather, tall buildings, and a freewheeling urban culture can be an overwhelming learning experience in itself.

Today's immigrants are arriving from Asia, Africa, and South America, and most come from diverse areas of the developing world. Teachers can no longer count on any kind of common cultural base as a starting point. Teachers appear to be working harder but accomplishing less.

Changes in curriculum and teaching methods to better support a student population with limited English skills must be considered. Our challenge is to make literacy and the love of reading an absolute priority. Schools should have a rich and appealing supply of children's books aimed at a vast range of ability levels. Remember, students don't just read, they look at text, pictures, and language. Students should be required to think and respond. Teachers should be required to rethink the ways students might relate to texts. Singing, movement, and art can become bridges to the written word.

Group work can allow students with stronger English skills to help language learners and create bonds across different ethnic groups. At the same time, use of individual projects (allowing children to write their own books) allows each child to work at his or her own pace.

These changes are not easy. Teachers will need to be both more structured and more flexible. They must adapt to the perspective of students who may never have lived in a house with doors and windows before they came to the United States. Most students learn English quickly but continue to lack background knowledge that their peers naturally acquire. Our new immigrant students didn't go to preschool, didn't have play dates, and have never seen snow. References in textbooks and classroom lessons may pass them by. Parents may need extra attention. Many parents do not understand the concept of homework, much less helping their child with schoolwork.

Learning to accommodate the new population can be a struggle. Discussions of world events have a new depth. Somalia and Laos are no longer just countries on a map or globe. Immigrant children offer a gift to our schools. They have energy and optimism often lacking in their U.S. counterparts. Ask immigrant children about school and they say, "School is great," "School is my future," "School is my life." Nonimmigrant children are more apt to say, "I hate school," or "School is boring."

Listen to the following words: "I came into this school expecting, as well as fearing, a lot. A lot of everything. This is a new start, a new beginning, and a new experience. I have been taught to expect the most from myself, as a scholar, a friend, and a member of my community. I expect to do as well as I can in every class, every day. I expect of myself not to become discouraged. I expect my fellow students to be supportive to me and I will be supportive to them. I expect my teachers to be respectful to me and to listen to me and every student as equal and to be fair." These are the words of a ninth-grade Nigerian student as she entered an American school for the first time. We must never forget the students' voices as we, the professional educators, plan for the academic success of all students.

Teachers must remember that the first day of school is scary because many children cannot speak English. Many have not ever seen a white student or a student with blond hair. Many have never seen a playground. Introduction to coloring can be a major issue. Have the students ever seen a crayon? Do they know how to hold a crayon or what it is used for? Teachers may need to show students how to color. Have our immigrant students ever seen toys, a playhouse, or a Barbie doll? What are snacks? Have they seen or tasted cookies, chips, or sodas? We cannot assume every child knows about these simple items.

We have our jobs cut out for us. Students are failing in America's schools. But failure has a history. Einstein failed in language, Schubert in mathematics, George Bernard Shaw could not spell properly, and Tolstoy displayed a severe learning disability during his school years. Delius, Gandhi, and Nehru showed no promise in school. Edgar Allan Poe and Einstein were expelled for serious misbehavior, while Thomas Edison was taken out of school after three months on the grounds that he was "unstable."

School failure, dropping out, and underachievement are too familiar in schools. Students of all ages and from all backgrounds and racial groups are wrestling with issues that threaten academic survival, cultural differences, learning styles, negative peer pressures, poor relationships, family difficulties, fiscal problems, and conflicting goals and priorities.

Middle-class and white students, however, are least likely to have negative school experiences. It is unfortunate that far too many culturally diverse students are overrepresented among poor achievers, dropouts, and pushouts, in the lowest ability groups, and among the educationally disenfranchised and disillusioned. In essence, these students are falling victim to educational suicide. Evidence indicates that culturally diverse students are first and foremost victims of issues both inside and outside of the schools. Curricular and instructional issues, testing practices, teacher-student relationships, classroom climates, cultural differences, and social and environmental factors all take their toll, either in isolation or collectively, on the educational, psychological, and affective (socioemotional) well-being of culturally diverse students.

FACTORS INHIBITING PERFORMANCE

Many factors inhibit the performance of culturally diverse students on school-mandated achievement tests. We must be aware of the following:

- *Environmental factors*: For economically disadvantaged students, scores tend to decrease with formal schooling. This may be due to qualitatively different and fewer educational opportunities. Many items on tests assess moral rather than cognitive development and are extremely biased. For example, on one test students are asked what they "should" do if they find a wallet containing money. Students must choose between returning the money and keeping it. For an economically disadvantaged student, this may be a difficult decision that is based on economic need and survival rather than cognitive or moral development. On another test, students are asked to choose common items found in a restaurant. Many students have never been to a restaurant, so the items listed are irrelevant. The degree to which such questions predict academic success is questionable.

- *Psychological factors*: Students who have poor internal motivation and an external locus of control and are easily distracted are not interested in tests. These students make errors because they take less time to understand the questions.
- *Instrumental issues*: Because life experiences and educational opportunities vary considerably, the reliability of most tests may be questionable. Content validity is unreliable because many culturally diverse students have not been exposed to the information on which the tests are drawn. Other tests simply lack cultural sensitivity. How valid are test results if a culturally diverse student takes a pictorial test in which all the people represented are white?
- *Grading practices*: The validity of grades is also questionable given that grading practices vary by the particular teacher, school district, and scales used as well as by course difficulty and the quality of the school and district.
- *Teachers as identifiers*: Teachers frequently emphasize such behaviors as cooperation, answering correctly, punctuality, and neatness as critical behaviors. These may not be the behaviors demonstrated by culturally diverse students.
- *Parents as identifiers*: Parents are an excellent and reliable source of information about their children's strengths and weaknesses. Use them!

There is no "one size fits all" test of intelligence or achievement. There is a need to progress from a culture of testing to a culture of assessment. In fact the move is long overdue. Assessment requires making an evaluation on development, the end product being a discussion about what intervention would be the most appropriate to facilitate a student's development. Assessment conveys expectations about what is important for students to learn, provides information about progress, and helps guide and improve instruction. Cultural, experiential, and environmental backgrounds provide important data. In addition, assessment must be ongoing. Culturally diverse students are in jeopardy of not reaching their potential in school and in life, particularly if their academic, psychological, and socioemotional needs are not adequately addressed.

PSYCHOLOGICAL PROBLEMS OF
CULTURALLY DIVERSE STUDENTS

The following should be addressed:

- *Isolation*: Students feel alienated from, unaccepted by, and unconnected to peers.
- *Anxiety*: This problem comes in many guises: test anxiety, perfectionism, procrastination, and other manifestations of stress. It is a state of perceived helplessness and being unable to cope
- *Self-esteem and self-concept*: The value we place on our worth varies from culture to culture and within cultures
- *Racial identity*
- *Survival conflict and guilt*

Every child enters the classroom with different characteristics and needs. These needs are a function of their membership in cultural groups.

Learning environments have a significant impact on students' achievement, motivation, and attitudes toward school and teachers. School and classroom environments, their culture, climate, ethos, and ambience set the psychological and affective milieu for students' learning. Teachers' expectations of students, their attention to individual student needs, and curriculum and instruction are also critical.

I would recommend that teachers, administrators, and staff take the following steps:

- Be open to the existence of culturally sensitive values and attitude among students.
- Avoid stereotyping cultural groups (retain the uniqueness of each student), recognize stereotypes, and teach all students how to challenge biases and injustices.
- Ask questions about culturally and racially diverse students, talk positively with students about their physical and cultural heritage, and

make sure that students understand that race and ethnicity are never acceptable reasons for being rejected.

- Hold high expectations for all students.
- Participate in the communities of culturally diverse students, learn about their cultures and values, and share this information.
- Recognize the contributions of cultural groups.
- Learn about your own culture and relate your values to your students.

With these guidelines, tolerance and acceptance of differences can become commonplace in schools.

INSTRUCTIONAL CONSIDERATIONS

Three considerations are important to the success of culturally diverse students: learning styles, the art of asking questions, and selecting high-quality literature. Consider the learning style of the student. The term *learning styles* refers to the highly individualistic ways we take in, process, and organize information. Our preferred learning style is the natural channel we use to learn more quickly, easily, and effectively.

White students are abstract and deductive thinkers, while culturally diverse students tend to be concrete and inductive thinkers. White students are individualistic and independent learners; culturally diverse students are interdependent, cooperative, social learners. White students prefer/ require less structure and direction; culturally diverse students require more structure and direction. White students seek academic meaning; culturally diverse students seek relevance and personal meaning. Most white students are kinesthetic, verbal, and auditory learners, while culturally diverse students are tactile, visual, and spatial learners. To reach all students, to stimulate and engage all students, teachers must adapt their teaching styles to students' learning styles. Teachers should use discussions, social learning, independent projects, group projects, role-playing, drama, music, dance, and other instructional techniques to meet students' learning preferences and needs.

Use the art of asking questions. Effective questioning focuses on depth rather than breadth, is explicit and precise, promotes cultural thinking and problem solving, and is cohesive. In essence, effective questioning cues and directs the students' thought processes and facilitates classroom discourse.

Select high-quality literature. Language, and hence literature, is the communication currency of the world. Literature should be personally meaningful and culturally relevant.

Culturally diverse students are hungry for a curriculum that reflects diversity, pluralism, equity, and the unacceptability of racism, sexism, and discrimination. Because of cultural differences in learning styles, changes in instruction are essential if all students are to succeed. In many cases students are required to assimilate, to give up their learning style preference in order to fit into the classroom, in order to succeed in school. For instance, most schools cater to students who prefer lecture-based instruction and are passive, abstract, and auditory learners. Yet many culturally diverse students prefer hands-on experiences and they are often visual, concrete, tactile, and experiential learners. Teachers do not modify their instruction, so students are forced to modify their learning. This "sink or swim" approach is reminiscent of the old melting pot philosophy.

Our curriculum must be changed to enable students to view concepts, issues, themes, and problems from several ethnic perspectives. We should not simply add a long list of ethnic groups, heroes, and contributions; we should instead infuse various perspectives, frames of reference, and content from culturally diverse groups that will extend to understanding of the nature, development, and complexity of U.S. society. We must not emphasize how various ethnic and cultural groups have contributed to mainstream American society; rather, the emphasis should be placed on how American society emerged from a complex synthesis and interaction of the diverse cultural elements that originated in the culturally diverse groups that make up American society. Educators must advocate for the hiring of teachers, administrators, and counselors of color so students can see a variety of adults teaching such a diverse curriculum.

Changes in attitude and teaching and management habits can raise the achievement level of every child. Education is not a neutral profession. Teachers are human; they are not immune to racial and cultural biases. For instance, a teacher who believes that culturally diverse students are not as competent as white students might communicate this by assigning easy tasks to these students and assigning more difficult and challenging tasks to white students. The message is sent that culturally diverse students are incapable of mastering challenging work and that white students are more capable and competent. Culturally diverse students are often given fewer opportunities to speak in class, are seated at the back of the classroom, are ignored, and are given less praise. Teachers must focus on academic factors, community factors, socioeconomic status, and families in order to help their students.

Schools who work effectively with culturally diverse students have the following:

- Ethnic and multicultural curriculum
- Teacher training in multicultural education
- Strong instructional leadership
- High expectations for all students
- A safe and orderly learning community including showing warmth, concern, and appreciation for students
- An emphasis on basic skills
- Continuous monitoring of student progress
- Clear and well-balanced goals
- High teacher and student morale
- Respect for individual differences

It is also the leadership of the school (vision, dedication, energy) that makes the difference between mediocrity and excellence. Successful administrators have clear and informed visions of what they want their schools to become, visions that focus on students and their needs. They also are friendly, good-natured, knowledgeable, and go out of their way to help and mentor their teachers. These administrators place an emphasis on basic skills, assessment of progress, and student achievement. Their school becomes a community. Most of all they are aware that ethnic, geographic, and socioeconomic groups differ in achievement levels from the school's average-middle-class white students. The bottom line is that school structure, organization, leadership, climate, values, policy, and practices have an impact on school achievement.

REFLECTIVE PRACTICE TO
IMPROVE LEARNING

The pivotal question is how to make the total educational enterprise more responsive to the histories, heritages, life experiences, and cultural conditioning of culturally diverse students in all of its policy making, program-planning, and instructional practices.

Teachers, materials, and teaching environments that work well for European American students do not necessarily work equally well for culturally diverse students. To believe that they do is to assume that African American, Latino, American Indian, Asian, Arab, African immigrants, and European origin students are identical in personal, social, cultural, historical, and family traits. In addition, most graduates of typical teacher education programs know little about cultural traits, behaviors, values, and attitudes that culturally diverse students bring to the classroom and how they affect the ways these students act in and react to instructional situations. They do not understand and use the school behaviors of these students, which differ from the normative expectations, as aids to teaching.

We also know that, like teacher education, most curriculum designs and instructional materials are Eurocentric. As such, they reflect the middle-class experiences, perspectives, and value priorities in which the macro culture of the United States is grounded. These educational initiatives are likely to be more relevant to life experiences, aspirations, and frames of reference of European Americans than to those culturally diverse students who are not part of the mainstream culture. Therefore, culturally diverse students must divide their energies and efforts between coping with curriculum materials and instructional methods that are not culturally relevant to their learning styles or reflective of their life experiences and mastering the academic knowledge and tasks being taught.

School environments in which students live and learn do not mean the same thing to comparable culturally diverse students and European students. When students and their teachers arrive at school, they do not leave their cultural backgrounds at home. This is not a problem for most European Americans, since school culture and rules of behavior are reflections and extensions of their home cultures. A high degree of cultural congruency exists between middle-class European American culture and school culture. These students do not experience social-code incompatibility or the need for cultural style shifting to adjust to the behavioral rules and expectations of schools. The converse is true for the culturally diverse students. Many of the social codes for succeeding in school are unfamiliar to them or are opposed to the codes they have learned from their home cultures. When learning situations do not reflect the culture of the students, gaps exist between learning and performance. These gaps are greatest for students from ethnic cultures and communities that are not part of the mainstream culture and can militate against effective teaching and learning.

Most educators do not think to teach students skills for how to survive and succeed in school. Our students need to be taught how to study across ethnic learning styles. Several educators suggest that ethnicity plays a major role in learning styles as well as prior knowledge (Landsman [2001], Takaki [1993], and Lemieux [1994] have all suggested that ethnicity is an important focus in prior knowledge and the development of learning styles), how to adjust language styles to accommodate school expectations, how to interact appropriately with school administrators and classroom teachers, and how to identify and adjust to the procedural rules for functioning in different instructional classrooms. For example, in order to function as empowered citizens, culturally diverse urban teens also need to be able to deconstruct and reinterpret messages that are sent to them through the media.

Educators tend to operate on the assumption that school codes of behavior are universal and commonly understood and are acquired from simply living in the broader culture that surrounds schools. What we forget is that many students live only marginally in mainstream culture. Interviews with a group of culturally diverse high school students reflect that they are grappling with issues of marginalization, discrimination, and racism in their schools. There needs to be a relationship between subject matter and the racial and ethnic experiences within the classroom. Furthermore, the parents of culturally diverse students may not be able to pass on to them a legacy of how to "do" schooling successfully because they did not experience it themselves.

Students must learn how to survive in school while simultaneously learning what is taught. The most inclusive curriculum we can construct makes student voices the center of the class. Educators are also increasingly aware that the values, attitudes, and ideas that children receive through literature, as well as through other media, are powerful influences on how children view themselves and their role in the society to which they belong. Toni Morrison argues that literary critics have been silent about the "Africanist" presence in 19th- and 20th-century literature. Morrison argues that literature holds more power and sovereignty today than ever before. We need to weave literature from a multiplicity of cultures into our English classes throughout the year, then allow students ample time to respond to and write from themes in this literature. However, if students fail to master the social codes, they may never get a chance to try the academic tasks.

Clearly related to school success is the role of teacher attitude, expectations, and competencies in perpetuating learning. Most teachers know little about ethnic groups' lifestyles or learning habits and preferences. Too many teachers still believe that culturally diverse students are academically and socially deprived and should be remediated by using middle-class whites as the appropriate norm, or that they do not have the aspirations or capacities to learn as well as European Americans. Many white teachers have the mind-set of a "white savior." These teachers must become aware of their whiteness and whether or not the savior mentality can be transformed to one of respectful, successful, culturally relevant practice.

Some Asian groups (Chinese, Japanese, and Koreans) are exempt from these negative expectations but are still treated unfairly. Many teachers form their expectations about children based directly on race and social class. Expectations are more influenced by negative information about student characteristics than positive data. Teachers transmit these attitudes and expectations in what they say or do in the classroom. Students respond accordingly and many believe they are destined to fail.

Look at the typical classroom in the typical school, urban or suburban. Instruction for culturally diverse students tends to be remedial; European Americans get enrichment. If students defy expectations by performing well, they are suspected of dishonesty and even cheating. Classroom interactions are reinforced further by culturally biased tests and diagnostic assessment.

Schools prize verbal learning and written demonstrations of achievement. These styles of demonstrating mastery are consistent with the cultures of mainstream American and European students, but they are contrary to the performance styles of many culturally diverse groups. For African Americans, whose cultural socialization emphasizes aural, verbal, and participatory learning, and for American Indians, who are accustomed to imitative learning in their home cultures, it is difficult to transform what they know from one performance style to another. Do not force or expect culturally diverse students to demonstrate mastery in culturally incompatible styles and formats.

A colleague once said, "The body is the hardware and culture is the software." How true this statement is when we look at student achievement. We are living in a nation (and world) of unparalleled diversity. Given the nation's changing demographics, issues of diversity must occupy center stage in much of what is currently being discussed, written, and taught in education. Demographic data indicates that culturally diverse students represent an increasingly large proportion of the school population. In many U.S. cities and schools, "minority" groups are actually the numerical majority. The National Center for Education Statistics projects that by year 2020 minority students will comprise almost half (46%) of all public school students.

More than two decades ago educators began encouraging the expansion of ethnic cultures and their incorporation into the mainstream of American socioeconomic, political, and academic life, exploring alternative and emerging lifestyles and encouraging multiculturalism.

An eighth-grade boy remarks: "You get tired of learning about the same white people and the same things. We need to learn about other people, even other countries. The white people are just trying to advance other white people and leave blacks behind and ignorant. I feel like being in class more when I learn about blacks and my heritage. It gives me encouragement and lets me know that I have rights. Learning about white people doesn't help me know about myself. I want to feel good about who I am. Why shouldn't I want to learn more about black people?"

Students' comments reveal their displeasure with and disinterest in the traditional curriculum in their schools. Their comments reveal that the students desire an education that is multicultural. They seek self-affirmation and self-understanding from the school and its curriculum. Educational engagement increases when the curriculum is relevant.

Interviews conducted with students reveal that culturally diverse students feel that they are not being educated to live in a racially and culturally diverse society. They say that the curriculum does not enhance their racial and cultural identities and that school subjects lack relevance and meaning. These negative attitudes toward school help to explain why culturally diverse students are represented disproportionately among under-achievers. The lack of educational relevance can decrease student motivation and interest in school.

Teachers must listen to students and work to provide a learning environment that promotes multicultural philosophy as well as curricular changes, instructional changes, assessment, and structural changes. Education must provide all students with mirrors and windows. In terms of mirrors, students must see themselves reflected in the curriculum; likewise, in terms of windows, students must see others reflected in the curriculum. Neither mirrors nor windows need to be distorted images of culturally diverse groups. Students must not be devalued, ignored, or negated. An honest and open portrayal of culturally diverse groups empowers children by giving them a vision of hope. Thus education must also provide ropes and ladders so culturally diverse students can pull themselves up and rise to the challenge that education has to offer. These apparatuses—mirrors, windows, ropes, and ladders—help all children succeed.

Too often students are presented a homogenized curriculum, one that is most likely to meet the academic and affective needs of white students in upper income brackets. In this type of curriculum, little (if any) material and discussion address multicultural perspectives. Cultural groups are ignored, trivialized, or negated in various ways. This treatment of diversity affirms, directly or indirectly, white students, while devaluing culturally diverse students. Likewise, homogenization espouses a color-blind philosophy, which is equally offensive to the students.

Our efforts must not be color-blind, which robs culturally diverse students of essential opportunities to be valued and respected as unique ethnic groups. When we seek such blindness, equality is equated with sameness, but students are not the same; they are equally human, but they are different.

The question becomes, how can we implement multicultural education so that it becomes not an add-on but an integral and integrated aspect of the educational process?

REFLECTING ON MULTICULTURAL EDUCATION

According to Maya Angelou, "Education brings breaking dawn; ignorance a long, long night." As a teacher you must continue to develop your multicultural knowledge base. The following are the problems and issues we still need to address:

- *Knowledge about multicultural education*: We still need to emphasize cultural diversity in our teaching programs.
- *Stereotyped thinking and prejudice*: We all grew up within a culture surrounded by beliefs and behaviors that we accepted without question. We must learn to accept culturally diverse thinking as a normal state of affairs.
- *The preschool curriculum*: We must reinforce the worth of every person in our diverse population.
- *Fear of handling controversy*: Teachers tend to avoid topics that invite controversy in the classroom. However, dealing with real topics in the classroom adds vitality and stimulates student involvement in learning.
- *Communication with parents*: Direct communication and involvement in their child's learning is critical.
- *Censorship efforts*: Have a plan if some parents want certain reading materials removed from the classroom.
- *The "English Only" movement*: This movement can wreak havoc with efforts that support instruction in children's native languages.
- *Assessment, testing, and effects of bias*: Students need to experience various methods of assessing mastery. Lean toward portfolio assessment, a method that is highly individualized.
- *Resistance to multicultural education*: The argument for total assimilation still exists.
- *Violence*: Children of all ages and all cultures are exposed to violence and abuse in their lives. Let's offer strategies to help them cope with life.

Once we acknowledge the existence of these issues related to multicultural education, we will be able to deal with differences of opinion and strive to find solutions. With regard to multicultural education, many schools in America today are also making visible efforts to deal with the following:

- *Self-esteem—the bottom line*: Currently there is renewed interest in the student's role in the learning process. All students need to feel a sense of worth, the "I can" attitude, if they are to succeed.

- *Writing, "thinking"*: We need to encourage students to think. Thinking leads to writing, and writing extends thinking.
- *Literature-based reading instruction*: Use literature to support instruction in all subject areas. We need to use literature to encourage and teach students how to discover, question, think, analyze, evaluate, and reflect.
- *Educating teachers for empowerment*: Teachers need more control and autonomy. Empowerment comes from within.
- *Schools as centers of inquiry*: We need to encourage teachers to utilize the discovery methods that engage students in inquiry. Self-motivation is a by-product of inquiry.
- *Reflection/thinking*: Center your instructional program around this essential aspect of learning.
- *Early childhood education*: Attitudes and values are firmly rooted in what is learned during the child's early years. Without learning opportunities, these children enter kindergarten and first grade with a disadvantage. We also know that some children require more time (and some less) to achieve the basic foundation of learning.
- *Growing concern for at-risk students*: Develop strategies and programs that will lower the drop-out statistics.
- *International and global issues*: Americans (of all cultures) must learn how to operate in a rapidly changing world. Children who are brought up with limited perspectives of the world will be at a disadvantage, unable to move beyond the narrow environment in which they were raised.

Teaching needs to be grounded in humanity and a sincere desire to make the world a better place. Education offers the only route to the empathy for others that is necessary to achieve harmonious living on our planet. Education can empower, and teachers are the enabling agents who can make it happen. Our cultures, our values, and our views color the way we see differences in other people. If we are to help culturally diverse students to become more successful, we need to look at how we define and see differences.

One strategy to promote self-understanding and awareness of who we are and how we see others is to use literature. The reader sees similarities between himself or herself and the character in the story. Emotions surface and there is insight and connection with the characters in the story. We understand that we are not alone and our issues are not unique, which leads to behavioral and cognitive change. All literature is multicultural and has concrete application to multicultural themes, concepts, and issues. Let's use this very crucial strategy to help our culturally diverse students.

Drama, music, dance, and art are additional effective strategies for engaging students. These creative outlets address learning styles and aesthetic appreciation. Poetry can be used to promote identity. Works by Langston Hughes, Rita Dove, Zora Neale Hurston, Maya Angelou, Nikki Giovanni, and Pleasant De Spaon often focus on self-determination, hope, identity, and achievement. This serves to empower students.

Biographies can also enhance students' racial identity, motivation, and achievement. Most books on Malcolm X depict his life in various stages of racial identity. Students witness Malcolm X's transformation from self-hatred to self-love, socially imposed identity to self-imposed identity, and they learn coping strategies for trials and tribulations. Also include journaling, which makes invisible thoughts visible. Write about an issue, think about it, and then let it go.

Mentors and role models can promote hope, faith, and optimism. Also, given the value many cultures place on families and social relationships, family and group counseling may be appropriate.

Finally, allow teachers to be more than just teachers. Allow them to be advocates, mentors, role models, and sometimes, surrogate parents for our culturally diverse children.

As we move forward we need:

- To be more involved in the families of culturally diverse students and their communities.
- To gain a more in-depth understanding of the cultural differences and similarities of our children.
- To explore how to develop and use teaching techniques that are not culturally biased.
- To build bridges of understanding that promote better cooperative learning experiences.
- To offer multicultural training that gives specific information about teaching culturally diverse students, training that explains the current issues and problems of the native countries of the students. This

training should include information about the structure, cultural habits, values, and taboos found in the families of our students.

Following these suggestions will ensure that we will continue to make progress in developing our ability to meet the needs of the growing population of culturally diverse students in our nation's schools.

REFLECTIVE PRACTICE TO IMPROVE OUR CLASSROOMS

The process of reflection influences the reality we perceive, feel, see, and hear. Humans don't get ideas, they make ideas. Our surrounding culture does little to support time out for thinking and learning.

Our own view of the world is so much a part of who we are that it serves as a filter for our thinking. Examine your beliefs. They stem largely from our experiences and influence the way we think and act. Beliefs create the lens through which we view our world. Reflective practice provides the way to understand and make sense of those worlds. We must become aware of our biases and make a conscious effort to see things from another's perspective. Be open to other points of view. Recognize that representation within a group is a way to view particular circumstances or events. Be open to changing viewpoints and let go of the need to be right or wanting to always win. The purpose is to be understood. Self-knowledge involves what and how you are thinking. Often a period of unlearning precedes new learning. Remember, students cannot be taught what they need to know, but they can be coached. They have to see on their own behalf and in their own way the relationships between the means and methods employed and the results achieved.

We must make culturally diverse students'—indeed, all students'—voices the center of the classroom. We must develop and use a child-centered approach. If we abandon the student in the name of test scores, if we eliminate a celebration of dialect and poetry in the name of standard English, if we do not combine both skills and creativity, we will lose our students to the streets, to despair, to boredom. As educators we must do it all, teach skills at the same time we make students' voices an important part of the core of a curriculum.

Children come fully equipped with an insatiable drive to explore, to experiment, and to inquire. Unfortunately, the educational process often is oriented toward controlling rather than learning, rewarding individuals for performing for others, rather than cultivating this natural curiosity and impulse to learn. From an early age, our fragmented curriculum teaches competitiveness and reactiveness. We are trained to believe that deep learning means knowing accepted truths rather than developing capacities for effective and thoughtful action; acquiring knowledge is for passing tests rather than accumulating wisdom and personal meaning. We are taught to value certainty rather than to doubt, to give quick answers rather than to inquire, and to know which choice is correct rather than to reflect on alternatives.

Schools are busy, active places in which students and teachers are pressured with high-stakes testing to learn more, learn faster, and be held accountable to others for achievement of specific standards and mastery of content. Students therefore confront learning opportunities with fear rather than mystery and wonder. They seem to feel better when they know, rather than when they learn. They defend their biases, beliefs, and storehouses of knowledge rather than welcoming the unknown. Life experiences are viewed as separate, unrelated, and isolated events rather than as opportunities for continuous learning.

Schools become barren climates where some teachers and administrators grow depressed. Their once vivid imagination, altruism, creativity, and intellectual powers soon succumb to the humdrum, daily routines of unruly students, irrelevant curriculum, impersonal surroundings, and equally disillusioned coworkers.

There is an educational movement today that says that time and effort invested in reflection will yield a harvest of greater student learning, higher teacher morale, and a more collaborative community. Reflecting enhances meaning. We learn by conversing with ourselves, with others, and with the world around us.

To be reflective means to mentally wander through where you have been and try to make some sense out of it. Emotion controls the gateway to learning. Trust must be present for individuals to share their thoughts and to be open to expanding their ways of thinking and doing. We must connect information to previous learning. If educators do not reflect and learn more from their practice, they are likely to continue doing what they have been doing. Recall the old adage, "If you always do what you've always done, you'll always get what you've always gotten." Learning requires change, and change involves risk.

A goal of education should be to recapture, sustain, and liberate the natural, self-organizing, learning tendencies inherent in all human beings: curiosity and wondering, mystery and adventure, humor and playfulness, inventiveness and creativity, and continual learning. Experience by itself is not enough. Reflection on experience is the pathway to improvement.

LET'S TALK ABOUT RACISM

Join me in looking at racism as a challenge to be overcome, not as an obstacle to be used as an excuse for not doing our best.

Salim Muwakki wrote the following statement in his article "Racism and Our Heritage" that appeared in the magazine *In These Times*: "When we first came here it was against the law to practice our rituals, to recognize our heritage. Even the drum was forbidden. So now, when Black people are just beginning to embrace their ethnic identity, White look at it as some kind of threat. It's simply that Black people are just beginning to realize how much they've been deprived of knowledge of their own selves. We must begin to realize that we are Americans of African decent and be comfortable with that identity" (pp. 15–16).

I observed a social studies class in which the teacher was reading a letter a man had written to his wife in 1944 after he and a small group of American soldiers had liberated one of the Nazi death camps. He told his wife that he hoped never again to see what he had seen this day, never again to witness the evil that human beings are capable of doing to each other. The teacher then asked the students to write, "I never again . . ." and "I wish . . ." at the top of their papers. They were to make one list of things they hoped would not happen again and another list of things they wished for.

Some said that they hoped never again to see poor people living in shelters, see old women knocked down and kicked, or hear gunfire at night. Some wished for money, food, or world peace. Tamika said it all, "I hope never again to feel the kind of prejudice I feel everyday when I walk down the street, or go into a store, or stand in line somewhere." She had only one wish, "I wish I was an American." Tamika's family has been living in this country since the mid-1600s. They came with the slave trade, were freed, and migrated north in the middle 1900s, centuries after their arrival on our shores in chains. She does not feel American after all this time. None of the other kids (white, Asian, Hispanic, American Indian, or black) in the class questioned her last statement. They all nodded their heads in understanding.

I believe that Tamika can come to feel like an American by seeing and hearing her ancestors' stories as part of her school experience. We must celebrate Tamika's culture, her history, and her life as well as every other student's life in every subject in our classrooms.

In order to hold our students' attention, I believe the continuum of history, its influence on present-day economics, politics, neighborhoods, and the law, must be presented in all its multifaceted complexity. We must present the truth in all its difficult and troublesome entirety. Contrary to a picture of history as a sequence of great events undertaken by great individuals, ordinary people every day act out the more powerful force of history and culture. One cannot sit on the fence of history but rather creates history by being alive. Inaction or following along with the tide has at least as much historical force as conscious action.

I have been an administrator in schools where at least 80 to 90% of my students were not of European American decent. More and more our public schools are dominated by students who are black, Asian, Latino, American Indian, and new immigrants or refugees. I have had students whose families have been in the United States for many generations and students who have arrived only a month ago. Many of my students do not speak English as their first language. The diversity of the culture in our buildings, the mixture of clothing, dialects, and music, can only increase our knowledge, our joy, and our excitement. It can add to the quality of our lives. At the same time, culturally diverse students will develop skills that will assist them in reading, writing, math, and science as well as in compassion, cooperation, and global knowledge.

Our classrooms must inspire and challenge all students. They must be places where students can bring their lives, their concerns, and their abilities into the school. Parents, businessmen and businesswomen, community agencies, and those in legal and medical fields need to be involved in the classroom.

We must get rid of the "color-blind" notion of the 1950s and from the Reagan years when it was considered wrong to recognize our differences.

We do not acknowledge the experiences of culturally diverse groups because of their skin, black, brown, yellow or white, dark or light.

I believe that it is among the students who are African American, Asian American, Arab, Latino, and American Indian, not only those who are white, that we will find important role models to lead us into a new era. In our urban classrooms are students who are willing to have important dialogues, interactions, disputes, and differences with each other that allow each one to understand other cultures. These students have learned to get along.

We can't get away from the term *race*. Old cultures, Western and non-Western—Greece and China, for example—have always distinguished between themselves and outsiders. It is a universal phenomenon. But the term *race* used today is more than that. It is part skin color, part privilege, and part social construction. White people do not usually think of themselves as having a race. Race is a marker for the "other." When we refer to a person without further description, the social norm is white (and male and straight, and not disabled). We typically refer to the "black lawyer" or the "woman doctor." The assumptions embedded in the language shout white privilege. If you are white, you need no further description. Our culturally diverse students have figured this out.

Eunice, a young Ukrainian immigrant, will be treated differently than Mai, her Hmong classmate, even though both young women arrived in this country about the same time. Eunice will find doors opening for her because of her white skin.

Susie is a street kid, often living on the streets, homeless, in condemned buildings near the tracks. Yet when she and Shanna (who is black) go to a bookstore, Shanna is followed and watched closely, while Susie can wander freely without surveillance.

Students tell me their fears of being "the only." Shanna does not like being the only black student at any gathering. Kamari will not go into a restaurant if there are no black people sitting there. Tyrone refuses to consider living in a white suburb because of how he has been treated. Kou rarely leaves his neighborhood.

There are certain things I cannot know. I cannot know what it is like to be any other color than my own, but I can imagine, and if I can imagine, I can understand. Of course, the more I experience what others experience, including the feeling of exclusion and separation from the mainstream, the more I can understand others' feelings the more I can empathize. We can all experience what it is like to be "the other" for a short while.

Culturally diverse students rarely see their own culture reflected in anything they hear or see in the school. They tell me that they tune out. That is how these students survive. Sometimes, when they are angry at what they are told or insulted by a condescending tone of voice, they think about objecting. However, most culturally diverse students give up and leave the classroom as soon as possible.

Culturally diverse people experience exclusion and discrimination. If this does not kill a person, it can lead to critical thinking about language, culture, oneself, and others. Though often damaging and painful to acquire, the wisdom and skill that arises from this type of experience is valued for survival.

We tend to remake language and culture each generation and each day, shaping it according to our current beliefs and vision. When we begin to leave behind racially biased language and thought, and to make our language more precise and accurate, our mistaken assumptions begin to dissipate. We begin to see that racial labels tell us little about a person, including his or her cultural identity. We begin to look beyond the traditional racial structure to see who is standing in front of us. We can then provide our children with a language capable of fairly reflecting the full spectrum of humanity.

Communication is the key. It is important to know *what* you think or want to communicate about cultural diversity and *why*. An understanding of other views and information allows one to respond effectively (as opposed to defensively) when confronted. Good communicators must ground their messages in an understanding of their own multiple positions in the world, and how these positions relate to others. It is time to formulate and share your own personal views about cultural diversity and use information and dialogue with others to expand understanding. The skills required are:

- Critical listening, reading, viewing, questioning
- Research and reflecting
- Thinking, reasoning, analyzing
- Judging and decision making
- Writing, speaking, expressing, creating
- Leadership

We must overcome the fear of difference. Ways that we can do this are as follows:

- *Examine your media.* What news program do you watch? What paper do you read? What sort of leisure reading do you choose? Read a novel by an African American author, or a mystery by a Latino mystery writer, or American Indian poetry.
- *Examine your own culture.* What are your personal beliefs and ethics? Traditions? How do you celebrate your culture? What do you give to others? What do you really know about other cultures? Ask questions and learn from community members. Where do you shop? Eat? Hang out? Where do you avoid shopping, eating, and hanging out? Why?
- *Examine your socialization.* How do you speak? Write? Think? Do you use inclusive language? Do you use color-coded language?
- *Keep a journal.* Set goals for yourself. Check your progress. Confronting bias and fear is personal.

Conscious shifts in our thought processes are necessary so we can stop making assumptions. These shifts involve reframing closed questions to open ones, gaining information about values, family, culture, and beliefs. Remember, language and culture are living things that are shaped by the choices we make every day.

In the past many people developed perspectives that reflected the limitations of isolation: by geography, culture, language, economics, politics, socialization, education, religion, belief systems, gender, ability levels, and many other factors. Interchanges across human differences have taken place for centuries.

Amidst a technological revolution, many people have unprecedented access to information and increased exposure to global, multicultural, historical dynamics. However, has our capacity to interpret information, and use it wisely, kept pace? Currently, the technological revolution has not led to a widespread recognition of what is now obvious: the destiny and interests of all humans are linked. Instead, infighting among groups rages on, while the environments we all depend on deteriorate. We must respect the rights and values of all groups. Difference gives us an opportunity to learn and grow. Difference needs to be viewed positively.

An awareness of one's own perspective provides an important basis from which to communicate with similar and dissimilar people. When we mistake our viewpoints as universal, we not only err, we lose the unique resonance of our own voices. Educators must look within, whatever "within" may be, for grounding and direction when teaching the issues revolving around cultural diversity. We then can look outward in search of better solutions, information, and connections.

RACIAL PRIVILEGE

The following is a "white" person's conscious observation of racial privilege: Whether I use checks, credit cards, or cash, or when I need legal or medical help, my color will not work against me. I can swear in public, or dress in secondhand clothes, or not answer a letter, or be late to meetings without having people attribute these behaviors to the bad morals, poverty, or illiteracy of my color. I can remain oblivious to the languages and customs of persons of color without suffering any penalty. I can speak in public without putting my color on trial. I can take a job without having coworkers suspect that I got it because of my color. White privileges also extend to receiving the benefit of the doubt with all types of law enforcement officials.

Recognized or unrecognized, continuing racial privilege reinforces "white" people's feelings of superiority and entitlement. Tragically, "white" self-esteem continues to be biased, at least partially, on a dynamic of *power over* other cultures. White children do not just get up one morning and decide to become racists. They learn about race through position and experience. At least four features of the English language promote this and are worth noting.

Color bias in English. Unequal value is attributed to different colors. Because the concept of race is based partly on skin and hair color, it shoulders a strong color bias in the English language, the association of badness or danger with darkness, and the association of goodness with light. Color-bias sayings permeate the language: "A dark cloud hung over the event," "She is a brownnoser," "He is a redneck," "He flew into a black rage," and so on. By default, speakers of English are taught that white or light things are usually good: "She is as pure as the driven snow," "The good guys wear white hats and ride white horses," "He's in the pink," etc. An overview of current thesaurus entries for lightness and darkness looks like this: Dark and black mean somber, gloomy, evil, vile, angry, sullen, bleak, dismal, etc. Light and white mean merry, luminous, innocent, pure, happy, amusing, effortless, untroubled, etc.

Whiteness as the norm. Common usage assumes the race of a person to be white unless otherwise indicated. There are scholars and *black* scholars, women and *black* women. Saul Bellow and John Updike are writers, Ralph Ellison and Toni Morrison are *black* writers. Whites easily forget, indeed are seldom aware, that they are also a part of a group. People identifying with different culturally diverse groups literally see a different "reality" at times. Each view is culturally specific and influenced by many other factors (gender, expectations, economic resources, education, belief systems, etc.).

Whiteness gains its character indirectly, by negative references to other races. In the act of defining African Americans as "uncivilized blacks" and Indians as "savages," and thereby excluding them from their world, Europeans in the 18th and 19th centuries were representing themselves as "white" and "civilized." Traditionally, whiteness has been held superior to other races.

Whiteness is now presented as a generic racial status. In addition to mistakenly treating whiteness as the "norm" and as better in comparison to other races, whiteness is now also presented as *generic* in English. European American scientists continue to fuel the legacy of white supremacy by claiming "whites" are intellectually superior to other races.

It is this world that our immigrants and people of other cultures are forced to live in and deal with.

MY PERCEPTIONS

As an educator I must acknowledge the perceptions of the world that culturally diverse students bring to me: perceptions about the difference their skin color makes in the way they are considered by store owners, teachers, policemen, and employers. It does not mean that I have to excuse students for behavior that is harmful or treat them as though they are victims. It does not mean that I have to change what I expect of them.

It does mean that I have to believe what they tell me about their lives, the way they might be accused, and the experiences that they have on the streets. I cannot deny their perception of the world. I need to understand their perception and go on from it and help them study, explore, research, make it in college, and remain employed. I also see more and more students who are recent immigrants to America. These students need to know the social codes, the ways to dress, and the protocols of white power culture.

An immigrant parent (a Hmong mother) sums it up for all immigrants/ refugees in the United States today: "In America, life is different. We must use our heads, our intelligence, and our knowledge to the fullest. I regret that I never got a chance to go to school, as you children have the opportunity to do now. Without any education I cannot go to work and bring home money. If you children love me and want to show your gratitude to your father and me for bringing you here, then please try to complete the highest level of education you can. Do it for your father and me. Do it for you. All we have now are you children. If you children do not do well in school, then all the hardships we have suffered to get here will have been in vain. We have suffered so much to gain so little." The tricky part is to be able to help students succeed without asking them to give up anything of their own culture and their own language.

A Hispanic American (a young man from Cuba) had this to say: "When I came to America my life began to change. I discovered a whole new world. Not all things are what I thought they are. Not all people are what I thought they are. Not all people are racist. Whether we are white, black, brown, or yellow, we all hate racism."

Another parent (an African American) said: "It is important that we teach our children about each other and about each other's customs and values. We are not going to survive if we don't." A young Somali woman simply said: "Together we have the power to transform the future."

Often schools are places where, because teachers lack cultural understanding, some children are reprimanded or criticized when they try to express themselves. Others are told to look the teacher in the eye when in their culture this is a sign of disrespect, yet many times teachers interpret this looking away as a sign of insolence. And many times children are put into competitive situations when they have been raised to work much harder and more effectively in cooperative groups. Those of us who are raised to speak quietly, to face our teachers directly, or to work on our own assume that the way we learned is the best way for all students to learn. Because we are comfortable with learning in silence and solitude, we assume our students are comfortable like this. Because we have been encouraged to think of ourselves first and our community, or even our family, second, we assume the same values on the part of the culturally diverse students we teach.

So why are we here? I can only conclude that somewhere along the line, our community and our system have not found ways to reach culturally diverse students. We cannot discount the importance of parents, home life, money, and street influences, and I do not expect any school system to act as surrogate parents, ministers, and guardians for all the students who come through the doors. I do believe we can reach these students and keep them coming to school by making them feel welcome.

Engaging all students in learning is our primary mission as educators. All stakeholders, colleagues, parents, students, and the larger community are necessary to reach this goal. Articulating clear standards for student learning enhances the quality of students' work and the students' sense of purpose. As John Dewey said, "Education enables *all* individuals to come into full possession of all their powers."

Every teaching situation is unique. Each day, in each classroom, a particular combination of factors defines the events that occur. The environment must be one of respect and rapport. Students take pride in their work as they engage in the task at hand.

Students want direction. Julie Landsman, in her book *A White Teacher Talks About Race* (2001), says that many students of color feel their white teachers are afraid to tell them to be quiet. These students quote their teachers as saying, "Would you please be quiet now so we can get some work done in here?" The students would prefer their teachers to just tell us, demand it. Don't ask us. The students feel there are too many choices. "Tell us what to do," the students say. Most of all students feel that the teacher needs to be in control, to make it safe (Landsman, 2001, p. 114).

Students are enormously diverse, and they arrive at school with a full range of academic preparation, interests, cultural norms, and preferred approaches to learning. Any given technique is bound to be more effective with some students than with others. The instructional goals must be valuable and suitable to the students.

CULTURAL SENSITIVITY

Students may arrive at school with traditions that are different from or antagonistic to those of many U.S. classrooms. Children in some cultures are taught different values about the methods of questioning. The ways questions are raised in many classrooms is foreign to some students. When teachers use questions that these students know the answer to as a way of checking, for example, whether students have done the assigned reading, these students are baffled. Why would a teacher ask a question to which he or she already knows the answer? Clearly this is not a real question, but if it is not a real question, then what is it? Such thoughts interfere with a student's ability to participate fully, and the teacher may well conclude that the student is a slow learner.

Teachers who are sensitive to the various cultures will learn about students' backgrounds and ensure that they are aware of relevant information about cultural traditions, religious practices, and patterns of interaction that may affect a student's classroom participation.

Too often culturally diverse children are rejected: for the way they speak, for the fact that their parents do not come to conferences, for the clothes they wear, and for the way they learn. I believe we reject them whenever we overcorrect those who are enthusiastically trying to tell us a story in their language or dialect. We reject them when we fail to include a discussion of black poets when we talk about famous "Southern writers." We reject them when we make generalizations about American Indians, Latinos, Arabs, and Asians based on what we see in the media. It happens every hour in every city and suburb in this country.

A very wise Yupek Eskimo once said that the purpose of education is to learn to die satisfied with life. That is what we need to bring to our culturally diverse students and all students, experiences that are full of the wonder of life, full of connectedness, embedded in the context of our communities, and brilliant in the insights we develop. All of us, educators and students alike, must learn to live lives that leave us truly satisfied.

So often we mouth the words "celebrating diversity, celebrating our differences," almost flippantly. It is easy to pay lip service to such words as *diversity*, *difference*, and *culture*. This is because we tend to stop on the surface of things. We want a quick fix, a tell-all session that will give us the secret and let us move on and get to the *real* business, whatever that is. We are used to messages, commercials, and talk shows that tell us there are easy solutions, recipes, pat answers, formulas that always work. Just like finding the right carpet, the right colors to wear to enhance your skin, or saying the right things. Just like all the quick fixes, you, too, can learn to become "diverse."

This is not true. Celebrating difference can cause tension and complications for both white and culturally diverse people. We are bothered by difference, by a language we cannot understand, by a way of dressing that is not usual to us, a veil or a yarmulke, a way of worshipping, a place of worship different from our own. We tend not to talk about it because it may be uncomfortable to do so.

Our classrooms have a long way to go before we encompass a greater definition of celebrating diversity. We must allow for friction, edginess, dissension, and discomfort in our environment. At the same time teachers, parents, neighbors, and students can find ways to celebrate our coming together in common cause in spite of our differences and because of our similarities.

We must accept differences and we must accept what we have in common. America is not a one-size-fits-all country. Such homogeneity is not going to happen. Celebration of difference involves not trying to change others to become like us, but rather taking pride in the fact that we are not like each other.

Schools are the best places to celebrate that we are not color-blind, to recognize differences in positive ways, in ways that teach us to see the different shades of brown, red, and coffee color that are in front of us. Why is recognizing color such a negative thing? Celebrating our place in the universe as part of a community of cultures is important for all students. It is not hard to find ways and things to celebrate with the students in our classrooms. They bring these things to us all the time.

Many policy leaders and educators now agree that our educational goals for the past 100 years are inadequate for students to meet the challenges of today and tomorrow. Traditionally, schools emphasized rote learning, memorization of facts, and recall of information with little emphasis on conceptual understanding and reasoning. The global economy, the technology revolution, and the rapidly changing nature of the workplace are strong incentives for schools to produce graduates who are knowledgeable, flexible thinkers and capable of understanding complex ideas.

USEFUL STRATEGIES

There are several strategies that we can employ: reflection and self-assessment, mentoring a student, utilizing peer coaching, and making sure that teachers are content specialists. We cannot teach what we do not know!

We must recognize that students come to the school environment with social and cultural characteristics that influence how they see the world (as Vine Deloria says, "Before correcting a child's perception of the world, we must understand what that perception is."), participate in learning activities, and absorb new information. Classroom goals must be appropriate for diverse students. We must realize that not all goals are equally suitable for all students.

Teaching is a matter of relationships among individuals, grounded in rapport and mutual respect. Trust needs to be earned. It takes time. Trust grows when people do what they say they will do. We must set standards of behavior that are appropriate, consistent, and clear to all.

We must also create a comfortable physical environment and then be willing to be flexible and make changes. If it is not working, don't use it. Most of all, utilize teachable moments. Teaching does not always need to be done in a formal classroom setting. Some of the best memorable teaching moments can be on a boat fishing in the sunshine or on a neighborhood walk.

Remember the old African proverb, It takes a whole village to raise a child? We must enlist the participation of students' families and community members in the educational process. You will find that student learning will be enhanced. Sensitive and respectful communication with families and community members can provide an important avenue for success.

SCHOOL REFORM

Reforming schools so that all students have a level playing field for success requires a new vision of education and social actors who are willing to advocate for and participate in change. How students and their families view their status in schools and society must be considered. School performance gaps exist because the forces of racial inequality continue to dominate our schools. Conditions such as inequitable school financing, unrepresentative school governance, and large class size play a powerful role in promoting student underachievement.

Let us focus on achievement. There are five conditions that promote student achievement within a multicultural perspective. Schools should:

- *Be antiracist and antibiased.* This perspective is at the core of multicultural education. Being antiracist means paying attention to all areas in which some students may be favored over others, including the curriculum, choice of materials, and teacher interaction and relationships with students and their communities. To become antiracist, schools need to examine how curriculum may perpetuate negative, distorted, or incomplete images of some groups while exalting others.

- *Reflect an understanding and acceptance of all students as having talents and strengths that can enhance their education.* Teachers should consider how the language spoken by the students may influence their academic achievement.

- *Involve those people most intimately connected with teaching and learning (teachers, parents, and students).* Such involvement can dramatically improve student learning. Programs must have family empowerment as a major goal and state a desire to reduce the gap between home and school. Designing programs that respond to and build on the values, structures, languages, and cultures within students' homes can reduce this gap.

- *Be based on high expectations and rigorous standards for all learners.* Many students cope on a daily basis with complex problems including poverty, violence, racism, abuse, and lack of health care and proper housing. Many speak a language other than English. Unfortunately, these conditions are often used as a rationalization for low expectations of what students are capable of learning. We must begin with the assumption that all students can learn. I believe that before fixing what may be considered problems with student learning that schools should change their perceptions of these perceived conditions and view them as potential benefits.

- *Consider reform within the parameters of critical pedagogy.* Students need to learn decision-making and social-action skills. Since no curriculum can be truly neutral, it is the responsibility of the school to present all students with a broad range of information that will help increase reading, writing, and math skills.

These five conditions can help provide an important framework for rethinking school reform. We can help students learn effectively and successfully and also help schools become places of hope and affirmation for students of all cultures.

STUDENT ACHIEVEMENT AND REFORM

Student learning is the primary purpose of education. Therefore, we must look at school reform in light of how students learn and to what extent. We should look at culturally responsive education, which is an approach based on using students' culture as an important source of their education. This approach can go a long way in improving the learning of students whose cultures and heritages have been maligned, denied, and omitted in the school curricula. However, we must note that by itself, culturally responsive pedagogy cannot guarantee that all students will be successful. We must move beyond isolated lessons in sensitivity training or prejudice reduction, or ethnic holidays. We must explore alternatives to systematic problems that lead to academic failure and develop a deeper awareness of how culture and language differences can influence learning.

PARENTS AND TEACHERS, PARTNERS IN REFORM

Educational reform needs the support, influence, and activism of parents and community groups. Schools are highly dependent on and vulnerable to citizens who can support or impede change.

Parent involvement is important because it acknowledges the importance of parents in the lives of their children, recognizes the diversity of values and perspectives within the school community, provides a vehicle for building a collaborative problem-solving structure, and increases the opportunity for all students to learn. Students arrive at the school door with knowledge, values, and beliefs they have learned from their parents. Parents directly or indirectly help shape their children's value system and view of the world in which they live. Parents can help teachers extend their understanding of the students.

To create a harmonious environment between the school, home, and community, teachers need to understand and be knowledgeable about parents' expectations for their children, languages spoken at home, and family values, as well as how the children are taught in their homes. Parents, in turn, need information about their school, what the school expects their children to learn, how they will be taught, and the required books and materials that will be used in the classroom. Most important, parents need to understand how their children will be assessed and how they can support their children in the process. Parent involvement allows parents and teachers to reinforce skills and provide an environment that has consistent learning expectations and standards.

TO PROVIDE THE BEST ENVIRONMENT FOR LEARNING WE MUST REFORM OUR SCHOOLS. WHERE DO WE BEGIN?

Reform efforts should begin with a redefinition of educational equality for culturally diverse students as access to a variety of instrumental processes that are informed by and responsive to their cultural learning styles. This means affirming that problems in student learning are not tied so much to the inabilities of the students as to culturally unequal, insensitive, educational practices used in the schools they attend.

Reform must continue to encompass changes in teacher preparation, curriculum design, classroom instruction, grouping of students, school climate, how students' needs are diagnosed, and how their achievement is assessed.

I believe that all forms of tracking should be eliminated entirely. Even under the best of circumstances, tracking denies equal educational opportunities to culturally diverse students as well as others who populate the lower academic levels. Tracking should be replaced with flexible and frequently changed cooperative groupings for specific instructional tasks on skill development purposes.

We should place less emphasis on norm-referenced standardized tests for evaluating student achievement and place more emphasis on evaluating students against their own records, with range of improvement between different points of reference being the focus of attention, as opposed to performance at isolated points in time. This means that our classrooms should use multiple techniques and procedures, including verbal, visual, observational, participatory, and kinetic means to assess students' school performance. The techniques should be administered frequently and instructional programming should be changed according to the results obtained. Thus, culturally diverse students should be placed on self-referenced and self-paced programs to complete their education.

School curricula, too, must be reformed if equal educational opportunities are to be assured for culturally diverse students. What schools consider to be essential knowledge and skills for all students may need to be revised to incorporate cultural pluralism. These revisions should reflect the comprehensive demographic, social, cultural, and linguistic realities of American society and the world around us, not just the technological, economic, and political sides of life. This means, first, that school curricula should demonstrate and emulate the interdisciplinary nature of human life, knowledge, values, skills, and experiences. Second, they should teach and model the interdependence of the world, a world in which whites are a small numerical minority, and one in which the control of natural resources, social aspirations, and power negotiations is gradually shifting from Western to non-Western, nonwhite nations. Third, a concerted effort should be made to achieve a greater balance between technological developments and humanistic concerns, where skills in ethics, morality, and aesthetics are as important as cognition. These kinds of curricular reform methods increase the possibility that the experiences, cultures, and contributions of culturally diverse groups in the United States will be included across subject matter content areas, that students will relate and identify with the curriculum, and that they will have a greater sense of ownership in their education.

Because teachers play such a central role in the kinds of educational opportunities culturally diverse students receive in the classroom, their reeducation and training are fundamental to providing educational equality. Teacher training should include self-knowledge, training on understanding differences, development of technical instructional skills, and development of public relations skills.

Teachers need to become conscious of their own cultural values and beliefs and how these affect their attitudes and expectations toward different ethnic groups (self-knowledge). Teachers may need to be shown how they behave toward their students in and outside of the classrooms. Teachers must learn how to analyze from the perspective of "others."

Teachers need to understand differences in cultural values and behavioral codes between themselves and their students (black teachers working with Hmong students, Hmong teachers working with Somalia students, white middle-class teachers working with all cultures, etc.), and how instructional processes can be restructured to better accommodate all students.

Teachers need to learn about ethnic learning styles and then develop strategies to diversify teaching techniques to create more supportive environments for learning (select high-quality appealing materials, develop and use learning activities that are meaningful, involving, enabling, and empowering).

Major reform is needed in how educators are prepared to communicate and interact with parents. We must stop blaming the academic failure of students on the perceived lack of involvement of parents in school affairs. This buck-passing is counterproductive to improving the education of our students. In the past, educators usually approached parents only when the children were in trouble. Adversarial posture is not conductive to cooperation among educators and parents. Instead of always expecting the parent-school interactions to take place in schools (which are alien and hostile territory for many parents), we should locate our efforts to increase parental involvement more within the community or at least on neutral territory. Parents always have to go to the school at the educator's convenience. This conveys an implicit message of school power and parent subordination. We must develop more constructive and cooperative relations with parents and their diverse communities.

A crucial focus of reform efforts should be on improving the quality of instructional interactions that occur between culturally diverse students and classroom teachers. As educators we should all heed the Teacher's Credo, "A child is not a vessel to be filled, but a lamp to be lighted."

The lack of teacher understanding and acceptance of cultural styles and the unwillingness or inability to use these styles as instructional tools mean that the culturally diverse student does not have comparable access to high-quality instruction as his or her white counterpart. It is not surprising, then, that disparities in educational access produces disparities in achievement outcomes. These situations will be reversed only when educators accept the fact that culture is a critical, if not ultimate, factor in academic achievement.

We must ensure that the delivery of all of the students' educational services—whether curriculum, instruction, materials, assessment, or leadership—are culturally embedded. In other words, culturally responsive strategies must be used to educate culturally diverse students. Improving educational equality for these students must be centered in the systematic implementation of multicultural education. As Tatanka Iotanko (Sitting Bull) of the Lakota Sioux said in 1877, "Let us put our minds together and see what life can make for our children."

CONCLUSION

Somewhere between 8th and 10th grade in most states there are a series of tests: high-stakes tests, low-stakes tests, pseudo-high tests, etc. No diploma will be issued until there is proof that these tests have been passed.

Our students need a range of services and supports. Some may need basic academic support, while others may need ESL support. Still others may need skill development support, which includes Internet research, library research, theme writing, test-taking skills, note taking, completing homework, and time/self-management.

Within that same period many students may need to develop high-level thinking and problem-solving skills and gain exposure to new ideas. Courses need to contain challenging new experiences. Time needs to be allowed to explore. The goal is to have all students proficient and prepared for programs by exhibiting depth and concentration.

We need to accelerate the learning process for all students and look into career opportunities of their choice. This means offering high-level learning opportunities and preparation for the next levels of learning.

Courses may need to be modified, and we may even need to create new courses to enhance learning.

We ponder the question, "How are culturally diverse students going to be guided and assisted as they move through school?" As educators we need to develop a continuing base for marketing accountability and new learning opportunities. Our top priority must be to find the time and the resources to accomplish these goals.

The United States is a multicultural nation of persons of different ethnic backgrounds, classes, religions, and native languages. In addition there are natural differences based on gender, age, and physical and mental abilities. Educators and their students are exposed to a social curriculum that makes positive and negative statements about these differences through radio, television, and newspapers, as well as through family attitudes. Often, distorted messages about people who are ethnically or religiously different from oneself are portrayed in the social curriculum. We learn that Italian Americans control organized crime, African Americans are on welfare, the homeless are dangerous, females are weak, hard hats are racist, and individuals with disabilities are helpless. Decisions made by employers, educators, politicians, and community members are often based on such misconceptions. As educators we must help students interpret and analyze the cultural cues that are forced on them daily.

Riots in Los Angeles pitted some Asian and European Americans against African Americans. Some of the nation's leaders led name-calling against persons from the Middle East during the Persian Gulf War. Some individuals declare that the Holocaust never occurred. Some individuals are nearly paralyzed by fear of persons from a different religious, ethnic, or language background.

Multicultural education provides an environment that values cultural diversity and portrays it positively. Gender, age, ethnicity, language, religion, class, or disability does not limit students' educational and vocational options. Educators have the responsibility to help students contribute to and benefit from our democratic society. Diversity is used to develop effective instructional strategies for students in the classroom.

Multicultural education can help students increase their academic achievement through the use of teaching approaches and materials that are sensitive and relevant to the students' cultural backgrounds and experiences. Their voices and those of the community must be heard in order to deliver multicultural education. Educators should develop skills for individualizing instruction based on the needs of the students. No longer can we afford to teach all students the same knowledge and skills in the same way. Individualizing instruction is the one way to help all students reach their potential and develop their unique talents. Teachers must make an effort to know all of their students, build on their strengths, and help them overcome their weaknesses.

Multicultural education can help students to think critically, deal with social and historical realities of American society, and gain a better understanding of the causes of oppression and inequality, including racism and sexism. Multicultural education must start *where the people are* and incorporate resources from the local community.

Positive student and teacher interactions can support academic achievement, regardless of gender, age, ethnicity, religion, or language. Oral and nonverbal communication patterns are analyzed or changed to increase student involvement. Learning styles of the students and teaching styles of the teachers are used to develop effective instructional strategies.

Educators should be aware of the biases that exist in most classroom materials and be able to draw on supplementary materials to reflect cultural diversity more accurately.

Educators will face a tremendous challenge in the next decade to effectively use the cultural diversity that the students bring to the classroom. For students to function effectively in a democratic society, they must learn about the inequalities that currently exist. Otherwise our society will never be able to overcome such inequities.

As educators, we must teach all children. The ultimate goal of multicultural education is to meet the individual learning needs of each student so that all students can progress to their fullest capacity. This goal has not been reached in the past, partly because educators have been unable to effectively use the cultural backgrounds of students in providing classroom instruction. Acceptance of the challenge to multiculturalize the schools is vital to the well-being of all citizens.

However, it is an unfortunate reality that schools are not changing sufficiently to meet the dramatic changes that have occurred in the United States. Schools continue to operate as if conditions and demographics are the same as when the common school was first created. Yet it is within our reach and within our power to bring about change. Tinkering and Band-Aids are inadequate.

At its best, education accomplishes its mission of meeting the needs of its students. To date this mission has not been met; too many culturally diverse students have been denied their right to an appropriate education, an education that prepares them to succeed inside and outside the school.

Students continue to be taught an ethnocentric curriculum, one that presents mirrors for white children and windows for others. The curriculum sends devastating messages that wreak havoc on the self-perception, motivation, and achievement of culturally diverse students while affirming those of white students.

Educators must realize that although each culture is distinctive in its own right, many cultures share common values and characteristics. In fact, the similarities seem to outweigh the differences. Every group has confronted racial discrimination, and all share the burden of poor educational outcomes, high unemployment rates, and high poverty rates. Conversely, they share cultural values that can serve as strengths, such as the value placed on family bonds and the preference for cooperative and social learning. Expressive communication and physical and creative expressiveness are also important values for each group.

Public schools were originally designed for a homogeneous group of children with a common culture, values, morals, ambitions, and parental expectations. Thus immigrants and cultural groups in the United States were thrown into the "melting pot" where their differences were expected to boil away as they melded into true-blue Americans, living the American way. The dream has proven elusive, even a nightmare for many. Giving up one's cultural identity to achieve success is too high a price to pay for some.

In later years the image of the melting pot was replaced by another image, that of a salad bowl. More recently the salad bowl has given way to the tapestry. This metaphor recognizes that each group has its distinctive qualities and says that different people can come together to create a new whole.

The issue is not whether our society is comprised of many cultures. It always has been and is becoming more so. The issue is whether we will create a new vision for how our society will function effectively. As Takaki (1993) noted, "America's dilemma has been our resistance to ourselves, our denial of our immensely varied selves. But we have nothing to fear but fear of our own diversity" (p. 3).

We must acknowledge the strong belief among culturally diverse groups that they must hold on tightly to their uniqueness, to their heritage, to their values and language. Rather than resist diversity, educators should embrace it. This is the first step toward helping to ensure that culturally diverse students reach higher levels of achievement in schools and other social settings. We can't let these students get caught in the battle between excellence and equity. These students, as do all students, deserve the best education can offer, excellence *and* equity.

As an advocate for change, I want to help students, teachers, and other stakeholders in the community become more aware of themselves as individuals and cultural beings. I want to help the school community become more culturally aware and competent. I would like to see multicultural education integrated throughout the academic process. Most importantly, I want all children to have the opportunity to reach their full potential. A mind is a terrible thing to erase.

Schools have a crucial role to play in helping create a society that is inclusive and pluralistic, one that goes beyond merely tolerating diversity and adopting color-blind philosophies. A color-blind philosophy ignores not only color but also culture. A color-blind goal to view all children in the same manner often has the reverse effect. When differences are ignored, problems associated with them may be exacerbated. When a color-blind philosophy prevails, all groups are expected to conform, to assimilate into the mainstream. In essence, the richness of this nation's diversity is a treasure, a treasure that must not be buried. Educators must celebrate and honor diversity. As with the rainbow, all colors of the human race illuminate the magnificence of the human experience.

Culturally diverse communities must understand that it is a waste of time hating a mirror or its reflection. Instead we must stop the hand that makes glass with distortions.

Teachers, as adults and classroom leaders, play the most significant and powerful role in shaping students' identities and providing an environment where diversity thrives. Culturally diverse groups can retain much of their original culture and be multicultural at the same time. These groups need to learn how to accommodate rather than assimilate, so that they can walk that line between two cultures that may be very different in terms of norms, values, and beliefs.

Students will live up to our expectations or they will live down to them. It is very simple: Make education relevant to the students. Confront the fact that we live in a society where race matters and that this society has a long history of white supremacy. We must work together to reduce the ignorance that breeds racism and work to develop understanding.

Our primary goal as educators is to foster the intellectual, social, and personal development of students. We must provide all students, not just some, with an equal opportunity to learn and achieve. As the old saying goes, "We may not all hit home runs, but everyone should have a chance at bat." Teachers are compelling figures in the lives of students. Teachers are both role models and change agents. Let these children have a chance at bat.

All students must have the opportunity to dream. Martin Luther King Jr. dreamed that one day the nation would rise up and live out the true meaning of its creed, that all men are created equal. He dreamed that the "sweltering heat of oppression" would be transformed into an "oasis of freedom and justice" (King, 1963, p. 25). Our schools must share this vision of what the United States and its schools *can* be for every child.

I am proud to be part of a long history of academic success. I am proud to be an administrator at a school that stresses quality education, demands parental support, celebrates cultural diversity, is tolerant and accepting of differences, and cultivates outstanding student achievement.

I realize that the tasks before us are challenging. We must continue to demand of our students and ourselves even greater levels of achievement. We must have courage (the ability to act on what we know is right and good) to dare to do what we should and must. Fear paralyzes; courage is what helps us move ahead. Courage does not conquer fear, it simply renders fear ineffective. It gives us a confident assurance that we can succeed. Cultural diversity, technology, pressing global issues, and instantaneous information have brought about new levels of learning and understanding. What was a level of success even ten years ago is now antiquated and no longer useful. We are preparing our students for employment and careers that do not currently exist.

This means that we cannot rest on our laurels or stand on what might have been successful in the past. This means that we must question what we are doing. This means we must not be satisfied with the educational process as it stands today. This means we might shake things up a bit. For some that will not be comfortable. For some that will be frightening. For some that will be outright blasphemy.

We must emphasize communication and involvement. We need learning communities that address the needs of all students. We must accept the possibility that what we are currently doing might need to change. Heed what Maya Angelou said: "We cannot change the past, but we can change our attitude toward it. Uproot guilt and plant forgiveness. Tear out arrogance and seed humility. Exchange love for hate, thereby making the present comfortable and the future promising" (Angelou, 1992).

Little will change unless we change ourselves. Think otherwise. Fly the cage. Make your presence felt. Leave your mark and have some fun while the window of opportunity is admitting fresh breezes. For soon it will close. Our classrooms must become meaningful for all our students and their families. Learn from a child how to open your eyes. Students, parents, community, and staff, I urge you to become part of this exciting new future.

I leave you with this final comment: *It is always your next move.* The keys to the universe lie within the choices you make. You don't have to buy from anyone. You don't have to work at any particular job. You don't have to participate in any given relationship. You can choose. The choice is always yours. You hold the tiller. You steer the course you choose in the direction of where you want to be today, tomorrow, or in the distant time to come. You can at any time decide to alter the course of your life. No one can take that away from you. All students should have the opportunity to be nurtured, to belong, to be heard, to be valued, and to have their needs met. You have the power to make the difference.

References

Abbott, L. (1888). *Education for the Indian*. (Keynote Address). Lake Mohonk Conference of 1888.

Ackland, L. (1983). No place for neutralism: The Eisenhower administration and Laos. In J. Adams & P. McCoy (Eds.), *Laos: War and revolution* (p. 143). New York: Columbia University Press.

Acuna, R. (1981). *Occupied America: A history of Chicanos*. New York: Prentice-Hall.

Angelou, M. (1992, October 11). Speech at Moorhead State University, Moorhead, MN.

Baldwin, J. (1981). *Go Tell It on the Mountain*. New York: Dell Publishing.

Black Elk. (1988). *Black Elk speaks: Being the life story of a holy man of the Oglala Sioux*, as told to G. Neihardt. Lincoln: University of Nebraska Press.

Brown v. Board of Education of Topeka, Kansas. (1954). 347 U.S. 483.

Chan, S. (1994). *Hmong means free*. Philadelphia: Temple University Press.

Chin, T. (1968). *Chinese in California*. Chicago: University of Chicago Press.

Cohen, E. (1994). *Designing group work: Strategies for heterogeneous classrooms* (2nd ed.). New York: Teachers College Press.

DeLeon, A. (1983). *They called them greasers: Anglo attitudes toward Mexicans in Texas, 1821–1900*. Austin: University of Texas Press.

Deloria, V. (1969). *Custer died for your sins: An Indian manifesto*. Norman: University of Oklahoma Press.

Dewey, J. (1902). *The child and the curriculum*. Chicago: University of Chicago Press.

Donnelly, N. (1999). *The changing lives of refugee Hmong women*. Madison: University of Wisconsin Press.

Espina, M. (1988). *Filipinos in Lousiana*. New Orleans: A. F. Laborde and Sons.

Eyes on the prize: America's civil rights years. (1987). Series I and II. Alexandria, VA: PBS Home Video Collection. 57 minutes.

Fadiman, A. (1997). *The spirit catches you and you fall down.* New York: Farrar, Straus, and Giroux.

Fuentis, C. (1988). *Myself with others: Selected essays.* New York: Farrar, Straus, and Giroux.

Garcia, E. (1994). *Understanding and meeting the challenge of student cultural diversity.* Boston: Houghton-Mifflin.

Goldstein, B. (1995). *Schooling for cultural transitions.* Madison: University of Wisconsin Press.

The Great World Atlas. (2004). New York: DK Publishing.

Hamilton-Merritt, J. (1993). *Tiger mountains: The Hmong, the Americans, and the secret war for Laos, 1942–1992.* Bloomington: Indiana University Press.

How the West was lost. (1993). Landover, MD: Discovery Enterprises Group. 100 minutes.

Kazuo, I. (1973). *Issei: A history of the Japanese immigrants in North America.* Seattle: University of Washington Press.

King, M. L. K., Jr. (1963). *I have a dream.* New York: Scholastic Press.

King, M. L. K., Jr. (1964). *Why we can't wait.* New York: Harper.

King, R. (1992, May 2). Statement to the press, *New York Times*, p. 6.

Lai, L. (1924). *Island.* Stanford, CA: Stanford University Press.

Landsman, J. (2001). *A white teacher talks about race.* Lanham, MD: Rowman & Littlefield Education.

Lemieux, R. (1994). *A study of the adaptation of Hmong first-, second-, and third-graders.* Minneapolis: University of Minnesota Press.

Little Soldier, L. (1997, April). Is there an Indian in your classroom? Working successfully with urban Native American students. *Phi Delta Kappan,* 650–653.

Los Angeles School District. (2004). Annual Report. Los Angeles, CA: Los Angeles School District.

Matsui, R. (1987, September 17). Speech in the House of Representatives on the 442 Bill for Redress and Reparation. *Congressional Record,* Washington, D.C., p. 2584.

Melville, H. (1849). *Redburn.* Chicago: University of Chicago Press, 1969. (Original work published 1849).

Miller-Lachmann, L., & Taylor, L. (1995). *Schools for all: Educating children in a diverse society.* New York: Delmar Publishing.

Minneapolis Star Tribune. (2004, March 22). "Minnesota welcomes the states newest members," 1A, 12A.

Montejano, D. (1987). *Anglos and Mexicans in the making of Texas: 1836–1986.* Austin: University of Texas Press.

Moss, M., & Puma, M. (1995). *Prospects: The congressionally mandated study of educational growth and opportunity.* (First year report on limited English proficient students). Washington, D.C.: U.S. Department of Education.

Muwakki, Salim. (2003, April 13). Racism and our heritage. *In These Times,* 15–16.

National Association for Bilingual Education. (n.d.). *Fact sheet: Need for additional funding for the Federal Bilingual Education Act.* Washington, D.C.: Author.

Reed, I. (1988). America: The multicultural society. In R. Simonson and S. Walker (Eds.), *Multicultural literacy.* St. Paul, MN: Four Winds Publishing.

Sithoff, H. (1978). *A new deal for blacks: The emergence of civil rights.* New York: Prentice-Hall.

Sithoff, H. (1981). *The struggle for black equality, 1954–1980.* New York: Prentice-Hall.

Slavin, R. (1995). Cooperative learning and intergroup relations. In J. Banks & C. Banks (Eds.), *Handbook of research on multicultural education* (pp. 228–234). New York: Macmillan.

Squire, J. (1982, September). The ten great ideas in the teaching of English during the last half century. Speech given at the Central California Council of Teachers of English Conference, San Francisco.

Standing Bear, L. (1973). What the Indian means to America. In W. Moquen (Ed.), *Great documents in American Indian history.* New York: Harper.

Stevenson, C. (1972). *The end of nowhere: American policy toward Laos since 1954.* Boston: Beacon Press.

Suarez-Orozco, C., & Suarez-Orozco, M. (2001). *Transformation: Immigration, family life, and achievement motivation among Latino adolescents.* Stanford, CA: Stanford University Press.

Takaki, R. (1993). *A different mirror: A history of multicultural America.* New York: Little, Brown.

Tanaka, C. (1982). *Go for broke: History of the Japanese American infantry.* Los Angeles: University of California Press.

Tatum, B. (1997). *Why are all the black kids sitting together in the cafeteria?* New York: Basic Books.

Uba, L. (2000). *Asian Americans: Personality patterns, identity, and mental health.* New York: Guilford.

USA Today Weekend. (2005, May 13–15). America the Diverse.

U.S. Census Bureau. (1993). *Statistical abstract.* Washington, D.C.: U.S. Government Printing Office.

U.S. Census Bureau. (1999). *We the Americans: Our education.* Washington, D.C.: U.S. Government Printing Office.

U.S. Census Bureau. (1999). *We, the first Americans.* Washington, D.C.: U.S. Government Printing Office.

U.S. Census Bureau. (2000). *Census 2000 summary, File 14.* Washington, D.C.: U.S. Government Printing Office.

U.S. Census Bureau. (2001). *Statistical abstract of the United States.* Washington, D.C.: U.S. Government Printing Office.

U.S. Department of Education. (2000). *Characteristics of the 100 largest public elementary and secondary school districts in the United States: 1998–1999.* Washington, D.C.: U.S. Government Printing Office.

U.S. Department of Justice. (1993, October). *Statistical yearbook of the Immigration and Naturalization Service.* Washington, D.C.: U.S. Government Printing Office.

Walker-Moffat, W. (1995). *The other side of the Asian American success story.* San Francisco: Jossey-Bass.

Weinberg, A. (1963). *Manifest destiny: A study of nationalist expansionism in American history.* Chicago: University of Chicago Press.

Whitman, W. (1958). *Leaves of grass.* New York: Columbia University Press. Originally published in 1855.

William, H. (1990, April 9). Beyond the melting pot. *Time,* 28–31.

Wilson, R., & Hosokawa, B. (1980). *East to America: A history of the Japanese in America.* New York: Columbia University Press.

Wolters, R. (1970). *Negroes and the Great Depression: The problem of economic recovery.* Westport, CT: Brown Press.

Woodson, C. G. (1933). *The miseducation of the Negro.* Washington, D.C.: Associated Publishers.

Yamada, M. (1983). Invisibility is an unnatural disaster: Reflections of an Asian American woman. In C. Morago and G. Anzaldua (Eds.), *This bridge called my back: Writings by radical women of color.* New York: Little, Brown.

Yung, S. (1946). *Chinese women of America.* Chicago: Chicago University Press.

About the Author

Darlene Leiding is K–12 principal at Oh Day Aki (Heart of the Earth Charter School) in Minneapolis, Minnesota, working with inner-city American Indian students. She is an expert in the realm of charter schools and alternative education and has created an elementary and high school alternative program.